Buber on God
and the
Perfect Man

◆

PAMELA VERMES

London · Washington
Littman Library of Jewish Civilization
1994

The Littman Library of Jewish Civilization
74 Addison Road, London W14 8DJ, UK

1640 Rhode Island Avenue, NW
Washington DC 20036–3278, USA

First published 1980 by Scholars Press in the
Brown Judaic Studies series.

A catalogue record for this book is available from the British Library

Library of Congress Cataloging in Publication data
Vermes, Pamela.
Buber on God and the perfect man / Pamela Vermes.
p.   cm.
Originally published: Missoula, Mont. : Scholars Press. c1980.
Includes bibliographical references and index.
1. God (Judaism)—History of doctrines—20th century.
2. Man (Jewish theology)—History of doctrines—20th century.
3. Buber, Martin, 1878–1965.
I. Title
BM810.V47 1994   94–1377
ISBN 1–874774–22–6 (hardback)
ISBN 1–874774–23–4 (paperback)

Copy-editing: Gillian Bromley
Proof-reading: George Staines
Design: Pete Russell, Faringdon, Oxon
Typeset by Footnote Graphics, Warminster, Wiltshire
Printed in Great Britain on acid-free paper by
Bookcraft Ltd, Bath

In Memoriam

Pamela Vermes
2 December 1918–10 June 1993

WITH the death of Pamela Vermes, the *Journal of Jewish Studies* has lost one of its pillars. She became literary editor in 1976, when *JJS* was acquired by the Oxford Centre for Postgraduate Hebrew Studies, but had already fulfilled the same function without any formal title since 1971, when Geza Vermes was appointed editor by Jewish Chronicle Publications. She introduced elegance and style into the pages of an academic periodical. Hundreds of contributors, and not just those whose mother tongue was not English, have benefited from her remarkable editorial skill, and many generously expressed their gratitude for an assistance which she modestly considered as her duty.

Grand-daughter of Sidney Dark (1874–1947), an eminent editor of the *Church Times* (1924–41) and a prolific writer, Pam, as she was generally known,[1] had journalism and literature in her blood. In her youth, she was employed in the Berlin office of the *Daily Telegraph* where one of her seniors was Hugh Carlton Greene, subsequently Sir Hugh Greene, Director General of the BBC. Geza Vermes's acceptance, twenty-two years ago, of the editorship of the *Journal of Jewish Studies* coincided with Pam's rising interest in the work of Martin Buber. Over the years, she published in the journal several preliminary studies on the thought of the man whom she considered to be the greatest religious thinker of our age. They developed into two books, *Buber on God and the Perfect Man* (1980, released 1981) and *Buber* (1988)—the 'little Buber', she used to call it—later published also in Italian (1990) and French (1992) translations, the latter with a prefatory essay by Emmanuel Levinas. She received numerous invitations to lecture on Buber, but decided that the spoken word was not her medium.

First published in the *Journal of Jewish Studies*, Sept. 1993.

[1] During the last few years, graduate students seemed to be reluctant to address Geza Vermes by his first name and usually spoke of Professor Vermes and *Pam*, which she found both delightful and amusing.

In the 1980s, Pamela Vermes switched her attention to that other great twentieth-century figure, Dr Albert Schweitzer, and the relationship between him and Buber, but progressive ill-health prevented the completion of her next major literary project, a study of Schweitzer's famous ethical principle, 'Ehrfurcht vor dem Leben', or reverence for life. She managed, nevertheless, to publish in 1986 an annotated edition of the correspondence between Buber and Schweitzer.

She wrote a fair amount of book reviews, mostly in *JJS*. They were always well researched, severe on pompousness or careless style without being unkind, and quite often marvellously witty. Re-read, for instance, the opening paragraph of her presentation of *Major Themes in Modern Philosophies of Judaism* by E. Berkovits: 'Not one of the "major themes" considered in this book is commended. From Hermann Cohen's *Der Begriff der Religion* and *Die Religion der Vernunft aus den Quellen des Judentums*, published in 1915 and 1919 respectively, to A. J. Heschel's *The Prophets* issued in 1962, the principal contributions to Jewish religious thought covering a period of almost half a century—including of course those of Franz Rosenzweig and Martin Buber—are measured against the standards of the Professor of Philosophy at Hebrew Theological College, Skokie, Illinois, and rejected.'[2] The PS appended to her review of *Martin Buber. A Centenary Volume* caused quite a few chuckles in libraries and common rooms: 'As our enigmatic translator gives Lorenz Wachinger to say, quoting the Bishop of Aachen: "Buber is a kind of suture in dialogue, an inexhaustible impulse, a challenge" (p. 453). Puzzle that one out.'[3] Or else, savour her comment on Jochanan Bloch's 'high peak of gossip' that Buber had an affair with Naemah Beer-Hofmann who, as a physiotherapist, treated him in a Swiss sanatorium after the death of his wife: 'It may not be out of place concerning this tale to note that at the time of the friendship [somewhere between 1961 and 1963] Buber was eighty-three to eighty-five years old, and the lady cannot have been over-young either, considering that [Richard] Beer-Hofmann's [her father's] *Schlaflied für Miriam* [Naemah's sister] was published in 1898.'[4]

Pam's poetry was known only to members of her inner circle. Presence, 'being with' and love of nature were among her central themes, and so also was death, for which she was fully prepared. 'This woman admirably managed her illness and her death,' remarked her doctor, whom she was teasing a few hours before she stopped

[2] *JJS* 29 (1978), 103.   [3] *JJS* 35 (1985), 259.   [4] *JJS* 40 (1989), 272.

breathing. A poem written in 1984 was prophetic of her own passing:

Going away

Remembering the gathering in
of a gentle friend
by the long and loving Arm,
she went very sweetly, you said,
she very sweetly went away,
as though from one room to another.

Yet o no no no no no
wasn't it more like passing
from one familiar corner
to another familiar corner
of the same familiar room?

Another piece, combining the themes of death, presence and a 'lovely lovely world', and splendidly equivocal concerning the meaning of 'you', was read during her funeral on 15 June 1993, and made many a mourner cry:

with you

peering ahead
into the pitchy depths of deadness
where I'll not be
where I'll not be me
where I'll not be me with you
where I'll not be with my greatly loved
whom I may no longer see

peering ahead into the pitchy depths
where being perhaps with Him
I'll nevertheless no longer be me
no longer be me with you

how shall I not express
reverential happiness
for your being with me now
for my being with you now
o lovely lovely world

bearing in mind the day
when I may possibly be with Him
I notwithstanding clap my hands
ten thousand times
for presently being with you
for presently being with you

Bibliography of Pamela Vermes

1971

'Martin Buber: A New Appraisal', *Journal of Jewish Studies* (*JJS*), 22, 78–96.

1973

'Buber's Understanding of the Divine Name related to the Bible, Targum and Midrash', *JJS*, 24, 147–66.

Literary editor of E. Schürer, *The History of the Jewish People in the Age of Jesus Christ* (*HJP*), rev. and ed. G. Vermes and F. Millar, i. Edinburgh: T. &. T. Clark.

1974

Review of Franz Rosenzweig, *The Star of Redemption*, trans. W. W. Hallo, *JJS*, 25, 344–5.

Review of Martin Buber's Correspondence (*Briefwechsel aus sieben Jahrzehnten*, i–ii), *JJS*, 25, 444–50.

1977

'Man's Prime Peril: Buber on Religion', *JJS*, 28, 72–8.

The Dead Sea Scrolls: Qumran in Perspective by G. Vermes, with the collaboration of Pamela Vermes. London: Collins.

1978

Review of Eliezer Berkovits, *The Philosophies of Judaism*, *JJS*, 29, 103–5.

Review of Martin Buber, *Briefwechsel aus sieben Jahrzehnten*, iii, *JJS*, 29, 200–3.

1979

Literary editor of *HJP*, rev. and ed. G. Vermes, F. Millar, and M. Black, ii. Edinburgh: T. & T. Clark.

Review of Kees Waaijman, *De mystiek van ik en jij*, *JJS*, 30, 257–60.

1980

Review of Rivka Horvitz, *Buber's Way to 'I and Thou'*, *JJS*, 31, 123–4.

1981

Buber on God and the Perfect Man (Brown Judaic Studies 13). Chico, Ca.: Scholars Press, 1980; released 1981.

Review of Jochanan Bloch, *Die Aporie des Du: Probleme der Dialogik Martin Bubers*, *JJS*, 32, 115–17.

Review of *Martin Buber: Dialogue et voix prophétique. Colloque international Martin Buber 30–31 Octobre 1978*, *JJS*, 32, 118–19.

Review of Arthur A. Cohen (ed.), *The Jew: Essays from Martin Buber's Journal, Der Jude, 1916–1928*, *JJS*, 32, 224–5.

1982

'A Buber–Lukács levelezés (1911–1921) [The Buber–Lukács Correspondence (1911–1921)]', *Évkönyv* [Year Book] *1981/82* (Budapest), 525–38. (The letters are reproduced in the original German.)

'The Buber–Lukács Correspondence (1911–1921)', *Leo Baeck Institute Year Book*, xxvii. 369–77. (The letters are printed in English translation.)

1983

Review of Maurice Friedman, *Martin Buber's Life and Work: The Early Years 1878–1923*, *Times Literary Supplement*, 7 Jan., 22.

Review of Maurice Friedman, *Martin Buber's Life and Work: The Early Years 1878–1923*, *New Blackfriars*, 64/752, 86–7.

Review of Arthur A. Goren (ed.), *Dissenter in Zion: From the Writings of Judah L. Magnes*, *JJS*, 34, 231.

1984

Review of Martin Buber, *Der Glaube der Propheten*, 2nd edn., *Journal of Semitic Studies*, 29, 306–7.

Review of Werner Licharz (ed.), *Dialog mit Martin Buber*, *JJS*, 35, 231–2.

Review of Martin Buber, *Des Baal Schem Tov Unterweisung im Umgang mit Gott*, *JJS*, 35, 236.

Review of Paul Mendes-Flohr (ed.), *A Land of Two Peoples: Martin Buber on Jews and Arabs*, *JJS*, 35, 237–8.

1985

Review of Steven T. Katz, *Post-Holocaust Dialogues: Critical Studies in Modern Jewish Thought*, *JJS*, 36, 135–7.

Review of Haim Gordon and Jochanan Bloch, *Martin Buber: A Centenary Volume*, *JJS*, 36, 256–9.

1986

'The Buber–Schweitzer Correspondence', *JJS*, 37, 228–45.

Literary editor of *HJP*, rev. and ed. G. Vermes, F. Millar, and M. Goodman, iii. 1. Edinburgh: T. & T. Clark.

1987

Literary editor of *HJP*, rev. and ed. G. Vermes, F. Millar, and M. Goodman, iii. 2. Edinburgh: T. & T. Clark.

1988

Buber (Jewish Thinkers). London: Peter Halban; New York: Grove Press.

1989

'Buber, Martin (Mordecai)', in *The Blackwell Companion to Jewish Culture*, ed. Glenda Abramson, 116–18. Oxford: Blackwell.

Review of Haim Gordon (ed.), *The Other Martin Buber: Recollections of his Contemporaries, JJS*, 40, 272–2.

1990

Martin Buber (Tempi e figure). Turin: Edizioni Paoline. (Italian translation of *Buber*.)

'Buber Re-Introduced' (bibliographical survey of M. Buber, *The Tales of Rabbi Nachman*, intr. P. Mendes-Flohr and Z. Gries; *Eclipse of God*, intr. R. M. Seltzer; *Moses*, intr. M. Fishbane; *The Origin and Meaning of Hasidism*, intr. D. B. Burrell; *The Knowledge of Man*, intr. A. Udoff; *Hasidism and Modern Man*, intr. M. Jaffee; Rivka Horvitz, *Buber's Way to 'I and Thou': The Development of Martin Buber's Thought and his 'Religion as Presence' Lectures*), *JJS*, 41, 145–6.

1992

Martin Buber (Présences du Judaïsme). Paris: Albin Michel. (French translation of *Buber* intr. Emmanuel Levinas.)

1993

The Riddle of the Sparks, published posthumously. Oxford: Foxcombe Press.

Contents

Preface to the First Edition

THIS book records my struggle to determine the meaning and relevance to the predicament of the present-day world of the message of Martin Mordechai Buber, one of the outstanding religious thinkers of our age.

As a first step, I had to make certain of Buber's platform; hence the scrutiny in Part I of his major publications, interspersed with biographical data and extracts from his correspondence. (The survey is also intended to be helpful to students unacquainted with Buber.) Once it was established that he was essentially an exponent of Scripture and of the teachings of Hasidism, and that his explicit wish was to communicate a vision of man made perfect, in the image of God, the way led inevitably to the Hebrew Bible for the divine Prototype, and to Hasidism for the ideal of human perfection.

The biblical enquiry of Part II and the subsequent follow-on into Jewish traditional literature are crucial to a proper grasp of Buber's concept of God. In this connection, I would like to reassure specialists that, although not myself an expert Semitist, I have at every moment been able to consult a patient and learned husband, Geza Vermes, who with much generosity—this not being his main field of interest—has answered every question and guided my research into the right channels. Without him, Part II would have been impossible. Nevertheless, the argument developed there and the conclusions at which it arrives are entirely my own responsibility.

Part III deals with Hasidism—more exactly with Hasidism as Buber represents it—and with the neo-Hasidism of his own compositions, chief among them *I and You*. A full summary of this key work is appended. I take the opportunity here to thank Mr Rafael Buber for his permission, communicated through Professor Ernst Simon in a letter dated 9 May 1974, to use my own translation provided it includes no consecutive lengthy excerpts.

Each of these sections will, I trust, contribute to a new understanding of Buber as a guide to the religious life. Or rather, I hope that singly and together they will generate fresh interest and insight into the demands and effects of life lived religiously today.

Oxford
28 October 1979   PAMELA VERMES

Prologue

THE Bretons, Buber wrote in 1924, a year after the publication of *Ich und Du*, believe in a daemonic book known in the vicinity of Quimper as *Ar Vif, The Living One*. It is very big, as tall as a man, and has red pages inscribed with black letters. Yet to those who approach it the letters are at first invisible. To read them, they must struggle with *Ar Vif* and conquer it. Using the word 'real', which occurs again and again in his writings, Buber then comments:

I think every real book is *Ar Vif*. Real readers know this, but real writers know it far better since the writing of a real book is above all danger, fight and conquest. Many lose courage midway, and their script, which began in a reading of the signs of mystery, finishes in the empty letters of their own arbitrariness. In a world rich in books there is but little reality of the mind.[1]

Was he thinking of his own work when he wrote these words? The parallels are in any case apt. *Ich und Du* is short, yet it too can be said to be as big as a man: indeed bigger, for in addition to its insight into human nature it extends to accommodate the mystery known as God. It too asks for an authentic endeavour on the part of a real reader. As for the real writer, it must surely be rare that a man stays as true as Buber did to his 'signs of mystery' once he had read and deciphered them. Everything he wrote after *Ich und Du* is in essence an enlargement of what appears there; and he went on writing for another forty years and more.

Yet when we look to see the effect of this massive effort, which fills four volumes of approximately twelve hundred pages each,[2] we mostly find no more than an often misinformed familiarity with its idiom, one that entails talk of 'the you', 'dialogue', 'meeting', and the like. People are aware that *Ich und Du* in particular constitutes an important

---

[1] Martin Buber, 'Das dämonische Buch', in *Nachlese* (Lambert Schneider, 1965), 23.

[2] Martin Buber, *Werke*, i: *Schriften zur Philosophie* (1962), 1128; *Werke*, ii: *Schriften zur Bibel* (1964), 1235; *Werke*, iii: *Schriften zum Chassidismus* (1963), 1270 (all Kösel–Lambert Schneider); *Der Jude und sein Judentum* (Melzer, 1963), 837; also three volumes of Bible translation in collaboration with Franz Rosenzweig: *Die fünf Bücher der Weisung*, rev. edn. (1956), *Bücher der Kündung*, rev. edn. (1966), *Bücher der Geschichte*, rev. edn. (1956); and one translated by Buber alone: *Die Schriftwerke*, rev. edn. (1962), all published by Jakob Hegner.

contemporary landmark in the progress of religious thought, but so far, only their peripheries have been stirred. Buber's lesson, and lessons, in the life of dialogue have as yet certainly not gripped on any large scale what he would call the 'whole man'.

Obstacles undeniably exist to the understanding of *Ich und Du*. The German language seems for some reason to lend itself readily to translation into clumsy and impenetrable English. But if, in addition, translators have to cope with neologisms, and a terminology purposely chosen to suit the work before them, the likelihood is not only that they will fail to find the correct English equivalent for a given term, but also that the one they select will not be used consistently throughout. On both counts, great damage can be done to Buber, for whom the right word and the right use of language was all-important.

One of the most obvious examples of the misinterpretation that can ensue from lax translation is the English title, *I and Thou*.[3] If, as is usually the case, one assumes from it that the book is concerned with 'I' and 'God', a crucial part of its thesis is sabotaged before even the first page is turned. The German word *du* is a pronoun in the mouth and mind of *ich* expressing closeness and intimacy and is applicable to everything—every thing, creature, and person addressed, God included. Thus *Ich und Du* conveys the idea of a certain kind of relation in itself. It was certainly not intended to refer to relation between 'I' and 'God' as distinguished from relation between 'I' and the rest.

Again, *du* is inseparable from *ich*. *Du* is thought, felt, and uttered by *ich*. *Du* has no existence in itself except as it issues from *ich*. '*Thou*', by contrast, with its archaism and by now exclusive association with the Deity, has very largely lost its pronominal character and can almost be said to stand in independence of 'I' as another divine Name. This is in direct conflict with Buber's pointer to him who is beyond every name by which God is known, to him who for us can be only *You*, the everlasting *You* of perfect *I–You* relation.

I take this opportunity to mention that in the present book, and disregarding the fact that *Ich und Du* has been known in English as *I and Thou* for at least the last forty years, it will be referred to throughout as *I and You*. I hope this will cause no confusion, but '*thou*' would be quite out of place here, and anyway, a start has to be made somewhere in getting rid of this anachronism.

[3] Walter Kaufmann's version of *Ich und Du* (Scribner, 1970; T. & T. Clark, 1971) introduces the correct form into the text but unaccountably retains the inaccurate translation for the title: *I and Thou*.

Another possible barrier to understanding may be the *I–you* jargon
which Buber employs—*'I–it'*, *'it-world'*, *'you-world'*, *'you-saying'*, etc.
Some readers, as we have said, take to it, and flourish it from then on
as evidence of their own sagacity. Others tend to be antagonized by it,
and even frightened off. If they were to persevere, they would quickly
become used to these contractions and would appreciate that, without
them, the text would become bogged down in most tedious repetition.

On the whole, these are petty hindrances rather than genuine difficulties. The real stumbling-block to comprehension in a first encounter with *I and You* is probably the terseness of its construction.[4] It
is as though Buber wrote it under pressure, like a dream pinned down
before the memory fades. The beginning is there, and the end, and all
the main points from one to the other. But the very fact that he was
able to continue elaborating on them for so long proves how much is
left unsaid in that initial breakthrough.

This is not to imply that *I and You* cannot stand alone, and that it is
useless to attempt a struggle with this *Ar Vif* of our age unless one is
also prepared to embark on a wider study of Buber's writings. It is a
seminal work and, as such, able of and by itself to move the mind and
awaken new ideas. At the same time, it is also true that without taking
into account the rest of his publications, we cannot hope properly to
grasp what he meant by his 'new answer to everything',[5] as he himself
described it, and may even be led, as has happened frequently already,
to conclusions quite foreign to him.

Without this longer and wider perspective, that is to say, the hurdles
of language and style may be cleared yet the book may still not bring
home Buber's own message. It may be seen that it draws attention to a
basic dichotomy of attitude towards life roughly translatable as relation
and irrelation. It may be realized that it postulates a readiness for
relation and a capacity for exclusive love as the *sine qua non* of human
health and effectiveness. It may be understood that according to
Buber, the disappointment resulting from the transience of loving
encounter, the high peak of relation, leads to a longing for a *you* that is
everlasting, one never by nature capable of withdrawing to the remoteness and separateness into which every other *you* inevitably, even
though intermittently, fades. The whole scheme may, in short, be
appreciated as a life of dialogue conducted, not only with what may be

[4] Kaufmann finds on the contrary that the style of *Ich und Du* 'is anything but sparse
and unpretentious, lean or economical': *I and Thou*, 24.

[5] Hans Kohn, *Martin Buber: sein Werk und seine Zeit*, 3rd edn. (Melzer, 1961), 310.

seen and heard in the world, but through it, with a supreme *Vis-à-Vis* simultaneously in and beyond it. But then, having absorbed the ideas and been stimulated by them, the reader will very likely return *I and You* to the shelf where it will be, not forgotten perhaps, but gradually overlaid by other ideas of other thinkers.

Why should this be?

Because no true contact has taken place between himself as a 'real reader' and the 'real writer'.

In one of Buber's Hasidic tales, two Talmud students come to their rabbi complaining of confusion. How can they possibly learn anything, they grumble, when one teacher, Abaye, says one thing, and another, Raba, says the opposite? The rabbi answers: 'Whoever wishes to understand the words of Abaye, must first bind his soul to the soul of Abaye. He will then learn the words in their truth as Abaye utters them. And if he then wishes to understand the words of Raba, he must bind his soul to the soul of Raba.'[6] This was, of course, all well and good for the Talmud students, who knew in which direction to look for the souls of Abaye and Raba. In the case of Buber, the matter is not so simple. For the point is this. The level on which he chose to express his thoughts in *I and You* is that of a sort of no-man's-land of philosophy-cum-sociology-cum-psychology-cum-anthropology, one that in itself gives little indication of his soul's true place.

In this connection, the Jewish reader acquainted with the literature and history of his people is naturally at an advantage as compared with his non-Jewish counterpart in that he will have heard of Buber as a great contemporary Jewish figure and will know of his links with the Bible and Hasidism. At the same time, he can also be at a disadvantage. One of the most important prerequisites to understanding is an absence of bias, and Buber, with his not uncritical attitude towards institutional religion, his frequently unpopular views on the politics of Israel, and his refusal to judge the German nation as a whole for the atrocities committed by the Nazis, has by no means endeared himself to all his compatriots and co-religionists.

These particular considerations may carry no great weight among Christian readers, but it should not be inferred for that reason that they are innocent of prejudice compared with Jews. Theirs is of a different and even opposite kind inasmuch as Buber has appealed to them because of his admiration of Jesus of Nazareth, and in their

[6] *Werke*, iii. 207–8; Martin Buber, *Tales of the Hasidim: Early Masters*, trans. Olga Marx (Schocken Books, 1947), 91.

gratitude for this rare Jewish testimony to the stature of their Lord they have tended to overlook the sharp distinction Buber has always made between Jesus' teaching and that of the church. Theirs is a bias towards sympathy, which, if it is based on the assumption that Buber was a crypto-Christian, will dispose them towards no closer contact with him than an inclination towards straightforward antipathy.

How then can we achieve this binding of souls of which the rabbi speaks?

Primarily by establishing his soul's situation. We have to find out where Buber stood, what was his platform. Was he a mystic? A prophet? An existentialist philosopher? A Hebrew humanist? A philosophical anthropologist? Each of these roles, and many more, has been assigned to him at one time or another.

We cannot bind our souls to his, in the sense the rabbi intended, until we know the place he occupied. But once we do, we shall be able, if we wish, to take our stand there beside him and hear his words 'in their truth'. It will be possible, if that is what we want, to discern what, essentially, he is saying to the world of today.

PART I
IN SEARCH OF THE REAL BUBER

I

Formative Encounters (1878–1903)

'THE thought that I should say, this is what I am, disturbs me. I do not have that sort of relation to myself. Will you understand what I say if I tell you that I take no interest in myself?'[1]

The current vogue of exhibitionism among autobiographers was not favoured by Buber. He assumed that his interest to thinking men and women must lie in his work and in whatever was associated with its production. The rest was his own business entirely. If people wanted to know about him, they were to look into his publications and, for more intimate glimpses, to burrow no further than the limit he himself had set. Although a fluent and easy writer, he rejected any suggestion that he should reveal the shadows and brightnesses of his adult life in terms of its private loves, disappointments, pleasures, joy, and relationships. Instead, he composed seventeen anecdotes, each with a bearing on what he considered to be causes and sources of his developed religious and philosophical outlook. He then added the briefest of appendices and published the lot in 1960 as a booklet under the title, *Begegnung: Autobiographische Fragmente.*[2] His aim, he said, was to present not a life-story, but only 'an account of moments arising in my memory which may have had a decisive influence on the manner and direction of my thought'.[3] As it happens, we can now also turn to the three large volumes of correspondence which appeared between 1972 and 1975.[4] These letters, selected from a mass of papers kept in the

[1] Letter from Martin Buber to Maurice Friedman of 11 August 1951, *Briefwechsel aus sieben Jahrzehnten*, ed. Grete Schaeder, 3 vols. (Lambert Schneider, 1972–5), iii. no. 236.

[2] Martin Buber, *Begegnung: Autobiographische Fragmente* (Kohlhammer, 1960); published in English as *Meetings*, ed. Maurice Friedman (Open Court, 1973). Here, the subtitle has been omitted and the singular, *Begegnung*, changed to the plural. In P. A. Schilpp and M. Friedman, eds., *The Philosophy of Martin Buber* (Open Court, Library of Living Philosophers, 1967), the title is dropped, and the same piece is named by its subtitle alone, 'Autobiographical Fragments'.

[3] *Begegnung*, 5; see *Meetings*, 17.

[4] *Briefwechsel*, i (1972), 606; ii (1973), 722; iii (1975), 720.

Jewish National and University Library in Jerusalem, undeniably leave us more knowledgeable than we would otherwise have been concerning Buber's opinions, friendships, and career, but the same reserve rules here as elsewhere and everything judged too personal has been omitted, at the request either of his family or of his surviving correspondents.[5]

There is therefore little choice but to make do with what information we have: the autobiographical pointers provided by himself, whatever of relevance has been allowed to remain in the published letters, the admirable discussion of his life and work (until 1928) by his younger contemporary Hans Kohn, first issued in 1930 and not yet translated into English, but brought up to date in a third German edition by Robert Weltsch in 1961,[6] and, first and foremost, the substance of his own principal writings. For our present purpose, these sources are in fact all we need.

———

Martin Mordechai Buber was born in Vienna in 1878, the son of Carl Buber, and grandson of Solomon Buber, the celebrated Hebraist, and the latter's capable and gifted wife, Adele. For a reason so far unexplained, the marriage between Carl and his wife soon collapsed, and their only child was taken at an early age to live with his grandparents in Lwów, at that time the capital of the Austrian province of Galicia and called Lemberg.

Solomon Buber, besides being a scholar, was a landowner, a corn-merchant, and the owner of a phosphorus mine. He was one of the leaders of the local Jewish community, but also a prominent member of the larger non-Jewish commercial fraternity. In both these roles he performed his honorary duties conscientiously.

Adele exerted a particularly lasting influence on the young boy. A woman of character and intelligence, her efficiency was such that her husband was able to leave his business affairs in her hands and feel free to concentrate on his studies and writing. Yet in spite of her practicality, Adele was not without intellectual interests of her own. Her passion was for books and language. She had educated her two sons, Buber tells us, to use words accurately and in such a way that

[5] Needless to say, a large body of most interesting recollections has been published over the years by Buber's friends and opponents alike, but although they help to round out our image of him, none of them penetrates to any great depth into his character.

[6] Hans Kohn, *Martin Buber: sein Werk und seine Zeit*, 3rd edn. (Josef Melzer, 1961).

they needed no paraphrase. She did the same for him, with the result that before he was fourteen years old, when he moved out of his grandparents' house into that of his father and stepmother, he had discovered 'what it meant really to say something'. When his grandmother spoke to people, she 'really spoke' to them. 'My grandfather', he recalls, 'was a true philologist, a "lover of the word"; but my grandmother's love for the genuine word influenced me even more strongly than his, because that love was so direct and so devout.'[7]

All in all, the family environment was materially comfortable, enlightened, and stimulating, and Buber obviously looks back on these years with pleasure and affection. He nevertheless admits that they were also penetrated by an enormous sense of loss. Solomon and Adele never referred to his mother in his presence,[8] and although the little boy expected her to come for him at any minute, he dared not ask them about her. Then one day—he was four years old—he was told by an older girl in charge of him that his mother would never come back at all. The painful shock of that moment stayed with him throughout his childhood, and, one might venture to guess, throughout his life, but he accepted the truth of what the girl had said and from then on waited for his mother no longer. He suffered from her absence, though, and later invented a word, *Vergegnung* (mis-encounter?), to describe an encounter which should happen between one person and another, but does not. 'I suspect', he commented in his old age, 'that everything I experienced of genuine encounter during the course of my life had its origin in that moment on the balcony.'[9]

Carl was another member of the family who left an enduring mark. No scholar, as is plain in his letters to his successful son many years later, Buber's father was a farmer whose central concern was for fertilizers, breeding-stock, corn, and the like. He was a kind and simple man who not only involved himself in the troubles and happiness of the people around him but was also bound in a special relation to his animals and even to the crops which he grew. He would greet

[7] *Begegnung*, 6–8; *Meetings*, 19–20.
[8] In the context of Buber's own reserve, it is interesting to note that he describes both his grandparents as being disinclined to discuss things relating to their own lives.
[9] *Begegnung*, 16; *Meetings*, 18–19.

his horses one after another, 'not just in a friendly way, but really personally'. Buber also remembers him stepping from his car to bend over the ears of corn, consider them carefully, and test the grain between his teeth. 'For this wholly sentimental and wholly unromantic man, it was a matter of genuine human contact with nature, an active and responsible contact. The growing boy learnt something, as he accompanied him on his way, undiscovered in any of the many writers he had read.'[10] Is one not reminded of Adele here? Where she 'really spoke' to people, her son communicated 'really personally' with nature as well.

———

An experience of a very different sort, but equally important, must not be allowed to pass unmentioned. It was Carl who first introduced the boy to Hasidism by taking him to visit a community at Sadagora, a 'dirty little town' not far from a Buber estate in Bukovina. The great age of the *zaddikim*, the saintly Hasidic teachers, might have passed, and their high spirituality might no longer be what it was in the eighteenth and early nineteenth centuries, but as Buber recalled it, a 'shudder of deep awe' still gripped the pious community when the *rebbe* rose to speak. Young as he was, he was deeply moved by this reverence, and just as he had arrived at a general idea of *Vergegnung* from the personal experience of his loss of his mother, so—as a child and not as an adult—he reasoned to himself that this must be what the world was really all about. It had to do with the upright man, the perfect man, the *zaddik*.[11]

———

Buber was taught at home until he was ten, and afterwards attended the Franz-Josef-Gymnasium at Lwów, where instruction, and communication in general, was in Polish (the family language was German). At fourteen, his intellectual development was in full spate and he turned his back on the traditional religion of his elders.

At fifteen, precocious boy that he must have been, he was wrestling with Kant's *Prolegomena*, and specifically with the philosopher's proposition that time and space have no existence in themselves but are 'mere forms of our sensory perception'.

At seventeen, he was absorbed in Nietzsche's contention that time is

———

[10] *Begegnung*, 11; *Meetings*, 22.   [11] See *Begegnung*, 28–9; *Meetings*, 38.

an everlasting return of the same thing, an endless sequence of endless continua resembling each other in all things, so that their final phases overflow into their beginnings.

Without a doubt, Buber's early years were fortunate. He was not even subjected to the humiliations of anti-Semitism. He was obliged to be present at his school's daily Catholic devotions, but no one tried to make him take part in them or to convert him. His teachers were tolerant, or wished to appear so, and black though it was, the only real shadow to fall across his path was, as has been said, the anguish of his mother's apparent dereliction—without which *I and You* might perhaps never have come into being.

The year 1896 saw the metamorphosis of the eighteen-year-old schoolboy into a university student. Nominally, his faculty at Vienna was that of philosophy, but he attended lectures on so many other subjects—history of art, literature, psychology, German studies, classical philology, and even economics—that he was clearly quite unsure at this stage of what precisely he needed to know.

It is worth noting, incidentally, that he was also a 'zealous student in the psychiatric clinics'.[12]

Buber's great enthusiasm at this period was however for the theatre, to which he was drawn, one gathers, not so much for the acting as for the joy of hearing the true 'spokenness of language' (*Gesprochenheit der Sprache*).[13]

At twenty, he travelled to Leipzig for a course of study and was there overtaken by his next great love, the music of Johann Sebastian Bach. We are not told why or how this happened but only that in some indefinable way it affected him radically. He has tried to illustrate this. He had given a lecture on Ferdinand Lassalle, portraying him as a hero after the model of Carlyle. When someone subsequently congratulated him on depicting Lassalle as he really was, Buber was at first pleased, but later realized that the image he had conveyed was in fact untrue. Disgusted with himself, he struggled for days to re-cast it. Of Bach's part in all this, he reports simply: 'Slowly, timidly and

---

[12] Kohn, *Martin Buber*, 25.   [13] *Begegnung*, 21; *Meetings*, 31.

perseveringly, my insight grew into the reality of human existence and into the difficulty of doing it justice. Bach helped me.'[14]

———

The year in which Buber succumbed to the spell of Bach also saw him make his initial major step towards maturity: he joined the Zionist movement newly founded by Theodor Herzl and thereby re-embraced the Jewishness abandoned in his adolescence. He was still not concerned with its religious aspect. Zionism for him was primarily a vehicle for the renewal of Hebrew and of Jewish and Yiddish culture in general. Intoxicated with the rediscovery of his own inheritance, he threw himself into speaking and writing on Jewish themes—on Jewish authors, Jewish theatre, Jewish poets, Jewish painters, Jewish folklore and legend, everything in effect that had to do with Jewish artistic creativity. The material he and his friends collected and published at that time now seems rather poor stuff, but it was primarily as a result of their efforts that the unsophisticated Jewishness of eastern Europe was introduced to the intellectually advanced Jews of Germany and Austria.

———

In 1899, when he was still only twenty-one, Buber made a second fateful choice. He met and shortly afterwards married a Gentile girl from Munich by the name of Paula Winkler.

Paula, who acquired a reputation of her own as a writer and poet under the pseudonym of Georg Munk, was of inestimable value to her husband at the start of his career, and doubtless during all his life, though again, we know little detail of their relationship. Her letters to him in this early period are in any case outstanding for their good judgement, and her advice to him is surprisingly sound for such a young woman (she was a year older than he). She responded moreover to another of Buber's needs, as is evident from a message he sent her in 1901 during a spell of depression. He was, he told her, making a stand 'against all my unease, all my anxieties, all my knowledge, all my deprivation, all that desires to subjugate me. Every moment.' Her letters alone gave him strength. 'Everything else is too interwoven with anxiety and restlessness. Your letters are absolutely the only thing. Besides them, the thought, perhaps, that there is a mother in you, the belief that there is. Now I know: I have always and always looked for my mother . . .'[15]

[14] *Begegnung*, 23; *Meetings*, 33.   [15] *Briefwechsel*, 25 October 1901, no. 28.

In the field of work, we find him sending her rough outlines of translations and monographs with the demand that she should polish them for him, or even re-write them entirely if she should think fit.

I shall write to you again this evening. But now whilst the post-office is open, I am sending two manuscripts, 'Die Wanderschaft' and 'Die Fische', with the request that you improve both. 'Die Wanderschaft' is a bit too colourless; naturally, that has to do with the material but perhaps you will be able really to *renew* the story . . . With the fishes . . . whether you can make something of it, brighten it, lift it up, let your own nature flow into the narrow-minded stuff, I leave it to you to decide. Tell me your opinion by return, and what you wish to do, and can do, and do it please as quickly as you know how.[16]

Paula would seem, above all, to have brought her husband down to earth when he threatened to lose touch with reality. Simply by being herself, she helped him to distinguish true from false, real from unreal. 'You made me see,' he wrote of her in a poem composed on his fiftieth birthday.

> Made me see? You merely lived,
> You element and woman,
> Soul and nature.[17]

———

Buber's dedication to his own concept of Zionism eventually led him and some of his friends to oppose the movement's authoritarian leadership. Their aims were quite uncongenial to Herzl, who knew little and cared less either about Hebrew or about Judaism in its intellectual and spiritual manifestations. His one dream was to establish a homeland for the Jews. A couple of years later, another row developed, caused mainly by the keen criticism, endorsed by Buber and his colleagues, of a novel by Herzl flagrantly contradicting the Zionist ideals held to be basic by those who disagreed with him. Herzl's resentment led to some strong written exchanges between Buber and himself, in which each gave as good as he received.[18]

[16] ibid., December 1906, no. 110.
[17] Du wirktest dass ich schaue.
  Wirktest? du lebtest nur,
  Du Element und Fraue,
  Seele und Natur!
'Am Tag der Rückschau, 8 Februar 1928', in *Nachlese* (Lambert Schneider, 1965), 25.
[18] *Altneuland*. See *Briefwechsel*, i, p. 192, n. 2.

Shortly afterwards, the younger man retired from active participation in Zionist work, though not for these reasons.

———

Buber chose his early reminiscences so that they would be seen to prefigure his developed thought. Encounter and absence of encounter, 'really' speaking to people and 'really' communicating with nature, the *zaddik* of Sadagora, the idea of reality, preoccupation with the significance of time—all the anecdotes included were meant to throw light on the life of dialogue as it is expounded in *I and You*. From another viewpoint, however, the whole of his life and experience until this stage can also be regarded as leading to a certain moment which preceded the publication of that book by some nineteen or twenty years.[19] I have in mind the hour, after all the years of indifference, of his sudden understanding of the religiousness of Judaism, and specifically of its ancient belief that man is made in the likeness of God.

This was the first of Buber's most notable intuitions. (The second, which occurred to him much later, concerned the nature of the divine Prototype in whose image he believed the perfect man to be made.) The story must be told in his own words.

One day, I opened a little book entitled *Zevaath Ribesh: The Testament of Rabbi Israel Baalshem*,[20] and the words flashed out at me: 'Let him thoroughly grasp the attribute of ardour. Let him rise ardently from his sleep, for he is become holy and is another man and is worthy to beget,[21] and is become in accordance with the attribute of the Holy One, blessed be he, when he engendered worlds.' It was then that, instantly overwhelmed, I came to understand the Hasidic soul. I discerned that most ancient of Jewish insights flowing in the darkness of exile into newly-conscious expression: man's likeness to God as deed, as becoming, as task. And this most Jewish notion was a most human one, the content of most human religiousness. It was then that I began to understand Judaism as religiousness, as piety, as *hasidut*. The image of my childhood, the memory of the *zaddik* and his community, arose and enlightened me. I perceived the idea of the perfect man. Immediately, I was aware of the call to proclaim it to the world.[22]

[19] Though not the writing: the first draft of *Ich und Du* dates back to 1917.
[20] The founder of Hasidism, 1700–60.
[21] *Zeugen* means 'to beget, to procreate', but also 'to bear witness, to testify'. This is probably a pun. No similar dual significance is attached to *erzeugen*, 'to engender, to procreate', the verb applied here to God.
[22] Martin Buber, *Werke*, 3 vols. (Kösel–Lambert Schneider, 1962–4), iii. 967–8; Martin Buber, *Hasidism and Modern Man*, trans. M. Friedman (Horizon, 1958), 59.

2

Early Writings (1904–1923)

DEEPLY and permanently affected by the words from the *Testament* of the Baal Shem, Buber, 'began', as he says, at this time (1903–4) to understand Judaism as religiousness, piety, or *hasidut*. Grasping the germ of true religion as a deed to be done, a task to be discharged, as something to be brought into being by man in imitation of the one supreme Doer and Creator in whose likeness he is made, he responded to the summons of Rabbi Israel ben Eliezer and straightaway gave himself over to a study of Hasidism. From being concerned with Judaism in terms of art, literature, folklore, history, and language, he directed all his energies during the next five years to collecting all the Hasidic literary material he could lay his hands on. Increasingly convinced that the secret of true spirituality and sanity lay in the religious ideals and practices of the Hasidic communities, he applied himself to reformulating Hasidic doctrine for the benefit of the sophisticated Jewry of western Europe, but also—a great novelty—for the non-Jewish world.

It was a momentous *teshuvah* on Buber's part,[1] a 'turning' from an abstract and fairly detached concern with Jewishness to an involvement of himself with the God of his childhood. Nor was this all, for Buber's re-encounter with Judaism as religiousness also entailed a jump into the deep end of religion itself. In effect, the feverishness of his early preoccupation with Hasidism went hand in hand with an equally absorbing curiosity concerning mysticism in general. Mystics and their relation with God became of enormous importance to him. He was already planning in 1903 an anthology of Christian and Jewish mystical writings.[2] It did not appear, in the event, until six years later, and even then not in the shape originally planned; but the fact remains that for a relatively brief time Buber was strongly drawn to everything mystical

---

[1] See J. Petuchowski, 'The Concept of Teshuvah', *Judaism*, 17 (1968), 179.

[2] See Buber's letter to Gustav Landauer, *Briefwechsel aus sieben Jahrzehnten*, ed. Grete Schaeder, 3 vols. (Lambert Schneider, 1972–5), i, no. 48.

and found the outpourings of Sufi, Chinese, Christian, Hindu, and Jewish mystics perfectly acceptable.

This interest would no doubt explain why one of the first of his Hasidic publications, *The Tales of Rabbi Nahman*,[3] turns around a man whom Buber himself describes as perhaps the last of the Jewish mystics, and why in a foreword to *The Tales* he does not hesitate to present Hasidism as the 'last and highest development of Jewish mysticism'. Later, he tones down the mystical aspect of Hasidism, admitting that his early enthusiasm led him to re-tell Hasidic legends rather too freely and to read into them qualities they do not have. He corrects this bias, we are told, in his *Tales of the Hasidim*.[4]

Rabbi Nahman's mystical imaginings were mainly focused on the land of Israel, which he had visited at the cost of much discomfort in 1798. Israel is the place of the creation of this world, he held, and that of the world to come, in which all shall be good. It is the place of the spirit of life. It is where the world will be renewed out of that same spirit. Joy and perfect wisdom are there. The perfect music of the world is there. The bond between heaven and earth is there, and the unity of the world to come is to derive from there. Even the resurrection of the dead is to occur there, so the perfect grave is also there.

Such were Rabbi Nahman's mystical notions concerning Israel. But his lively intelligence must also have appealed to Buber, as well as his great love for the countryside and for animals.

In 1908, another book of legends was ready, with this time the Baalshem himself as the principal figure.[5] Again, the portrait of the founder of Hasidism is coloured to match Buber's mood at that time, and the man at the centre of these assembled tales of miracles and strange unearthly happenings differs somewhat from the 'real' teacher of 'real' life as Buber depicts him in after years. We meet him then as a powerful spiritual guide whose main distinction was that, after spending many years in the study and contemplation of the Bible and the method of mystical interpretation of Scripture known as kabbalah, he managed to construct a synthesis of doctrine and ethics applicable

[3] Martin Buber, *Die Geschichten des Rabbi Nachman, ihm nacherzählt von Martin Buber* (Rütten und Loening, 1906); published in English as *The Tales of Rabbi Nahman* (Souvenir, 1974).

[4] Martin Buber, *Die Chassidischen Bücher* (Schocken, 1927); published in English as *Tales of the Hasidim: The Early Masters* (1947), *The Later Masters* (1948), trans. Olga Marx (Schocken).

[5] Martin Buber, *Die Legende des Baal Schem* (Rütten und Loening, 1908); published in English as *The Legend of the Baal-Shem* (East and West Library, 1956).

to ordinary Jewish people earning a livelihood in their various trades in the villages and towns of Poland and the Ukraine. This was an unprecedented advance as far as an interest in the religiousness of the common man was concerned. Kabbalism until then had been closed to him. Concentrated purely on an esoteric manipulation of the words and sentences of the biblical text, and even on single letters, its aim had been to explore Scripture for hidden meanings. The kabbalist had removed himself as far as possible from the actualities and claims of everyday existence and directed all his attention to a system of extraordinary and fantastic complexity involving symbols, figures, numbers, and names.

The Baalshem's contribution to Jewish spirituality was that he broke with this pattern and with the tradition of separation from the 'world'. He rejected the pretensions of kabbalist intellectual endeavours devoid of any bearing on present existence but supposed to be meritorious simply in themselves. On the other hand, he preserved and breathed new life into kabbalist teachings which he knew would help his poor, insecure, and hard-pressed fellow-Jews by elevating their dignity as persons and by investing everything in their lives with a religious significance which even the most ignorant among them was able to understand and appreciate.

Little of this emerges from *The Legend of the Baal-Shem*, but it is well even at this early stage to have some idea of the character of the Besht as Buber eventually projects it.[6] For however much he may have enjoyed during these years an aspect of Hasidism about which he later preferred to remain quiet, he knew even then the real nature of the author of the *Tzeva'at Ribesh*.

Not everyone, by the way, was pleased with the way in which Buber's mind was moving at the start of his career. His father, simple and down to earth, was worried and disturbed. 'Dear Martin,' he wrote in February 1908,

accept for your birthday my most heartfelt wishes for your happiness; may your work from now on bring you the desired success and your life be free from worry and care.

I should be glad if you would drop the Hasidic and Zohar[7] business, which only ravages the mind and has an unhealthy effect, and it is a shame to use your

---

[6] The name Besht is a contraction of *Baal Shem Tov*. Similarly, *Tzeva'at Ribesh* = Testament of *Rabbi Israel Baal Shem*.

[7] The Zohar is a mystical commentary on the Pentateuch by the Spanish kabbalist Moses de Leon (d. 1305).

abilities and to spend so much work and time on such a fruitless theme, useless in itself and to the world . . .[8]

The Jewish farmer from Lemberg would have approved still less of Buber's *Ekstatische Konfessionen*, published a year later,[9] but maybe they were never shown to him. The principal reaction of the *Buberkenner*[10] to this collection of writings of ecstatics—some of them Hasidim but many of them Christian, especially Christian ladies, e.g. Mechtild von Magdeburg, Saint Hildegard, Adelheid Langmann, Jeanne Marie Guyon, and our own Julian of Norwich, but not forgetting also figures from other faiths such as Lao-Tse, Ramakrishna, Plotinus, etc.—is that, with the two books of legends, it represents an extraordinary difference of spirit compared with that of the productions of Buber's maturity. Eventually, he renounced mysticism and its search for union with God, but there is no point in denying that his first steps back to religiousness, when he 'began' to understand what it was all about, were made in the company of mystics of many persuasions. More importantly, they helped him. In fact, one or two of the personalities to whom he felt particularly close at this time continued to influence his outlook, chief among them the illuminating medieval German mystic, Meister Eckhart (*c.*1260–1327).

——

Strangely, Buber's original work on his return to public life in 1909 bears little resemblance to the re-writings he had been engaged on, and few signs, if any, of the spiritually exotic or whimsical. On the contrary, the talks he composed at the invitation of the Jewish student society of Prague University, the Bar Kochba Verein, are addresses worthy of any thoughtful and intelligent rabbi (which of course Buber was not). Yet if one listens to them attentively (and to his next work *Daniel*), one can hear him as it were tuning *up* his literary instruments of style and language, and, more significantly, tuning *in* to the major themes which will dominate his thinking for another fifty years and more.

Still reflecting the impression made on him by the call of the Baalshem, he uses his three addresses on Judaism, *Drei Reden über das*

[8] *Briefwechsel*, i, no. 124.

[9] Martin Buber, *Ekstatische Konfessionen* (Eugen Diederichs, 1909).

[10] *Buberkenner* means, literally, 'Buber-knower': i.e. Buber specialist, Buber student.

Judentum,[11] to hammer home the notions of renewal, deed, task, and becoming another man, and to stress, first and foremost, the ancient and traditional Jewish idea of unity, of the 'one'.

The first talk, 'Judaism and the Jews', deals with inner integrity. Do we call ourselves Jews because our ancestors did, or because we really and truly are Jews? Is there such a thing nowadays as genuine Jewish religiousness? The answer suggested is that, living in an environment at variance with his inner nature and tradition, the Jew is prey to a duality which tears him apart. To achieve personal integrity, he must choose between the claims made on him. He must become one person in face of the world in which he lives.

Carrying the notion of unity further, the next address, 'Judaism and Mankind', points out that integrity is necessary, not only *vis-à-vis* one's surroundings, but also in one's inner self. Jewish literature and history abound in characters in whom purest sincerity cohabits with deceit, grandest self-sacrifice with self-seeking. As Jakob Wasserman had written: 'This is certain: an actor or a sincere man, one capable of beauty and yet ugly, lustful and ascetic, a charlatan, a dice-player, a fanatic or a craven slave—a Jew is all this.'[12] Yet no people had fought more magnificently than the Jew for personal unity, for the unity of person and nation, of nation and nation, of mankind and all living beings, of God and the world. His God had himself

emerged from the struggle for unity, from a dark passionate struggle for unity. He was not inferred from nature but from the subject. The believing Jew 'asked not after heaven and earth if only he had him' . . . because he had not created him out of reality but out of longing, because he had not seen him in heaven and earth but had raised him up as unity over his own duality, as healing over his own injury. The believing Jew . . . found his unity in his God; he saved himself in him in that mystical time, that time of childhood, of original still undivided existence when, as Job says (29: 4), *God's understanding was over my tent*; he saved himself in him in that future messianic time of reunification; he *redeemed* himself in him from all duality.[13]

Redemption from duality is a Jewish idea, and the Jew's ability to fulfil his duty to mankind depends on his ability to achieve it. Unified, he can offer to the world ever-fresh possibilities of synthesis. At the time of the prophets, and of early Christianity, he presented it with a

---

[11] Martin Buber, *Drei Rede über das Judentum* (Rütten und Loening, 1911); also *Der Jude und sein Judentum* (Melzer, 1963), 4–46.

[12] Buber, *Der Jude*, 19.   [13] Ibid. 22–3.

religious synthesis; in the age of Spinoza, with a synthesis of ideas; in that of socialism, with a social synthesis. What synthesis is the spirit of Judaism preparing now?

Nowadays a great deal of this specifically Jewish analysis of a Jewish situation seems equally applicable to the non-Jew, but no wonder Buber's student audience was stirred by his words. Reading them, we can understand the feelings of Hans Kohn, himself a member of the Bar Kochba Verein and in later life responsible for an indispensable introduction to Buber's thought.[14] After expressing with some diffidence a few of his doubts and queries, Kohn ends his letter to Buber of 22 September 1911: 'You know, Herr Doktor, what your addresses have meant to us in the Bar Kochba Verein, but I can honestly say that to no one have they meant more than to me, and that in many respects they have become for me in every way a turning-point.'[15]

In the last of this initial group of lectures to the Prague students Buber pleads for a return to the realities of Jewish religious life, one that will transform not only Judaism itself but the world. Quoting Isaiah's words that heaven and earth are to be 'created anew', he insists that Judaism is not to be changed gradually, rejuvenated gradually, perhaps by rationalizing its beliefs or relaxing its observances. It must be caught up root and branch in a total *teshuvah* and altered utterly. Where it is now identified with prophetism and the teaching of unity, it has to make unity, and deed and future, the two concepts dependent on it, a reality.

The Jew's idea of unity, and his tendency towards it, spring from his ability to envisage an association of things more clearly than each thing individually. He is by nature more aware of the wood than of the trees. His idea of deed, and his tendency towards action, arise from the fact that his motor system is superior to that of his senses; his doing is more efficient than his perceiving. In religion, his deed rather than his experience is central. And his idea of the future, and tendency towards it, derive from the fact that his concept of time is stronger than his feeling for space.

If these talents and ideals are translated into reality they will result in a creative synthesis from which a new universalism will spring. But first, the Jew has to renew himself: or rather, the renewal of himself and the coming into being of the new universalism must be one event.

[14] Hans Kohn, *Martin Buber: sein Werk und seine Zeit*, 3rd edn. (Melzer, 1961); as yet unavailable in English.

[15] *Briefwechsel*, i, no. 173.

To conceive unity, the Jew must himself become unified. To prepare
the way for deed, he must realize his own capacities for it. To serve the
future, he must free himself from the attraction of lesser aims and
direct himself towards one great end.

Such is the recipe Buber offers his fellow-Jews in the paper entitled
'The Renewal of Judaism'.

———

Buber's homiletic style, which he favoured prior to *Ich und Du*, continues to be evident in the remaining work of substance to be published
before the outbreak of the First World War. *Daniel*, subtitled *Gespräche
von der Verwirklichung* (Conversations on realization), is an earnest,
romantic, but mercifully short work,[16] quite different in treatment
from both the re-written Hasidic legends and the addresses to the Bar
Kochba Verein, in which we nevertheless meet with some return of the
ecstatic mood of the former.[17] Paradoxically, we also lose sight here of
some of the biblical quality of the latter, Buber now widening his
approach to embrace Greek drama and religion, Hindu mythology,
and, of course, the cult of nature.

The main point to note concerning this book, which takes the form
of conversations between someone called Daniel and five partners, is
that its rather turgid debates mark the stage at which Buber begins to
feel his way out of one concept of Judaism, Hasidism, and mysticism,
into the infinitely more mature outlook eventually expressed in *Ich und
Du*. It would not be useful, but on the contrary confusing, to demonstrate subject by subject how, and in what respect, he modifies his
opinions and beliefs, but one or two small examples may be of interest.
In one of his discourses, Daniel urges his companion to fight free of
the 'many' and to find and follow the 'one direction' intended for her,
one that is not 'over things, nor around things, nor between things, but
in each thing, in the experience of each thing'.[18] If, that is to say, she
stands back from a tree as an observer, she will discover a great deal of
information about it, but she will not get to know it until she identifies
herself with it to the extent that she feels its bark as her own skin, its
roots as her feet, and its cones as her children. By the time the tree

[16] Martin Buber, *Werke*, 3 vols. (Kösel–Lambert Schneider, 1962–4), *Werke*, i. 12–
76; *Daniel: Dialogues on Realization*, trans. M. Friedman (McGraw-Hill, 1965).

[17] Though ecstasy itself is declared a 'false way', and unity is said not to be found by
means of 'unbecoming', *entwerden*. See *Werke*, i. 71.

[18] *Werke*, i. 14.

illustration appears again in *I and You*, these overtones of mystical union have disappeared. 'Experience' has also gone (though it returns later). Nevertheless, it is not difficult to recognize in the new tree parable the marks of Buber's earlier struggle to formulate what he understood as the knowledge that comes from a loving presence of one with the other.

In a discussion of reality and realization, Daniel warns that whoever fails to realize remains himself unreal,[19] an observation that Buber must have liked since he repeats it elsewhere. He then goes on to couple 'realization', by which he means the association of an experience with nothing other than itself, with an opposite which he terms 'orientation', signifying by this the investment of things and persons with qualities, values, and dimensions. Again, these two concepts drop away as a contrasting pair to be replaced by the stands of *I–you* and *I–it*. In fact, 'orientation' more or less vanishes altogether. 'Realization', on the other hand, remains of great importance in Buber's idiom.

Another of Daniel's friends tells him that his life seems no longer to possess any purpose, and that with no meaning to his existence he is afraid as though an abyss had opened up under his feet. Daniel's answer in this case is that if a person strikes out in the direction he believes to be right, and if he tries to experience every event and encounter as authentically as he can, he will become aware that each carries a message for him. The star of 'meaning' will shine always over him. Meaning is not made of planks like Noah's Ark. Meaning is constructed of the elements, like the fiery chariot of Elijah. Daniel does his best to encourage this person, exhorting him:

Danger, danger, danger! Let your motto be God and danger! For danger is the gateway to profound reality, and reality is the supreme reward of life and the everlasting birth of God . . . You have no security in the world but you have direction and meaning. And God who desires to be realized, the God of the daring, is near you always.[20]

The idea of God's 'everlasting birth' is *not* one that Buber discards.

A conversation with yet another companion, ruminating on polarity, is an argument stimulated by a play which they have just seen on the duality of being and anti-being.

The same theme reappears in the fifth and final talk, one that for all the artificiality and uncongeniality of its language contains much that is of abiding value and depth. Here Daniel, recounting how his father

[19] *Werke*, i. 21.   [20] Ibid. 45.

had sent him off alone to a remote village to recover from the death of a dearly loved friend, wishes his friend to know that it was in fact his very loss of joy and hope which saved him. Despair, he insists, 'is the highest of God's emissaries'.[21]

One day, he had woken from sleep on a mountainside and looking for the lake below found that he could not distinguish one thing from another. Everything, light and dark, colour and form, had seemed to him to be one nebulous mass. Indeed, his own body had felt as though buffeted in an ocean of chaos, not as a unity but as a duality, one half of himself being life and the other death. Searching for support, his soul rose up and reached into the world to see if it could find unity there, but all it had discovered was muddle and mixture. Instead, it was his body that had delivered him—by performing the 'simple deed' of assuming the attitude of prayer.

My two arms lifted, my hands folded in towards each other, my fingers interlocked: and the whole horror was spanned over by a God-powerful bridge. My body was unified, the world was unified for me. . . . I realized that I was not cut off. I had pulled down the everlasting walls, *the walls within myself.* From life to death, from the living to the dead, flowed a deep attachment. I could not go to my dead one, nor could he come to me, but we were bound together . . . because I was bound into one within myself. At that hour, Lukas, the teaching came to me, the one teaching needed . . . True unity cannot be found but only done.[22]

Later, Buber will argue that not unity alone, but everything, has to be 'done' if it is to be real and true, but here he confines himself to viewing his unified body as a symbol both of his own inner unity and of his unity with God, and hence with all things, including death and the dead.

———

Poor Carl Buber. Agitated and perplexed once again, though gratified that Martin was meeting with so much acclaim, he wrote to him in June 1913:

I have your dear letter of the first and your 'Daniel', and the proofs of the 'Neue Blätter' have also reached me. Many thanks for the friendly dedication.

We have read the latter with great interest and if the world acknowledges only a part of what Landauer says of your work, you can be very satisfied; it fills us with joy and happiness that your endeavours are having this success.

[21] Ibid. 68.   [22] Ibid. 69–70.

I only fear that the great intellectual work is over-taxing you and would be
content if you would concern yourself with less difficult problems and would
return to lighter work.

I have tried to understand 'Daniel' but have unfortunately not succeeded, and
the thought has even come to me that you are overworking intellectually at the
cost of your physical strength.[23]

Between 1913 and the end of the war, Buber published a few short
works but his activities were mainly journalistic. He wrote for the
Frankfurter Zeitung and specially for Jewish organs. In 1916 he founded
and assumed the editorship of a journal which, as Reinhold Mayer
observes, 'he pointedly and provocatively' called *Der Jude*.[24] Franz
Rosenzweig, who was later to become a close friend, was deeply
impressed by it, as is apparent from the frequent references to it in his
letters, though he could not always resist the temptation to poke fun at
Buber. '*Der Jude*', he wrote once, 'appears to be addressed to the
intellectual, but within it speaks Rabbi Martin Salomonides.'[25]

To those who know something of the tragic story of the Jews in
Germany it will come as no surprise to learn that besides the hat of a
rabbi, Buber wore another kind of headgear in those years—that of a
German patriot. In this, it must be repeated, he was by no means an
exception; it would be only too easy to assemble testaments of love for
Germany and its people published in those days, by some of Jewry's
best-known figures. There is the story, typical and true, of the newly
married orthodox couple from Odessa who travelled to southern Germany for their honeymoon and stayed in a strictly kosher hotel.[26] On
the day war was declared, the hotel-keeper, himself of course a Jew,
marched into the dining-room wearing a spiked helmet and brand-
ishing a flag and ordered the 'enemy aliens' out of the house forthwith.
That Martin Buber, one of the sages of our times, should also be
discovered striking attitudes which now appear tragically foolish must
therefore not depress us unduly. In this respect he was simply a man of
his period and place.

A whiff of the contemporary political atmosphere in Germany is
discernible in a letter written to Buber by a friend named Hermann
Stehr, a poet and freelance writer of roughly his own age, whom he

---

[23] *Briefwechsel*, i, no. 215.

[24] Reinhold Mayer, *Eine Philosophie der dialogischen Erfahrung* (Chr. Kaiser, 1973).

[25] Franz Rosenzweig, *Briefe* (Schocken, 1935), n. 211.

[26] These were the parents of Professor Chaim Rabin.

had known for about nine years and addressed as *du*. Buber had expressed fears that a barrier of some kind had come between himself and Hermann. It is impossible to tell for certain whether he meant the sort of barrier that might arise between Gentile and Jew, but from Stehr's reply, it would seem so. 'My dear Buber,' the latter assured him, 'O no, nothing, not half a trowel of mortar, lies between you and me, between your world and my world . . .'

A lyrical beginning but the best is still to come:

We Germans will conquer, undeniably, and the problem we shall then have to resolve has the dimension of a problem affecting the human race. We must build up mankind as once the Romans ruled over it and the Greeks permeated it. We can do so because we are the one nation for whom the conversion of religious claims into state facts, and the making of the state into a concern of society, is in the blood. We alone have the force to be a true democracy . . . We alone have the maturity to tolerate the separation of church and state because our metaphysics are not an outflow of instinct and because our order results from our inner organization.[27]

How does Buber reply to this awful letter?

Part of his answer has been deleted by the editor of *Briefwechsel*, but his reaction would seem to have been fairly blameless: thank you for your good words which have been taken deeply to heart, what very nice photographs of your children, plus a few vague remarks concerning community, the German nation, and the power of the spirit.[28]

On other occasions, though, he may be heard voicing opinions which in the wake of the Holocaust can only strike us as unfortunate, to say the least. The following passage from one of several addresses published as *Vom Geist des Judentums* is an example.

I would consider the oriental human type identifiable in records of Asian antiquity, as well as in present-day Chinese or Indians or Jews, compared with the western type represented by, say, the Greeks of the age of Pericles or the Italians of the Trecento or the Germans of our age, to be motor as opposed to sensory types.[29]

[27] *Briefwechsel*, i. 259.
[28] Ibid., no. 25. Paul Flohr nevertheless cites an almost equally ill-judged letter by Buber to Stehr condoling with the latter on his son's death at the front. It is not included in *Briefwechsel*. See 'The Road to I and Thou', in *Texts and Responses: Studies Presented to Nahum Glatzer on the occasion of his Seventieth Birthday by his Students* (Brill, 1975), 201–25.
[29] Buber, *Der Jude und sein Judentum*, 47.

Unable to contain himself, Gustav Landauer, the brilliant writer and thinker and a great friend of Buber, raged over the latter's *faux pas*. 'I confess my blood boils when I read how you place "the Germans of our age" . . . side by side with the Greeks of the age of Pericles and the Italians of the Trecento.'[30] Perhaps bravely, Buber did not in this instance remove the offending paragraph, even when the opportunity presented itself. He seems to have said to himself, *quod scripsi scripsi*.[31] But he did delete from the second edition of 1919 a call to the German nation to lead the way towards a *teshuvah* and to institute a new era of understanding with the spirit of the east. Landauer's fury had been enormous. That Buber should represent Germany as the one chosen redeemer-nation! The fact that it had assimilated more fully than the other nations of Europe the socialism of such degenerate Jews as Marx and Lasalle was, on the contrary, a discredit to itself and a tribute to the rest. Accordingly, we find affixed to the new edition: 'I have deleted the sentences at the end of the first address . . . The German nation has not taken on itself the function intended in those sentences and cannot now do so.'

That Buber and many others did not manage to preserve themselves from the Teutonic infection, from which the brave and independent spirit of Gustav Landauer kept itself free, should not be allowed to obscure the fact that Buber's great and overriding interests during this time were not the fortunes or misfortunes of the *Heimat*, but still the many aspects of *teshuvah*, the turning back to God in a life of real religiousness within the person and within the community. He was in fact attacked by Landauer on this point, too, for seeing 'community' as one of the finer outcomes of war itself![32]

A few minor pieces of writing came out just prior to the end of the war and immediately after it, among them 'My Way to Hasidism' and 'The Holy Way',[33] the latter dedicated to the recently assassinated

---

[30] *Briefwechsel*, i, no. 306.

[31] The expression of other such sentiments may be found if one wishes to look for them, e.g. in *Der Jude und sein Judentum*, 303.

[32] Paul Flohr sees in Buber's serious disagreement with Landauer over the meaning and purpose of the war the occasion of a profound change of outlook. It was then, according to Flohr, that Buber turned from his emphasis on *Erlebnis* (experience) to the notion of life as a continuing dialogue. See Flohr, 'The Road to I and Thou'.

[33] In Martin Buber, *Hasidism and Modern Man*, trans. M. Friedman (Horizon, 1958); 'Mein Weg zum Chassidismus', *Werke*, iii. 959–73; '*Der heilige Weg*', in *Der Jude und sein Judentum*, 89–143.

Landauer.[34] But the most fateful event of that period was the renewal of the acquaintance first made in 1914 between Buber and Franz Rosenzweig.

Best reached, perhaps, through his strong, reasoned, and often lengthy letters to his friends, Rosenzweig's mind and outlook would seem on the face of it, despite his interest and enthusiasm, to be not entirely in sympathy with Buber's. Yet as it turned out, the two became the closest of friends and collaborators.

How did their paths come together? Rosenzweig, after serving during the war in the German army, had taken over in 1920 the direction of the Jewish teaching establishment in Frankfurt-am-Main known as the Freies Jüdisches Lehrhaus. His work on his *magnum opus, The Star of Redemption*, was by that time more or less over (it was published in 1921),[35] and the illness which was eventually to kill him had not yet made itself manifest. Buber in his turn was also teaching, but in Frankfurt University, where he was offering a course on ethics and religion.

One afternoon, both Rosenzweigs, Edith and Franz, went over for tea to Heppenheim, the village in the environs of Frankfurt where the Bubers had their house. As Rosenzweig mentions to his friend Rudolf Otto, this was to be his last walk before sclerosis deprived him of the use of his legs. But the background to the visit must be fitted in first.

To celebrate the fiftieth birthday of Nehemia Nobel, the founder of the Lehrhaus, Rosenzweig organized a *Festschrift* in his honour. Ernst Simon had wished Buber to participate despite the fact that he had no great opinion of Nobel, which Simon did not know, and Rosenzweig had also thought it a good idea since Buber's name was bound to give the *Festschrift* greater weight. Buber as a good Zionist complied. For the introductory page, Rosenzweig chose selections from Nobel's curriculum vitae which he had composed as a 25-year-old when applying for a post in Cologne. A final sentence was then added which ran as follows: 'With these words written twenty-five years ago, you have, in the opinion of all of us, defined the essence and task of the rabbinical vocation.' The page was printed and despatched to the signatories. It was a mere formality.

---

[34] 'Ein Wort an die Juden und an die Völker: Dem Freunde GUSTAV LANDAUER aufs Grab.'

[35] Franz Rosenzweig, *Der Stern der Erlösung* (Lambert Schneider, 1921; 3rd edn. 1954); published in English as *The Star of Redemption*, trans. W. W. Hallo (Routledge & Kegan Paul for Littman Library, 1971).

A telegram, however, arrived from Buber: 'Cannot put my signature to the dedication.' Amazed and shocked, Rosenzweig immediately contacted Ernst Simon and with him re-read the page in question. To their great dismay, they discovered that, strictly speaking, at least three-quarters of the names appended, including their own, should not have figured there. Rosenzweig's tribute placed a far higher value on Jewish conservatism than most of the signatories actually believed it to possess. Hastily the piece was re-worded and the new version sent off to Buber. This time, the message came back: 'Agreed.'

Of this episode, Rosenzweig writes that it

was such a terrific symptom of what is great in Buber, whom the whole world thinks is a king in the land of the spirit, but is actually a true king, not also, but only, in his underpants, that I thereupon felt the strongest desire to renew the acquaintance made in the spring of 1914 (also under very remarkable circumstances).

As soon as the Nobel festivities were over, the Rosenzweigs decided to call on Buber. Again, the story must be Rosenzweig's own.

I had not had it in mind to invite him or not invite him to the Lehrhaus. I did not consider the possibility . . . Then in the course of conversation, while we were already at coffee, I suddenly realized that Buber was even intellectually not the mystical subjectivist people imagined him to be, but that even intellectually he had begun to develop into a solid and reasonable person. I was quite thrilled by the great honesty with which he expressed himself. When we came to his Hasidic books, he said he was surprised that in all these years he had only been questioned once about the sources. He was going to add a source index to his new book on the Maggid.[36] Thereby scoring a mark with me. I had always looked for the eastern-Jewish originals of his stories, so far without success . . . He said he would gladly present the sources to a few people, whereat I said I would be able to bring these few people to him . . . It was only on the journey home . . . that I realized it would be cheaper to transport one prophet rather than twenty of his students. And I wrote to him to this effect. I had already told him about the Lehrhaus and even shown him the programme. Whereupon I received the answer that to his great surprise, after years in which refusal had become a matter of course, my proposal had immediately aroused in him a definite feeling of acceptance.

Rosenzweig continues with a revealing portrait of Buber as a member of the Lehrhaus staff.

[36] The Baalshem's pupil, Dov Baer of Mezritch, known as the Great Preacher (Maggid).

It was his first lecture cycle. Till then, he had given only addresses. The peculiar nature of the Lehrhaus fascinated him, the questions, the fact that it was not just a lecture, and more a matter of teaching than of holding forth . . . Buber, precisely because he had understood the Lehrhaus from the beginning as a whole, immediately became one of its pillars, and at that, not the Buber of the past but the developing and future Buber . . . The lectures have demanded quite a big effort of him, and this because he has had to learn for the first time how hard of hearing the public is. Due to his absolute honesty, he is in the very difficult position of having used the paintbrush of Ming so successfully for decades that no one can believe that he no longer speaks as Ming but as Fu, so the words he utters as Fu, as his own mature self, are still misheard as the words of Ming.[37]

Ming, needless to say, was the Buber of the first books on Hasidism, etc. *Daniel*, the *Ecstatic Confessions* and zeal for the mystics. Fu was the Buber of the post-mysticism period.

Hans Kohn has listed the titles of Buber's lecture courses and classes at the Lehrhaus.[38] In 1922, he spoke on 'Religion as Presence'[39] and held classes on Hasidic texts as planned during the Rosenzweig visit to Heppenheim. In 1923 he discussed 'The Primal Forms of Religious Life' (magic, sacrifice, mystery, and prayer) and devoted his classes to 'Witnesses of Religious Life from Eastern Lands and from Judaism to Christianity'. Later in the same year, he chose prayer as the subject of his classes and worked on various psalms. During the first term of 1925, the Baal Shem was the topic of his lectures, and 'The First Sentence of the Bible in Hasidic Interpretation' that of his classes. Other themes followed, such as 'The End of Time', 'The Fourth Book of Ezra', 'The Anonymous Servant of God',

---

[37] Rosenzweig, *Briefe*, 461–3.

[38] Kohn, *Martin Buber*, 362–3.

[39] Buber may at first have wished these lectures to be called 'The Presence of God'. The following letter to him from Rosenzweig is in any case worth noting: 'Sehr verehrter Herr Doktor, I am very satisfied with the theme as you now formulate it. The word "religion" is, I admit, not to my liking because it has become too much of a fox's earth out of which idealistic prevarications fly when one thinks one has already caught the fox and it can no longer escape. But the public, precisely on account of this assurance of multiple exits prefers to venture into the cave of this word rather than into the lion's den without exit (from which tracks lead not out, but only in) of the word "God." So it had best be called, "Religion as Presence", even though it will afterwards in fact be concerned with "The Presence of God"', *Briefwechsel*, ii, no. 72. The lectures are published in full, in German, in Rivka Horwitz, *Buber's Way to 'I and Thou'. An Historical Analysis and the First Publication of Martin Buber's Lectures*, 'Religion als Gegenwart', *Phronesis* 7 (Lambert Schneider, 1978).

and 'The Manifestations of God in Genesis'. And in 1926, to the consternation of many, he collaborated with a Christian pastor, Hermann Schafft, in a debate before his Jewish students on 'Judaism and Christianity'.

Meanwhile, in 1923, *I and You* had appeared.

3

I and You (1923)

I and You is Buber's masterpiece. It is the receptacle into which he pours the learning and wisdom accumulated over the years, and the vessel in which he re-words them to express his own vision of the good life. Everything that he wrote afterwards can be traced back to it. Into it go the teachings of the Baal Shem, themselves drawn from the Hebrew Bible and from kabbalah; out of it flow the notions of relation, encounter, reality, meaning, and unity. Into it go Hasidic and biblical aims, principles, and virtues; out of it comes Buber's 'new answer to everything' in terms of response, responsibility, *I, you*, and the everlasting *You*. Into it go age-old and hallowed Jewish concepts of God, and out of it emerges a new form of the Deity for today and a new perfect man shaped in his image.

The overwhelming impression received in moving forward from Buber's earlier works to *I and You* is that with this book he arrives at maturity. The contrived argument characteristic of *Daniel* is no more. The romantic prolixity has gone. One feels that here Buber has to the best of his ability cleared his mind of its mystical impedimenta and pared his language to the bone (though it still provokes criticism). Possibly, a note of unreality creeps in now and again, as for instance in his speculation on metacosmic movement towards and away from the First Cause and on the reciprocity of relation in certain spheres. But on the whole, those concepts which he retains, and which were formerly somewhat loose and ambivalent, become as it were sensible and related as far as possible to actual human existence.

To judge from the text of the 1922 course of lectures referred to in the previous chapter, which were clearly a run-in for his book, the underlying lesson of *Ich und Du* was intended to do with the Presence of God, and with a representation of religion as an imitation of that Presence. But, more precisely and overtly, *I and You* has for its main topic relation interpreted as a helpful loving presence of one with the other. Or, more exactly still, it points to a pattern of life in which such relation necessarily alternates with irrelation, but in which, ideally, relation habitually takes precedence over its opposite.

Naturally, *I and You* has furnished material for meditation and comment continuously since it first appeared. Its importance to contemporary religious thought has been acknowledged world-wide. The theologians, in particular, have taken it to themselves and continue to this day to ponder heavily over how to assess the everlasting *You* and over the doctrinal nuances of 'word' and 'spirit' in Buber's lexicon. The philosophers have likewise mulled over chosen problems. And certainly, every one of these approaches is legitimate. Nevertheless, compared with Buber's own wide and masterly synthesis, and by comparison with his endeavours to reach into the four corners of life and into the heights and depths of man's spiritual, intellectual, and psychological existence, each seems so small. It is not too much to say that Buber's outlook has relevance to the very future of the world, to the actual continuance of man and the universe. But, so far, few appear to have realized this.

Moreover, if Buber introduces into this grand design relation between man and his Creator, it is important to bear in mind that it is meant to be inalienably and inextricably part of relational life as a whole. In no way is it separate. *You* cannot be uttered authentically in Buber's opinion—in ordinary language, God cannot be genuinely spoken to, prayed to, let alone lived with—until one has learnt to say *you*. And what *you*-saying entails will also receive an explanation of its own in due course.

Another aspect of *I and You* that has been greatly neglected is the *range* of the relational life as Buber envisages it. Mostly, commentators discuss its implications as they affect personal and social relationship, though they are of course specially fascinated by whatever is associated with relation between man and God. Man, in any case, man with man and man with God, occupies the all-important centre of their canvasses where he doesn't fill and even overflow them. Now this is not a correct reflection of what is conveyed in *I and You*. What Buber proposes there as the range of relational life, in which a person moves to and from positions of *I–you* relation to irrelation, reaches on the one extreme into the natural world—animal, vegetable, and even mineral—and, on the other, into the realm of ideas, into the affairs of the mind and the spirit. Furthermore, in pointing to this wide embrace of potential *I–you* relation, Buber has not in mind some kind of sentimental attachment to flowers or dogs, or to poetry, or to knowledge, or to holiness. Implicit in his concept of true relational life is a rigorous standard of loving responsibility, carried out, performed, executed, within the little circle of these relational spheres, as they occur within the little circle of each person's everyday existence. Relation between man and man is merely part of a whole system of relation with these others.

And if, next, such a great and effective armful of response and responsibility can be gathered up and included in a similar relation of response and responsibility to a *You* believed to be at once in and beyond them all—this is perfect relation, this is true religiousness, this is what makes man whole, this is what will save and redeem the world.

Paradoxically, this is at the same time what will save and redeem God's own Presence, Shekhinah, from its exile. But that too calls for another story later on.

In this connection, however, one other general comment is called for concerning *I and You*, namely that Buber's view of the interdependence of God and man admits of the possibility of God's non-existence. Such an acceptance, not so much of doubt as of room for doubt, would have been anathema to the Hasidim he so much admired. For them, it might have been right to confess ignorance of *what* God is, but never to ask themselves *whether* he is. By contrast, Buber (and probably, if the truth be known, most of the religious minds of the present day) was able to confront the hazard of faith, not carelessly and without trepidation, but as belonging by nature to the notion of perfect *I–You* relation. Refusing to commit himself to any doctrinal statement about knowledge of God's existence, he maintained that it is possible, with courage, to dispense with the spurious security that such knowledge brings. He was sure that shouldering the danger inherent in unknowledge, and 'walking in the way' outlined in *I and You*, we can work for the perfection both of ourselves and of our world: in religious terms, make a reality of the Kingdom of God on earth.

———

Nothing can take the place of reading *I and You* for oneself, *in toto*, and preferably in the original German. At the same time, it is probably safe to say that whereas many are interested enough in Buber to take up a book about him, quite a few will not be sufficiently familiar with *I and You* to follow the present exploration of its ideas merely with the help of an abstract such as has been given of his other major works. For the sake of clarity, therefore, and in order to lay bare its essentials, I have taken the liberty of 're-writing' it—not to the extent that Buber himself 're-wrote' his Hasidic material, but simplifying it (I hope) by means of abridgement, paraphrase, and quotation. It is placed at the end of this book as an Appendix in order not to interrupt the flow of the narrative and to avoid irritating readers who will not require it.

4

Bible Translation and Emigration to Palestine (1924–1939)

IF the first major turning-point of Buber's career was the re-identification of himself as a Jew through Zionism, and the second his discovery of Hasidism, the third most important step was his acceptance in 1925 of an invitation by the publisher Lambert Schneider to undertake a new German translation of the Hebrew Bible. He had been asked to do so once before, in 1914, but war had prevented the work from going ahead. Now he agreed, on condition that Franz Rosenzweig would be his collaborator, and after a few false starts the two men were soon deep in the Book of Genesis.

As Rosenzweig was now so gravely paralysed that he was unable to move, Buber used to visit him at his home at regular weekly intervals, taking with him the work done during the previous few days. Together, they would discuss the exact wording of their draft. In his drily humorous way, the younger man analysed their roles in June of that year when there was a question of what his honorarium should be. He told Buber: 'You are the poet, I the muse. Muses, even when milked hardest, do not enter into publishing contracts. That is our muse point of honour.' On further consideration, however, he came to the conclusion that 'my part of the work amounts to more than a sixth and less than a quarter. A fifth therefore.'[1]

The Buber–Rosenzweig translation of the Bible is generally held to be remarkable. In Hans Kohn's opinion, it fully reproduces the original, and in its fidelity furnishes a commentary which repeatedly throws light on profound meaning. 'It cuts an underground passage from the original to the language of the translation. It does not render something found into something found, but wrestles conscientiously with the German language for its uttermost possibilities.'[2] Nevertheless not everyone likes it. Many feel uneasy at the way it forces German into

---

[1] Franz Rosenzweig, *Briefe* (Schocken, 1935), no. 442.
[2] Hans Kohn, *Martin Buber: sein Werk und seine Zeit*, 3rd edn. (Melzer, 1961), 262.

unfamiliar shapes and sounds. As a brief illustration, the Hebrew word *ruah means both wind (Wind)* and spirit *(Geist)*. To Buber and Rosenzweig, *Geist* seemed to have lost the dynamism it originally possessed, so they substituted for it the noun *Braus* (from *brausen* = a roaring, raging, surging, etc.), dividing this again into *Windbraus* and *Geistbraus*. Thus where there is question in the text of spirit as a creative electrifying power coming from God, the word chosen is *Geistbraus*; and where the allusion is to a natural event, but one caused from above, one in which the creative *Braus* is at work, the word used is *Windbraus*. Where wind pure and simple is intended, *ruah* is translated into German as plain *Wind*.[3]

Another principle governing the Buber–Rosenzweig Bible is that since it was first meant to appeal to the ear as well as to the eye, the German text should also be adapted for recitation aloud. Hence the 'breath measures': i.e. no sentence is so long that it requires a fresh inhalation on the part of the reader.

Other novel features aimed at reflecting the characteristics of biblical Hebrew include the pun, and emphatic repetition such as 'dying you shall die', which in the Buber–Rosenzweig version read '*musst sterben du, sterben*' (Gen. 2: 17). Altogether, it is a Bible very different from those that had gone before, or for that matter have appeared since, and the two men suspected in advance that it would not find general favour. As Rosenzweig wrote to his friend in August 1926:

We are faced today with two kinds of readers, those who know nothing and those who know everything. If we do our work properly, the former will understand everything, the latter nothing. The former are those who have confidence in us and in themselves; those in other words who believe that what we have written, and what they have understood, is what is really meant. The others are mistrustful—mistrusting us, but themselves too. They always think that what is there, and what they may understand it to mean, is not what is meant; and then they 'compare' it. If they compare it with the original text, they go over to the other party; and since the other party includes one per cent of our readership, our support thereby increases to eleven per cent. The remaining eighty-nine per cent who compare our text with Luther and Kautzsch are lost to us; they can only die out. We should write solely and exclusively for the one per cent, with a side-glance at the ten per cent. The eighty-nine per cent do not concern us. If we had had to write for them, we should never have started. The one per cent understand immediately what is meant by *Braus* . . .

---

[3] See Martin Buber, *Werke*, 3 vols. (Kösel–Lambert Schneider, 1962–4), ii. 1164–5.

the ten per cent understand on reflection; the eighty-nine per cent never, for they look for a translation of 'spirit' . . . and there, admittedly, they can look for a long while.[4]

A year later, in September 1927, Rosenzweig was again impressing on Buber his opinion of their achievement.

Someone expecting a work of art *cannot* understand us. Yet it *is* one. But visible as such only to one not looking for it. In the same way that the elegance of a mathematical proof is apparent only to those who approach it with mathematical interests and not searching for elegance.[5]

Work of art or not, Alfred Jeremias, the Lutheran theologian and Assyriologist, greatly admired it. After studying fascicles 1–5 with 'burning interest', he asserted his conviction that the new Bible would be the number one German translation for religious Jews in the same way that Luther's New Testament was the number one translation for religious German Christians. Luther was able to do the work because he was in the Christian sense himself prophet, psalmist, and evangelist. 'I can think', Jeremias assured Buber,

that your translation of the Old Testament could be the same for believing Jews. I see in you and your colleague the Jewish-prophetic quality. Experience aroused in me long ago the greatest confidence that you have grasped what is most profound in Jewish spiritual life: the mysticism of the everyday, the holiness of the profane.[6]

Franz Rosenzweig's sufferings came to an end in 1929, and with them his collaboration on the work on the Bible, which by then had reached the Book of Isaiah. Individual biblical books nevertheless continued to appear until 1932, when Ezekiel was issued. But it was not until 1949 that Buber returned to the task, and not till 1961, when he was eighty-three years old, that the final volume of the revised *Die Schrift* was published. In the meantime, the ideas generated by these years of concentrated study stimulated the production of several writings on biblical subjects.

———

Before turning to them, it should be noted briefly that during the 1920s Buber was already thinking—negatively as it happens—of emigrating

[4] Rosenzweig, *Briefe*, no. 462.   [5] Ibid., no. 508.

[6] Martin Buber, *Briefwechsel aus sieben Jahrzehnten*, ed. Grete Schaeder, 3 vols. (Lambert Schneider, 1972–5), ii, no. 250.

to Palestine. He intended to visit the Holy Land in 1927 in connection with a *Volkshochschule* which he planned to establish there but, as he confided to Hans Kohn in a letter, he rejected the idea of staying there as head of the school. 'I cannot, in the sense of productivity, Hebraize myself, and must be content with living and dying as a frontier watchman [Grenzwart].'[7]

Buber's initial exegetical work, *Kingship of God*, was published in 1932 as part of a larger enquiry into the development of messianism in Israel. His wish (which went unrealized) was to trace the relation between God and Israel through the ages and to demonstrate how, from the concept of YHWH the King, the idea came into being of a human king who would be YHWH's Follower, his Anointed, his Messiah, his Christos Kyriou. As we have it, the study is in fact concerned only with God the King, but its great underlying importance is that it presents the first, though by no means adequate, explanation of the extraordinary Buber–Rosenzweig translation of Exodus 3: 14, where God answers the question put to him by Moses concerning what he should tell the Israelites when they asked him about the divine Name: 'I will be there such as I will be there,' *ehyeh asher ehyeh*. This crucial subject will be discussed in detail later, so no more need be added for the moment beyond remarking that whereas the first edition of *I and You* gives God as saying of himself, 'I am who I am' as the equivalent of *ehyeh asher ehyeh*, the second edition includes the new exegesis of Exodus. And with the re-translation of the Name, the whole governing theme of presence and Presence falls, as we shall see, into place.

More 'burning interest' was evinced in *Kingship of God* when it came out, this time on the part of a well-known Swiss theologian, Emil Brunner. At last! at last! he jubilates, a book on the Old Testament written with understanding instead of misunderstanding. Gerhard (Gershom) Scholem was more critical and expressed himself unconvinced by the Name argumentation. Buber should in any case have explained himself at greater length. To this he received the reply:

You are right, that *ehyeh* must be dealt with more thoroughly: I did not want to load the context any further. As far as the decisive issue was concerned, I thought I could confine myself to pointing to Rosenzweig,[8] from whom came

---

[7] Buber, *Briefwechsel aus sieben Jahrzehnten*, ii, no. 201.

[8] In the notes, which are copious.

the encouragement, and to my mind the highly important interpretation, *asher* = 'such as'. Jacob had discovered the treasure but failed to raise it.[9]

During the four years between the appearance in print of *Kingship of God* and the very different 'Question to the Single One',[10] a certain amount of correspondence had travelled to and fro between Heppenheim and Jerusalem in connection with the possibility—which despite Buber's remark to Hans Kohn about his inability to Hebraize himself, he had clearly not definitively rejected—of taking up a position there in the Hebrew University. Scholem was most persuasive. He would be very happy, both for himself and for the sake of the university, to have Buber in Jerusalem. It would be extremely valuable, he believed, to have a person there of Buber's authority and standing. In February 1934, he was even able to inform Buber that a formal application had been made in Council to establish a Chair in General Religious Studies and for a decision to call on Buber to fill it. There would undoubtedly be some lively discussion over the plan but at least the matter was under way.

Within a fortnight (unfortunately we do not have Buber's contributions to this interchange), another letter from Scholem reached Heppenheim, even more sanguine than before and clearly assured that the affair was settled. Buber might hear from Judah Magnes, the then Chancellor of the university, straight away, or Magnes might wait until after the meeting of the university governors. It was now up to Buber to make his final choice whether to move to Jerusalem that winter. Scholem ends his letter: 'I need not say how greatly I rejoice in the prospect of seeing you here . . . Let us hope it will not remain just a prospect.'[11]

In the event, Magnes confirmed the invitation a week later after the Council meeting. 'The Rubicon is crossed', he announced. After considerable reflection, it had at last been decided to appoint Buber to the Chair of General Religious Studies for two years in the first place.

Bearing in mind all the trouble gone to on his behalf, and the eagerness with which he was awaited, Buber's reaction strikes one as not over-keen. Ascribing his delay in answering Magnes's letter to a

[9] *Briefwechsel*, ii, no. 390. On Benno Jacob, see Part II, pp. 95–8 below.

[10] Buber, *Werke*, i. 217–65; 'Question to the Single One', in *Between Man and Man*, trans. R. Gregor Smith (Routledge & Kegan Paul, 1947), 60–147.

[11] *Briefwechsel*, ii, no. 467.

'stubborn influenza, with a relapse', he acknowledged the invitation with which he had been honoured and said he was 'considering' it. But he was obviously not favourably impressed by the shortness of the appointment, and especially not by the alternatives suggested by Magnes (dictated by a lack of funds) of a two years' tenure on a higher salary *or* a five years' appointment on a lower one.

By the end of that summer, the matter was in any case out of Buber's hands altogether and he was writing to Scholem to say so. For Magnes had meanwhile had to explain to Buber that the project had fallen through. He had written to him: 'For the problem of *Jewish* religion, the subject is not suitable or necessary, and for the subject, a brilliant writer is not enough of a scholar.'[12] Buber's ironical comment on the reasoning of what Magnes alluded to as the Hebrew University's 'clique scholarship' and 'clericalism' was that he did not understand the first point, and that the second seemed to indicate that the gentlemen in question had not noticed his academic activity in the philosophical faculty at Frankfurt. 'All in all, one more experience!'[13]

———

Published before the outbreak of the Second World War, in 1936, 'Question to the Single One' considers the constitution and role of the effective individual in the society of which he is a part, and enlarges on the notion, introduced in *I and You*, of the unified and integrated 'person'.

Kierkegaard's so-called 'single one' around whom the argument revolves, the individual withdrawn in isolation from the world and preoccupied with his torments and his God, is predictably deplored. So is Max Stirner's category of '*der Einzige*', the unique one. The ideal is not, as Kierkegaard would have it, to be concerned 'essentially with God and only relatively with others . . . absolutely with God and only relatively with public life.'[14] The ideal is to be a 'person' for whom the exclusive reality of relation with God includes and embraces reality of relation with *all else*.

In the human crisis of today, the 'person' is at risk, and so is truth. The 'person' is threatened by collectivization, and the truth by politicization. Yet it is imperative that 'persons' should exist, not simply representatives elected or appointed to take over responsibility from those they represent, but men and women who will not permit them-

---

[12] *Briefwechsel*, ii, no. 491.   [13] Ibid.
[14] Buber, *Werke*, i. 244; *Between Man and Man*, 88.

selves to be represented where their responsibilities are concerned. And faith in truth is necessary, as something independent of man, something that he cannot contain in himself but with which he can live in real living relation.

The 'person' must himself be responsible to the truth in his historical situation. He must hold his own *vis-à-vis* the whole of existence present to him, public life included. Indeed, true community and true community life will only become real to the extent that the 'person' becomes real out of whose responsible existence (*Dasein* = literally, 'being there') public life is renewed.[15]

Albert Schweitzer could not understand why Buber had bothered with Kierkegaard at all. He thanked him for his copy of 'Question to the Single One' but asked quite frankly: 'Why do you take issue with this poor psychopath? He is no thinker. I read him only with aversion. What does he actually want? . . . He has only been made into a thinker by everything people have written about him.'[16]

————

Life in Germany became from now on progressively more difficult for the Bubers. Passes were withheld. Teaching was forbidden. Paula Buber was banned from publishing. News however came from Jerusalem in January 1936, in a letter from Hugo Bergmann, rector of the Hebrew University, that after yet another debate, a Senate decision to nominate Buber to a teaching post had at last been ratified. He and Paula consequently travelled to Palestine in May 1937 to look for somewhere to live.

When they returned to Heppenheim to settle their affairs, they were obliged to endure more exasperating delays in connection with work permits and the disposal of their property, but after another of Martin's bouts of 'severe and stubborn influenza', not to mention an accident to Paula, who fell down the cellar steps and was unable to walk for a week, the Bubers finally set out for their new homeland in March 1938.

Martin Buber was by then sixty years old.

[15] Ibid. 265, 108.   [16] *Briefwechsel*, ii, no. 561.

5

War Years (1939–1948)

'YOU really should come here some time,' Buber urged his psychiatrist friend, Hans Trüb, from Jerusalem in the summer of 1938. 'What is to be experienced here of reality and of the Indwelling "in the midst of our stain" is probably to be experienced nowhere else.'[1] This may have been a reference to the Arab rioting of that time, and especially to the acts of bloody revenge, condemned by the Jewish Agency as a blemish on the moral achievements of the Jews in Palestine, executed on the Arabs, and later on the British, by the independent military organization Irgun Zeva'i Leummi, led from 1943 by Menachem Begin.

As far as his own career was concerned, the Chair eventually accepted by Buber in the Hebrew University bore the title 'Social Philosophy'; the orthodox veto had effectively barred him from a position more obviously suited to his gifts and attainments. But although the uprooting from Germany, and the necessary switch to another language with all the extra burden of work that this entailed for a teacher, were not easy for a man of his age, a preliminary period of depression was succeeded by a veritable onrush of energy and productivity evident in the series of important publications which followed one after the other. By 1945, several projects that had hung fire for years were either realized or on the point of being so. His academic work, which had needed a great deal of preparation, was progressing peacefully and well, and to add to his satisfaction, Paula, after her own period of acclimatization, was also able to continue with her writing.

———

Curiously, the first full-scale book of Buber's new life in Palestine, *The Prophetic Faith*, appeared initially in the Netherlands in Dutch.[2] The explanation is that soon after he took up his post in Jerusalem, he

[1] Martin Buber, *Briefwechsel aus sieben Jahrzehnten*, ed. Grete Schaeder, 3 vols. (Lambert Schneider, 1972–5), iii, no. 8, Jerusalem, 1 Aug. 1938.

[2] Martin Buber, *Het Geloof van Israel* (H. Meulenhoff, 1940); published in English as *The Prophetic Faith*, trans. from the Hebrew by Carlyle Witton-Davies (Macmillan, 1960).

was invited by Professor Gerardus van de Leeuw of Groningen to contribute to a planned collective study of the religions of the world. Buber at first demurred, but was persuaded to accept once he realized that he would not only be the only non-Dutchman taking part but also the only non-Christian. As might not be apparent from the English title, *The Prophetic Faith* is accordingly intended as an exposition of biblical religion, of the faith or religion of the prophets. It sets out to show in particular how the prophet acted as mediator in the living dialogue between men and God, promoting concepts of the Deity to fit the needs of the people and directing the people's attention to the demands made on them by the Godhead they had accepted. Each passing divine form was determined by its predecessors and influenced the shape of its successors, the God-idea evolving from a God of journeys, to a God of the fathers, God the King, the Warrior, the Husband, the Holy One, the Righteous, the Lord of the World, though not necessarily in that order. Each form entered history for a while as Israel's supreme Lord, played its part, and afterwards made way for another one perceived, on the part of God's people, by another of their prophets.

Buber is at pains to stress that although Israel has throughout history seen God in varying shapes and aspects, every divine form has held at its heart the same essential divine nature. The God of the Patriarchs, for example, may seem very different from the God of the Exodus tradition, but is not so in fact. It is the human partner that changes in man–God relation. Israel's God remains fundamentally the same. He is HE IS THERE, the meaning of his Name YHWH as it was expounded to his servant Moses on Mount Horeb.

This time, full advantage is taken of the opportunity to make good the insufficiency of explanation of the Buber–Rosenzweig interpretation of the burning bush episode. But it is pointed out in addition that if the Name provides the clue to YHWH's requirement of himself that he should 'be there' with his people for their help and guidance, it does the same in regard to the people's duty to God. As YHWH does to them, so—within the limit of their capabilities—must they do to YHWH. The religion of Israel as the prophets preached it was the true worship of YHWH by means of presence with him.

The final third of the book, 'God of the Sufferers', is rather different in tone from the rest. It considers the prophets' condemnation of the Sanctuary, the suffering of the 'righteous', and the mystery of the messianic redemption of the world.

The prophet Buber mainly stays with is Jeremiah. In particular, he appears to relish the latter's famous Temple speech (Jer. 7) calling on the people: 'Amend your ways and your doings, and I will let you dwell in this place. Never safeguard yourselves with the words of the lie, the saying, "HIS hall, HIS hall, HIS hall is this!"' By this, Jeremiah means, according to Buber,

that his God is not concerned with 'religion'. Other gods need a house, an altar, sacrifice, because without them they are not, because they consist only of what earthly beings give them. The living God and King of world-time [*Weltzeit*] needs none of this because he is. He desires no religion. He desires a human nation, human beings living with human beings, human makers of decisions to provide those who thirst for justice with their rights, strong to pity the weak (7: 5 f), human beings associating with human beings.[3]

Jeremiah, one of the martyrs of the ancient world, who bore the sufferings of his people and fulfilled in himself their purification and *teshuvah*, was witness and catalyst of one of the moments in which a new divine form took over from the old. He saw YHWH leave his 'house' and withdraw into the heavens to be a 'far' God there, though still remaining close to the needy and outcast.

And yet why, Buber asks next, does he allow the innocent to suffer? Or rather, why, as the Book of Job expresses it, does he *cause* the innocent to suffer? One of the views of God found there is that of a Being who permits Satan to wander round the earth tempting men to sin. Another, that of Job's friends, sees the Deity as an avenger; Job's troubles must be the result of his offences against God, who is now punishing him for them. A third is Job's own idea of God, which is that he is a Deity who contradicts himself. HE IS THERE denies his own essential nature in not being there with Job and in 'hiding his Face' (13: 24) from him. When Job says that he wishes to reason with God and to convince him of his blamelessness, what he really wants is for God to be there once again with him. 'O that I knew where to find him' (25: 3), he mourns. He fights against God's remoteness, and against his silence, against the God who rages and remains quiet. It is this very hiding of God's light that Buber sees as the source of Job's despair.

The fourth and last concept of God is God's own as the poet author of the Book of Job formulates it. Notwithstanding Job's accusations

---

[3] Martin Buber, *Werke*, 3 vols. (Kösel–Lambert Schneider, 1962–4), ii. 417–18; *The Prophetic Faith*, 171–2.

against him, God sees himself as a just God, but with a justice far removed from human justice. He is a just Creator who gives to each of his creatures 'its own', all that it needs to become entirely itself. He permits each to become wholly itself by distributing justly that which each one needs. Man, Buber explains, 'is deliberately deficient in this presentation of heaven and earth, which shows him that a justice exists greater than his own, and that with his justice which aims to give each "his due" he is called on merely to emulate divine justice which gives to each what he is'.[4] As for the enigma of suffering, the lesson to be read in the Book of Job is its association with revelation: not revelation in general, of course, 'but a particular revelation to an individual, revelation as *reply* to a sufferer concerning the question of his suffering; God's limitation of himself into a Person who replies to a person'.[5] For Job's pain that God's 'lamp' no longer shone over his head, and that his 'friendship' no more covered his tent as in the days when 'the Almighty was yet with me', was eased at last, not so much by his mind's recognition that the divine ways were totally beyond his understanding and that he had been complaining out of ignorance, as by his spirit's awareness of being once again in contact with God. He had heard with his 'ear' God's words to him, and now, after all the silence and the absence, he could again see God's Presence with his 'eye'.

In the final chapter in this section, Buber considers the teaching of Deutero-Isaiah that Israel's redemption and that of the world are to be two phases of the one great coming of the Kingdom. 'Turn to me and be saved, all the ends of the earth' (v.22) is YHWH's command.

Who is to be the agent of this universal *teshuvah*? Who was, or who will be, the Suffering Servant smitten—not for the sins of Israel, which God himself will carry, but for those of the 'nations'?

Buber's reasoning is that there will be not so much one Servant as a succession of them. He will come from the ranks of the prophets who mediate between heaven and earth. He will be God's *meshullam*, his 'perfected one'. Called on to work directly for the 'nations', he will establish God's Kingdom on earth. But in addition to this personal Servant—or, more precisely, *identical* with him—there will be the corporate Servant, Israel. Israel is to be God's *meshullam*, his stricken and afflicted one and his Messiah. 'Insofar as Israel's great suffering in the Diaspora is a suffering not merely endured but truly borne and performed, it is to be interpreted in the image of the Servant. Whoever

---

[4] *Werke*, ii. 442; *The Prophetic Faith*, 195.
[5] *Werke*, ii. 442; *The Prophetic Faith*, 195–6.

in Israel does the suffering of Israel, is the Servant, and he is the Israel in whom YHWH is glorified.'[6]

———

Buber's ability to cope expertly and easily with a wide variety of subjects was admirable. Thus in the few years under review in this present chapter, he was able to pass with relative speed from the Bible, to Hasidism, and to philosophy, not to mention lesser writings on other topics still, such as politics and education. But also, in 1941, he published *For the Sake of Heaven*,[7] a book as different as could be from the biblical study preceding it. He had for a long time wanted to bring together Hasidic 'sacred anecdotes', each of them an adage linked to an event, so that they formed a readable and coherent whole, but the undertaking had proved so difficult that he had twice laid the project aside. Now, he at last discovered how to do it. It is the nearest he ever came to writing a novel—though a truer description of it is his own: 'a chronicle'. In combination, the originally separate stories present a portrait of nineteenth-century Hasidic life, with its magic tradition and its anti-magic school, with its great and saintly personalities such as Rabbi Jacob Isaac of Lublin, nicknamed 'the seer' (d. 1815), and Rabbi Jacob Isaac of Pzhysha, known as 'the Jew' and 'the holy Jew' (d. 1813), together with their women, children, followers, opponents, and friends. The canvas into which they are packed is held together mainly by dialogue but contains enough colour and incident to help it to do what Buber primarily intended: to show how the Hasidic community, gathered round its leader the *zaddik*, translated Hasidic teachings and beliefs into the reality of what is so frequently alluded to in Buber's writings as 'lived life'.

———

Two years later, another title appeared which in English became 'What is Man?'[8] Here, with the assistance of thinkers ranging from Aristotle

———

[6] *Werke*, ii. 483; *The Prophetic Faith*, 234.

[7] Originally published in Hebrew as a serial in *Davar* between January and October 1941, *For the Sake of Heaven* came out as a book in 1944. An English translation was issued in 1945 by the Jewish Publication Society of America, but the edition now in circulation is the Meridian Books and Jewish Publication Society edition, first published in 1958.

[8] *Werke*, i. 309–407; 'What is Man?', in Martin Buber, *Between Man and Man*, trans. R. Gregor Smith (Collins, 1961), 148–247.

to Max Scheler (d. 1928), Buber looks for man's changing concept of himself with the aim of proposing his own answer to the question.

There seems little point in reproducing in any depth his estimates of the opinions he consults, but broadly his conclusions are as follows.

It is a characteristic of the history of the human spirit that periods in which man feels isolated and out of place in the world alternate with others in which he is contentedly at home there. Another recurring feature is that it is during the times of estrangement, and not those of closeness to present existence, that he poses the question of what he is and answers it in varying ways. It is when he feels himself to be alone, in a world unfamiliar and strange to him, that he reaches out beyond it to something or someone who will mitigate his loneliness—God. But with each successive period of estrangement, God becomes more and more difficult to reach out to, and in the end he cannot be found at all and is pronounced 'dead'. At that point, the only remaining course is for man to reach out to himself. And this he does. Finding it impossible to communicate with a divine form, of whatever kind or shape, he is reduced to trying to enter into intimate communion with himself.

This approach to the problem of man is typified by the 'individualistic anthropology' of such thinkers as Hegel, Heidegger, Kierkegaard, etc., which is concerned with relation with the self and within the self (e.g. between mind and instincts). But man can never properly understand himself by this means. The problem of real man is comprehensible only within the context of his real relation with other beings.

On the other hand, it is also true that it is above all the solitary who is able to throw light on man's true nature. Consequently, a way has to be found to overcome his isolation without damaging his special ability to ask the question, what is man?, and to answer it. In effect, a new task has to be confronted for this means that a person 'who wishes to grasp what he is must preserve the tension of solitariness and the fire of its problem in a nevertheless renewed life with his world, and must think from out of that situation'.[9]

How can he do this?

Two methods in particular have been used in modern times to lessen human alienation—the application of the principles of individualism on the one hand, and of collectivism on the other. Individualism has laid the stress on man in relation to himself; collectivism has ignored 'man' altogether and emphasized 'society' at his expense.

Neither of these treatments of the human situation—both of them

[9] *Werke*, i. 400–1; 'What is Man?', 240.

essentially the outcome of a fear of the world and a fear of life, products of an existential solitariness of a magnitude probably never before experienced—has done anything to answer the world's need. Individualism, with its glorification of personal separateness, has done no more to diminish the misery of alienation than collectivism, with its submergence of the self in the group, the bigger the better. And the reason for this is that 'the fundamental fact of human existence is neither the individual as such nor the totality as such . . . What primarily distinguishes the human world is that something exists between being and being that appears nowhere else in nature.'[10] That something is speech, the medium whereby man is able to sustain relation with his fellows. It is speech that makes man into man, into a being who can commune with another being in a sphere common to them both.

Buber at this point introduces the concept of the Between already mentioned in *I and You*[11] (and due to reappear elsewhere, notably in *Paths in Utopia*). The Between, he says, is part of the existence of man with man but one that is still very little understood. It is where we should think of relation as taking place. It is not *in* the individual, nor *in* a general world that includes and determines it, but specifically and factually 'between' two partners. These three facts, *I*, *you*, and the Between, constitute the situation and the conveyors of what happens between two people.

Buber's own definition of man, although it is really not so much a definition as a suggestion, is a dialogical one. We may come closer, he proposes with diffidence, 'to the answer to the question, "What is man?", when we learn to understand him as the being in whose dialogic, in whose reciprocally present two-ness, encounter of one with the other is realized and recognized'.[12]

———

As he remarks in the Foreword to *Moses*,[13] Buber's wish in his second major biblical work published during the war years was to portray the prophet as a concrete personality and relate his historical achievements from the point of view of an unbiased critical investigation unaffected by any religious tradition or particular academic school of thought. As

[10] *Werke*, i. 404; 'What is Man?', 244.
[11] See e.g. the final paragraph.
[12] *Werke*, i. 407; 'What is Man?', 247.
[13] *Werke*, ii. 11–230; Martin Buber, *Moses* (East and West Library, 1946).

far as his own approach to the Bible was concerned, he rejected the theory that its text is assembled from various 'sources'. He believed that every biblical episode rests on the adaptation of a tradition which, during the course of time and under the influence of many differing tendencies, has undergone a variety of treatments. The scholar's task is to distinguish the early strata from later increments and to proceed from the tradition's adaptation to the presumed tradition itself. The first half is not difficult since additions can be identified both linguistically and by their content. But in the second, one can only hypothesize.

Moses, like *The Prophetic Faith* (with which it not unexpectedly over-laps in places), is an account of relation between man and God, this time not God in his changing forms, but specifically the God of Moses. It depicts relation with a God who delivers, leads, and fights for his people, who is his nation's Prince and Law-Giver, who sends them a great message. It portrays a God acting, on the level of history, upon and between nations, a God concerned with nations, a God who requires a nation to be entirely 'his' and holy, with its life sanctified through righteousness and faithfulness and to whom he stays close. He is a God

who appears, speaks and reveals. He is invisible and 'causes himself to be seen'—in whichever natural phenomenon or historical event he in each case wishes to be seen. He causes his word to be made known to the men he calls in such a way that it breaks out of them and they become a 'mouth' for God. He causes his spirit to seize whomsoever he has chosen, causes it to produce in him and through him the work of God.[14]

The biblical tale, unfolding in brief and succinct chapters, leads inevitably to the story of the burning bush, where once again the Buber–Rosenzweig exegesis of the Name is entered into and justified. This is followed by a discussion of the first Passover, which Buber interprets as a sacramental meal, a 'holy and ancient shepherd's meal', renewed for the sake of uniting with their God the people whom Moses was about to lead into freedom. The 'Passover for YHWH', celebrated in the family with shoes on the feet and a stave in the hand in readiness for a journey, was eventually to be transformed into the great feast held yearly in the Temple of Jerusalem.

To these two 'renewals'—a renewed understanding of the Name of God and a renewed sacramental meal—Buber adds renewal of the Sabbath. The Sabbath was not invented at the time of the Ten

[14] *Werke*, ii. 15; *Moses*, 8.

Commandments: by then it was already ancient. Moses renewed it to create 'a holy order of time'. Like other spiritual leaders, the prophet was not so much concerned to found a religion

as to order a human world under a divine truth, to unite the ways of earth with those of heaven; and it is an essential part of this that time, which in itself is articulated only through cosmic rhythms, through the sun's changes and the phases of the moon, should become consolidated in a supreme holiness, one extending even beyond the cosmos. Thus Moses institutes the Sabbath, and with it the week flowing into the Sabbath, as the divine measure regulating the life of human beings. But the God whose measure it is, is precisely he who accepts man, is with him, frees him and helps him to salvation. Thus the Sabbath week cannot be only an 'absolute metre of time'; it is also of necessity an ever-returning way to the peace of God.[15]

In his reflections on the Covenant, one of the observations Buber makes is that it was a contract between the various tribes themselves, as well as one between them and God. They became one nation, Israel, through being bound by their Covenant with the One God.[16]

Concerning the Commandments, Buber believed it must have been primarily Moses who 'raised imageless worship to a principle, or rather the imageless being-there [*Dasein*] of the Invisible who permits himself to be seen'.[17] Moses was the first to counter the tendency to drift into a cult devoid of content, as may be seen from his treatment of those who 'murmured' against him and rebelled. When his people, desiring security, wanted a God whom they could 'possess' and manipulate through the medium of a sacral system, he refused to accede to their wish. In place of a power to 'utilize' God, Moses substituted the sacral notion of consecrating all things—men, objects, times, and places—to him who grants his Presence to his people *if* they remain faithful to the Covenant made with their heavenly King.

Another problem confronted here is why the Decalogue contains these commandments and not others. Buber's explanation is that it is not some kind of catechism, a summary of Israelite religion. The 'soul' of the Decalogue is its 'you'. Its words are directed by the *I* of God to the *you* of the man who listens to him. Nevertheless, when the commandments are considered together, it is also clear that 'you' is not addressed to the individual in isolation but to a people living together.

[15] *Werke*, ii. 96–7; *Moses*, 82–3.
[16] Cf. *Werke*, i. 108 for Buber's definition of the 'true community'; see also Buber, *I and Thou*, trans. Ronald Gregor Smith, 2nd edn. (Scribner–T. & T. Clark, 1958), 45.
[17] *Werke*, ii. 146; *Moses*, 127.

If a community is to stand firm, its life, marriage, property, and social honour must be preserved. Further, its safety must be ensured not only by injunctions against *acts* of stealing, murder, adultery, and the like, but also against *attitudes* such as covetousness. Envy is a threat to the social body.

As for the stirring narratives of the acceptance of the tablets of the law by Moses from the hands of YHWH, the writing of the law by God's own finger, Moses' stay of forty days and forty nights on the mountain inscribing 'the words of the Covenant', and his descent with a face radiant from his proximity to God—in Buber's view, all these stories must be dispensed with in the interests of reality. We must do without

all these powerful images if we wish to envisage a course of events happening in our human world. Nothing remains for us but the image, perceptible only in faintest silhouette, of a man who withdraws into the solitude of the Mountain of God in order to write, far from the people and overshadowed by the cloud of God, the Law of God for the people.[18]

Meditation on the Ark, and on the Tent of Encounter or Assembly, allows additional expatiation on the divine Presence, but later, the prophetic spirit is examined in its two manifestations—ecstasy and prediction—with a view to determining with which of these two elements of ancient prophecy Moses should be associated. Buber's opinion appears to be with neither. Moses was one and absolutely special. The passage is cited from Numbers where the people express dissatisfaction with their inadequate diet, and Moses, in consequence, summons the elders to the Tent of Encounter. There, YHWH 'came down' in the cloud, and after speaking to him, 'took some of the spirit that was upon him and put it upon the seventy elders; and when the spirit rested upon them, they prophesied. But they did so no more' (Num. 11: 25). Afterwards, when Miriam and Aaron were finding fault with Moses, they referred to the incident in the Tent and argued that he, after all, was not the only prophet, for YHWH had spoken through them, too, when the spirit was on them. At this, God was very angry. The rest of them, he said, had heard him speak in a dream and perceived him in a vision. Not so his servant Moses. 'With him I speak mouth to mouth, clearly, and not in dark speech, and he beholds the form of YHWH' (Num. 12: 7–8). These words, Buber thought, hide some dim recollection 'of the man who recognized his God, "visually", in his natural appearances, the God who is each time there such as he

[18] *Werke*, ii. 159; *Moses*, 139.

is there, and experienced his word as breathed into his inmost self. This is classically Israelite, and yet in its purity and power, unique'.[19]

Moses finishes appropriately with the prophet's own end. He ascends another last mountain. He contemplates from there the promised land. He dies 'by the mouth of YHWH'. And as Buber remarks, from the fact that the text mentions that 'he' buried Moses in the gorge in the land of Moab, facing Beth Peor, it was obviously thought that YHWH himself dug his servant's final resting-place. Hence 'no man knows his grave until this day' (Deut. 34).

————

Buber's political stand at this time and always was one of passionate hope for the co-operation of Jews and Arabs in the development of a bi-national commonwealth. To this end he founded in 1942, with Judah Magnes, Ernst Simon, Leon Roth, and others, the movement called Ihud (unity). Its intention was to win sympathy from Arab and Jewish intellectuals for the protection of the rights of the Arabs and to further mutual understanding and compromise. Ihud as representing liberal thought was, however, not new. It had been preceded by Berit Shalom (Covenant of Peace), a group established in 1926, with among its members such well-known intellectuals as Hugo Bergmann, Hans Kohn, and Gershom Scholem. It was also supported on occasion by politicians such as David Ben-Gurion. Ihud temporarily ceased its activities with the outbreak of war and the death of Magnes in 1948 and, although it was revived in the 1950s, came definitely to an end in 1964.

As early as 1938, in any case, shortly after his arrival in Palestine, Buber was inveighing against terrorism and violence. He was against those people, he said, who announced that if they were to protect themselves against wolves, they must become wolves themselves. They were forgetting that they had undertaken this work in the land to become 'whole human beings' again.[20] In Palestine, where the Jew was at home, the 'Jewish problem' no longer existed. One must therefore expect the Jewish people, released from the need of nationalistic fervour, to remember their bond with humanity as a whole, and their membership of the community of man, not just their relation to their fellow-Jews. He wished to see entire equality between Jews and Arabs

[19] *Werke*, ii. 195; *Moses*, 169.
[20] See Robert Weltsch's 'Nachwort', in Hans Kohn, *Martin Buber: Sein Werk und seine Zeit*, 3rd edn. (Melzer, 1961), 413–79.

and to ensure that the fruits of Jewish enterprise in the land should benefit the Arabs also.

His admonitions were without effect. Violence continued to generate violence and preparations went ahead unilaterally for the foundation of a Jewish state. In October 1942, the so-called Biltmore Programme formulated by Ben-Gurion, proposing that 'Palestine be established as a Jewish Commonwealth integrated in the structure of the new democratic world', was approved by the Zionist General Council.

Buber published a reply to this in 1944, the year in which the Irgun Zeva'i Leummi initiated a series of assaults on the Arabs and the British in order to exert pressure on the government. Published in the form of a fictitious dialogue about the conference held in New York two years earlier, it asked how the Jews could form a state in a land where they were in the minority? (They constituted at this time approximately one-third of the total population.) The only outcome of the moves suggested and accepted in the Biltmore Programme would be the highly regrettable partition of Palestine.

With Judah Magnes and another representative of Ihud, Buber appeared before the Anglo-American commission convened in 1946 by Ernest Bevin to discuss a memorandum circulated by Ihud expressing the view that Palestine, by the very nature of things, should never become either a Jewish or an Arab state. It should be the homeland of both peoples, each possessing full autonomy. And even at this late hour, trying to place the problem on a plane more elevated than that of simple politics, Buber did his best to convey to the commission that the task of Jewry was to found and realize a 'true community'. The re-born Jewish people were not only to live with the Arabs in peace; they were to strive to make the prosperity of the land a co-operative venture with them. There should be an internationally guaranteed agreement between the two communities which would assure their corporate and individual existences.

All this was also in vain. In November 1947, the United Nations recommended partition. The Jews were to be allotted eastern Galilee, the northern part of the Jordan valley, the valleys of Beit She'an and Jezreel, the coastal strip from a point south of Acre to a point south of Rehovot, together with the Negev, including Eilat on the Red Sea. The Arabs were to get the rest. Jerusalem was to be internationalized.

It may be helpful in this search for the real Buber to read a letter he wrote a few months earlier to Judah Magnes disclosing his state of mind. Some years ago, he tells Magnes, when I was fighting for a Jewish–Arab treaty at the Zionist Congress, I had an experience that shocked me and was to determine my future life. I had outlined a resolution emphasizing the community of interests of the two nations and presenting a way of collaboration between them—the only way that can lead to the salvation of the land and its two peoples. Before the resolution was presented to the Congress for ratification it came before an editorial committee which was to establish its final form. Naturally, I was a member of this committee. Then something happened that is quite usual and ordinary for a professional politician, but so shocked me until this day I have not managed to recover from it. In the editorial committee, which for the most part consisted of old friends of mine, first one small amendment was recommended, and then another small amendment, and yet another amendment . . . Each one individually had no apparent significance and the reason for them all was that the resolution should be acceptably formulated for the Congress. Repeatedly, I heard the words, 'Do you just want to make a demonstration, or do you wish Congress to endorse the basis of Jewish–Arab collaboration and fight for it? If the latter, you must agree to the small amendments.' Naturally, it was not a case of demonstrating; I wanted a change in the attitude of the Zionist movement towards the Arab problem. I therefore struggled for my own proposed text, but gave in more and more, and waived it when the affair depended on it. When the editorial committee had finished its work and brought a fair copy of the agreed text to me in the hotel, I saw a series of fine and convincing sentences, but the marrow and blood of my original demand were no longer in them. I accepted the business and gave my consent for the resolution to be brought before the Congress. I contented myself, in a personal explanation prior to the reading of the resolution and the vote, with emphasizing the *fundamental* turn which I had in view with my motion. But I felt that my role as 'politician', i.e. as someone who takes part in the political activity of a group, was finished. I had taken up a cause and had had to bring it to an end. I could not take up a new cause in which I would again be placed before the choice between truth and realization. From then on, I had to renounce 'resolutions' and be satisfied with 'personal talks'.

Many years thus passed until I came to Eretz Israel and saw how you, my friend, were trying to promote the same radical struggle for Jewish–Arab collaboration which eventually assumed the form of our Ihud. The fact that you did so, and the way you did it, have been a great gift of life to me: you have made it possible for me to work politically once more within the context, and in the name of, a political group without sacrificing truth. You understand my meaning. I am not concerned for the purity and salvation of my soul; if ever it should be the case—which in the nature of things is impossible—that I had to choose between the saving of my soul and the salvation of my people, I know I would not hesitate. It is a question of not violating the truth, since I have come to know that truth is the seal of God (*BT Shabbat*, 55*a*), whilst we are the wax in which this seal seeks to be stamped. The older I grow, the clearer this becomes, and I feel that in this we are brothers. To you too, it becomes clearer every day. But from where we stand, there has for a long time been no longer any choice. There is no opposition between the truth of God and the salvation of Israel.[21]

The foundation of the State of Israel was declared in May 1948. The mass flight of the Arabs was encouraged by their leaders with atrocity stories. Horrors abounded on all sides. The seeds were sown and watered of the political conditions in the Middle East as we now know them.

[21] *Briefwechsel*, iii, no. 108.

6

The Last Two Decades (1949–1965)

DESPITE his involvement in the momentous political upheavals taking place in Israel, 1947 was the year in which Buber made a first return to Europe. He travelled to Paris to lecture in the Sorbonne, and to Holland, Switzerland, and London, and was in particular greatly moved by his reception among the English and the Dutch. The French reaction to him, he told Hugo Bergmann, was 'more intellectual', but the vigour of the spiritual life that he found in the west was all in all an agreeable surprise to him.

Paths in Utopia was published during the same year in Hebrew, and appeared two years later in English.[1] A German version came out in 1950. It is a work that has been greatly admired, even by those who for one reason or another are unable to get very far with Buber's other writings. It again breaks new ground: Buber meditates here on the theme of political idealism and surveys the historical development of what he calls utopian socialism with a view to proposing, as examples of a modern semi-success in putting genuine socialism into practice, the smaller communities in the State of Israel.

Utopianism he describes as characteristically a fantasy construed around a wish, an 'image of what should be, which the image-maker desires shall be'.[2] It is a desire for rightness which, if experienced philosophically as an idea, appears as an image of perfect *space*. Or it is a desire for rightness which, if experienced as revelation, is projected as an image of perfect *time* in the form of a messianic eschatology. In the first case, it is restricted by nature to human society, though it sometimes includes an inner transformation of the individual. In the second, it extends by nature beyond human social life. Both utopianisms are realizable only in the community.

Another even more important difference between the two visions of the right is that in the image of a perfect time the decisive action takes

---

[1] Martin Buber, *Werke*, 3 vols. (Kösel–Lambert Schneider, 1962–4), i. 836–1002; *Paths in Utopia*, trans. R. F. C. Hull (Routledge and Kegan Paul, 1949).

[2] *Werke*, i. 843; *Paths in Utopia*, 7.

place from above—although in its elementary prophetic stage a share in the coming redemption is allotted to man also. In utopianism as an image of perfect space, all is entirely dependent on the human will.

With the passage of the ages, the influence of the utopianism associated with revelation has been gradually eroded in that it has grown increasingly difficult to believe in any action from above which will save the world. By contrast, technology and the social inconsistencies of the present epoch have had such a profound effect on utopianism as an idea of perfect space that even the will on which the creation of a new social order was formerly seen to rely has now come to be understood technically. Society, like nature, is controlled by technical estimates and technical constructs. Furthermore, the forces of the displaced messianism have now all been directed into this new utopian social system, and the proclamation and summons which were formerly the prerogative of the religions are now heard issuing from modern socialism and communism.

Following a sensitive though critical outline of the teachings of the fathers of utopian socialism, Count Claude-Henri de Saint-Simon (1760–1825), Charles Fourier (1772–1837), and Robert Owen (1771–1858), and subsequently of Pierre-Joseph Proudhon (1809–65) and Prince Pyotr Alekseyevich Kropotkin (1842–1921), Buber turns to the theories of his friend Gustav Landauer, an anarchist rather than a socialist, and finally to Marx, Engels, and Lenin.

Landauer's utopian vision was of a revolution in which individuals would not require to be taught by a political party how to live in co-operation with each other but would learn from personal example. Thus, if socialism is to be regarded as a form of secular messianism, and the Marxists as apocalyptics foretelling the course of history and its catastrophes, Landauer and his predecessors were its prophets calling for *teshuvah*. He believed in the interrelation of all living beings (and shared with Buber his early enthusiasm for mysticism, especially that of Meister Eckhart), but it was his conviction that genuine religion would be the *outcome* of a regenerated society rather than its *cause*. His 'communities of love' were to be religion realized.

Buber's sympathy with Landauer's beliefs is obvious from his own reflections on community, which to be authentic must, he said, be a community of need and hence a community of spirit, a community of endeavour and hence a community of salvation.

After viewing some of the courageous but failed attempts to make a living reality of utopia, Buber moves on to discuss Marx, Engels, and

Lenin. Utopian socialism, he reminds us, looks for the replacement—
'to the highest possible degree'—of the state by society. Karl Marx
came close to realizing this, but in the end found it impossible to
renounce the concept of the state as such. He was also unable to
provide any answer to the problem of the interrelation of smaller social
units in the reconstruction of society as a whole. He approached the
reformation of society solely from the political viewpoint. Of the tragic
deformation of socialism which ensued, Buber writes:

It [Marxism] gathered the proletariat around it with great powers of recruit-
ment and organization. It acted with great pugnacity in attack and defence in
the political and economic field. But that for which in the last resort it had
recruited and organized and fought—the development of a new social form—
was neither the true object of its awareness nor the true goal of its action . . . It
did not look to the pre-forms of a new society already existing. It did not
bother itself seriously with promoting, influencing, leading, coordinating and
federating newly developed experiments or those in the process of formation.
It did not itself, with consistent work, call into being the cells, and associations
of cells, of living community. With its great powers, it did not lend its hand to
re-shaping the new human social existence which was to be liberated by the
revolution.[3]

The socialist idea involves the organic reconstruction of a new
greater society out of smaller societies linked by ties of common life
and work. In the hands of Marx and Lenin, it was not this idea which
provided the context for positive action. With them, the tendency
towards decentralization was displaced by the centralization of politics.
Marx demanded that the political principle should be superseded by
the social, but he persisted in steering in a political direction.

The one comprehensive attempt to create a new society with some
measure of success in the socialist sense is, Buber suggests, the *kibbutz*
and the *kevutzah*, the Israeli collectivist working community and the
village commune. Even they have not always witnessed a smooth
development of the three necessary processes of (a) a growth of the
sense of community in the smaller group; (b) a growth of federal sense
between one smaller group and another; and (c) a growth of the
federated groups into a transformed greater society. Nevertheless, by
contrast with Russia, they have not been failures.

One reason for this is that the Jewish *kevutzah* owes its existence to

---

[3] *Werke*, i. 946; *Paths in Utopia*, 98.

circumstances and not to a theory. Another is that in the Israeli communes, ideals have gone hand in hand with motives and have therefore remained flexible. A third, even more important than the others, is that a great external crisis aroused by way of response a powerful inner change which threw up an elite—the *halutzim* or pioneers. The *kibbutzim*, and the remaining form of settlement known as the *moshav*, or semi-individualistic work commune, are not failures, Buber repeats. But neither are they successes. Yet 'until Russia itself experiences an essential inner change—and we cannot yet guess when and how this will happen—we must designate by the mighty name of "Moscow" one of the two poles of Socialism between which we have to choose. The other pole, despite everything, I would venture to name "Jerusalem".'[4]

Buber had been publishing Hasidic legends, mainly in the journal called *Die Welt*, from 1905 onwards, and they appeared as a collection in German in 1927. Soon after the end of the war, however, he issued them in a final definitive form, first in English as *Tales of the Hasidim*,[5] and afterwards in German. It is probably correct to say that this anthology of Hasidic teaching in the form of brief anecdotes, simple and accessible as they are to every kind of reader, has been the most widely influential of all his publications.

On Buber's seventieth birthday, 9 February 1948, Judah Magnes published his good wishes in a special edition of *Ba'ayot*. The letter is very revealing.

I saw you for the first time in the 1900/1 semester, when I enrolled in the course of lectures given by Professor Simmel at the University of Berlin. The audience was so numerous that the lecture had to be held in one of the larger lecture-halls. Although the room was full to the last place, you entered at the head of a group of young people—boys and especially girls—through a side-door, and sat in the first row which was obviously reserved for you. Your black beard, your measured tread, and your way of walking ahead of the group like a *zaddik* ahead of his Hasidim, made me ask the student sitting beside me—a blond Aryan—who you were, and his answer was that this Jew was the founder of a new religious sect.

[4] *Werke*, i. 992; *Paths in Utopia*, 149.
[5] Martin Buber, *Tales of the Hasidim*, 2 vols., trans. Olga Marx (Schocken, 1947–8); *Die Erzählungen der Chassidim* (Manasse, 1949). See *Werke*, iii. 71–712.

Magnes, shocked to learn that Simmel had been baptized, stopped attending his lectures, and now expresses regret that he had allowed a whole lifetime to pass before seeing Buber again.

Of all the greatness that you have produced in this half-century from the treasures of your profound and noble spirit, especially since you came to the Land, people will speak among the circles of the wise and clever not only now but in the days to come. Today, I cannot restrain myself, but must devote my words to the tragic events which are taking place during these days as you enter the 'club' of the hoary seventies.

The tragedy of these days is not that after the dancing and jubilation over the UNO decision [of 29 November 1947, partitioning Palestine and inter-nationalizing Jerusalem] confusion and anxiety now reign, or the loss of dear and irrevocable human life, or the fighting and more fighting, the end of which cannot be foreseen. The tragedy is that today, as in the days of the prophet Micah (3: 9–10), the 'heads of the house of Jacob and the lords of the house of Israel build Zion with blood'—though with changes of nuance and definition corresponding to the circumstances of the time.

You thought and believed that Zion could be built, not with blood and fire, but with untiring creative work, and by means of mutual understanding with our neighbours. You know quite well that in the history of humanity, states have almost always been established only with blood and injustice. But you counted too much on miracles, for at least since the days of Rabbi Yohanan ben Zakkai until our own time, religious tradition, the tradition of Judaism, has considered the shedding of blood as the national arch-sin. The terrible suffer-ings which our people had to suffer were so unbearable that they robbed us of the ability to be patient. We were unable to be satisfied for a further length of time with daily creative work, and we became subject to the *fata morgana* of the state, as though it were a shield which could protect us against the enmity of the nations.

You see now the wreckage of almost everything that was dear to you. In Eretz Israel, out of the house of Israel a nation has come into being that is like all other nations; and it has no faith in election, or in the religion and ethical mission of the people of Israel. You see the younger generation, and their teachers, priests, and prophets going before them, as they create their gods in their own likeness and leaping and dancing proclaim the molten calf which they themselves have made. 'This is your God, O Israel.' You see with how much satisfaction the Holy Land is dismembered and the horse-trading over its parts. You see how all your efforts to instil into the nation a spirit of mutual understanding with its neighbours have come to nothing.

You, the man of spirit *par excellence*, must suffer spiritual torment when it becomes clear to you that in the people of Israel, your own people, spirit has no actual effect, but only the fist and violence. You unite in yourself two qualities which, viewed superficially, contradict one another.

You are able to see real reality as it is, but also spiritual reality as it is. Can these two realities be in fact reconciled? That is the question with which you are constantly occupied in life. The same problem concerned the prophets of Israel, Micah among them. On the one hand he prophesied concerning the sins of the leaders of the people: 'Therefore shall Zion on your account be ploughed as a field and Jerusalem shall become a heap of stones, and the mountain of the Temple a wild thicket' (3: 12). And that is in fact what happened. On the other hand, he had the magnificent vision of Zion's universal task at the end of days, when the teaching of righteousness should go forth from Zion, and nation should no more raise the sword against nation (4: 2–3).

Do you look into the future with extreme pessimism? God grant that there will be no new destruction. It is in any case my wish for you today that you do not allow your courage to sink; that it may be given to you to continue your struggle with true reality as ever; that you may be granted long life so that you may see HIS return to Zion in truth and mercy.[6]

Buber's popularity among his fellow-countrymen in Israel was at that moment not excessive. He had aroused the hostility of religious orthodoxy by his idiosyncratic approach to Jewish tradition, and political antagonism by his attitude on the Arab–Israel dispute. Yet his eighth decade was in many ways the richest and busiest of his life. He founded, and for four years directed, a training college for teachers specializing in adult education. He resumed his work on the Bible. He continued his journeys and lecture tours. And he published three new books together with a number of briefer writings.

In the foreword to the first of the books, *Two Types of Faith*,[7] he attributes to his friend Leonhard Ragaz, the Protestant theologian and writer and one of the four Christians whose helpful comments Buber acknowledges, sentiments which can just as properly be described as his own. A lover of Israel, Ragaz foresaw, according to Buber, 'a future and as yet unimaginable understanding between the kernel of the community of Israel and a genuine community of Jesus, which would arise, neither on a Jewish nor on a Christian foundation, but on the message common to both Jesus and the prophets concerning man's *teshuvah* and the Kingdom of God.[8] These very important few lines are

-----

[6] Martin Buber, *Briefwechsel aus sieben Jahrzehnten*, ed. Grete Schaeder, 3 vols. (Lamber Schneider, 1972–5), iii, no. 131.

[7] *Werke*, i. 653–782; M. Buber, *Two Types of Faith*, trans. N. P. Goldhawk (Routledge & Kegan Paul, 1951).

[8] *Werke*, i. 659; *Two Types of Faith*, 15.

not inserted into the foreword by accident. The whole underlying tenor of the work, concerned as the title indicates with two kinds of belief, emphasizes that Jesus' type of faith was not that of the Christian church but of Judaism; but also that while the followers of Jesus would do well to return to their master's belief, the faith of Christianity possesses virtues which Judaism should acquire if it is to remain a living and true religion.

Whatever the object of a belief or beliefs, the manner of believing falls into one of two basic categories, so Buber's argument goes. The first is *emunah*, a Hebrew word signifying belief *in* someone. The second is *pistis*, a Greek word meaning belief *that* something is true (or untrue). *Emunah*, typical of the religion of Israel, is an acceptance of God's sovereignty demonstrated by obedience to his will in everyday life. *Pistis*, a characteristic of early Christianity, involves first and foremost an act of the mind: Thomas the doubting disciple was one of the first to testify to it.

The religious position corresponding to *emunah* is that of a person who as it were finds himself through membership of a community whose bond with the Absolute includes him also. The religious position of a person professing *pistis* is that of an individual 'converted' to his faith. Thus, where in the first instance it is the community that generates *emunah*, in the second, it is *pistis* that generates a community of converted individuals.

Buber is careful to point out that his statements must not be taken to allude to Jews in general or Christians in general, but are intended only to mean that *emunah* and *pistis* are typified by Judaism and Christianity respectively.

One outstanding feature of *Two Types of Faith* is that its author opposes quite forcefully the faith and teaching of Paul to that of Jesus. The *pistis* of Christianity is to be traced to the former, he says, but the religion of Jesus was belief *in* God. Preaching *teshuvah*, a return to a spirit of trust, obedience, and love, Jesus did not ask for faith in statements relating to God's nature, but for a re-orientation towards doing God's will. In the translation of this doctrine for the Greek world, *teshuvah* as a concept lost its comprehensiveness, and instead of conveying the idea of a total personal return to God, became *metanoia*, a change of 'mind'. Paul, moreover, never speaks of the love of God as Jesus does. Paul never repeats Jesus' stress on immediacy of communion between man and God. Referring to Jesus' recommendation, ask and you shall receive, knock and it shall be opened, Buber observes that for Paul it is 'as though a wall were erected around the *deitas* since Jesus gave that instruction to the disciples, a wall pierced by one door only. To whomsoever opens it, God who has redeemed the world shows grace. Whoever remains distant from it is given up to Satan's angels, to whom man has been surrendered by the God of wrath.'[9]

Again, in the Sermon on the Mount, Jesus, in common with Pharisaic Judaism, speaks as though the fulfilment of the Law is possible literally, as well as in accordance with its inner purpose. Paul contests this, provoking Buber to assert:

That he thereby also contradicts the teaching of Jesus either did not enter his mind, or as seems more likely, is connected in some way which we cannot understand, since we lack the equipment, with his decision or necessity not to know Christ any longer 'after the flesh', and this would mean acknowledging that what Jesus taught was all right for the hour in which he lived, but not needed for the very different age that followed his crucifixion and resurrection.[10]

Paul's thesis is that the God of Israel, with the deliberate intention of making his people obdurate 'until the full count of the Gentiles has entered in' (Rom. 11: 25) in his planned salvation, gave them a Law on which they would certainly come to grief. 'When I contemplate this God,' Buber writes with barely concealed distaste,

I do not recognize the God of Jesus, nor if I contemplate this world do I see it as his. For Jesus, who was concerned with individual human souls and with each individual human soul, Israel was not a generality . . . Neither was it merely the totality of Jews living in his time and in relation to his message. All the souls who had lived between Moses and himself were *in concreto* part of it. In his view, *teshuvah* was assured for every one of them if they had gone astray, and each one making his *teshuvah* was the lost son returning home. His God was ever the same, who in all generations, though he might at times harden himself and at times even give a statute that was not good, answered the soul representing Israel with: 'I have forgiven in accordance with your words' (Num. 14: 20). In Paul's image of God, this characteristic is replaced by another where the generations of souls between Moses and Jesus are concerned. I do not dare to name it.[11]

Needless to say, Buber cannot omit mention of Jesus the 'son of God', or, as he puts it, 'the God Jesus'. Jesus' deification is seen by him

---

[9] *Werke*, i. 773; *Two Types of Faith*, 161.
[10] *Werke*, i. 709; *Two Types of Faith*, 80.
[11] *Werke*, i. 717–18; *Two Types of Faith*, 89–90.

to have been 'a process, a compulsion, not a caprice'—which is how all new forms of God emerge, ever and always. But a divine form such as this had never happened before. Israel in terms of religious history means direct relation between man and a Being who allows himself to be seen in events and natural phenomena yet remains invisible. To this form of God, Christianity opposed one with a particular human face, the face of a 'great Saviour God' (Titus 2: 13), of the 'other God' (Justin), of a 'suffering God' (Tatian). 'The God of Christians is at once imageless and imaged, imageless in the religious idea, imaged in the lived present. The image conceals the Imageless One'.[12]

Buber maintains that the periods of Christian history can be classified according to how much or how little Paulinism predominates. He finds our own age especially Pauline.

A Paulinism of the unredeemed exists, one therefore from which the stronghold of grace is eliminated. Here, the world is experienced as Paul experienced it, as in the hands of ineluctable powers, and only the manifest redeeming will from above, only Christ, is missing. The Christian Paulinism of our time is the fruit of the same fundamental view, though it weakens or removes the aspect of the demonisation of the government of the world. Nevertheless it sees life split asunder into an unbounded domination by wrath, and a sphere of expiation whence the call goes up clearly and vigorously for the establishment of a Christian way of life, but where the redeemed Christian soul *de facto* confronts an unredeemed human world in noble powerlessness.[13]

Pistis and *emunah* are both at present in a state of crisis. In Israel as a secular state, *emunah* has no longer any psychological foundation, and no vital one in an isolated religion. The essential spontaneity of personal religion consequently risks eventual impoverishment in a time of eclipse such as our own, and may be succeeded by elements of *pistis* by nature partly logical and partly mystical. The danger to *pistis*, on the other hand, lies in the divorce of personal holiness from national holiness. Whereas *emunah* is embodied in the *emunah* of a nation, *pistis*, with its origin outside the national experience in the individual himself, is a commitment *whereby* he sets himself apart from his nation. The idea of a holy nation has been displaced by that of the church as the one true 'people of God'. Christian existence is therefore divided into personal life, and life as a participant in the affairs of the nation. As long as the sphere of the person is able to hold its own against the

---

[12] *Werke*, i. 748–9; *Two Types of Faith*, 131.
[13] *Werke*, i. 773; *Two Types of Faith*, 162–3.

pressures of the public sphere, all will be well. The danger, Buber suggests, lies in the disparity between personal holiness and the accepted unholiness of the person's community, a disparity necessarily transferred to the 'inner dialectic of the human soul'.

Returning finally to the tone sounded at the very beginning of this book, he pleads that *pistis* and *emunah* need one another. Christianity and Judaism are essentially different. They will moreover remain so until mankind is gathered in from the 'exiles of the religions' into the Kingdom of God. But an Israel struggling for renewal of its faith through rebirth of the holy person, and a Christianity struggling for renewal of its faith through rebirth of the holy nation, may have help as yet unsuspected to render to one another and something as yet unsaid to say to one another.

———

Three talks delivered by Buber in New York at the Jewish Theological Seminary in 1951 were published a year later as *At the Turning*.[14] He notes in the last of them, 'The Dialogue between Heaven and Earth', that nowadays even believers deny the existence of a living dialogue between man and God in daily life. They maintain that he spoke to man in the past, that what was said then has been recorded once and for all in Scripture, and that since then he has stayed mute. But whoever reads the Bible with an open mind will realize that what happened once, continues to happen. By the same token, we will feel also that that fact of it happening now is a guarantee that it happened in the past.

We are spoken to personally; and we answer by way of personal actions, reactions, and abstentions from action. But biblical teaching indicates that we are also addressed nationally. The nation, too, is summoned to realize God's will on earth. Modern life is guilty in this respect because behaviour viewed as culpable in relations between individuals counts as praiseworthy in relations between nations. Similarly, personal life and public life obey quite different laws. Acts frowned on in personal conduct are acclaimed in public affairs. Privately, lies are judged reprehensible; publicly, very worthwhile.

Thus God speaks via personal and national channels. But his voice is not confined to these sources. It can be detected in everything.

[14] Martin Buber, *At the Turning: Three Addresses on Judaism* (Farrar, Strauss, and Young, 1952); 'An der Wende', in *Der Jude und sein Judentum* (Melzer, 1963), 144–83.

'Everything, whatever exists and whatever comes into existence, in nature and in history, is essentially an utterance by God, an infinite context of signs intended to be perceived and understood by perceiving and understanding beings.'[15] Nevertheless, a difference distinguishes one from the other, according to Buber, inasmuch as nature expresses in all her elements what may be termed a continuous divine self-communication, whereas what God says in history does not possess this quality. Times of revelation alternate with times of silence. Times when God's influence is recognized in a coincidence of events alternate with others seemingly empty of him, with 'nowhere a beckoning of his finger, nowhere a sign that he is present and affecting our historical present. In such times, it is difficult for the individual, and very difficult for the nation, to understand that it is being spoken to by God.'[16] How can we regain contact with God in such conditions? How should we live who believe in a living God and know him, and are nevertheless fated to pass our lives in an age when his Face is hidden? How above all is a Jewish life possible after the concentration camps? How can the Jew still hear God speaking to him? 'Dare we recommend to the survivor of Auschwitz, to the Job of the gas-chambers, "Give thanks to God for he is loving-kind, for his mercy endures for ever"?'[17] We should remember that Job's comfort, after all his disputes with God and after all his sufferings and agony of mind, was that God, from having been far from him, was present with him once more. He could again hear him and his 'eye' could see him. We should wrangle with God as Job did.

Do we stand defeated before the hidden Face of God like the tragic hero of the Greeks before faceless destiny? No. We too contend even now with God, with him, the Lord of existence, whom we here once chose to be our Lord. We do not resign ourselves to earthly existence, we struggle for its redemption. And contending, we call on the help of our Lord, of him who is ever and again hidden. In such a situation we await his voice, whether it comes from the storm or from the stillness which follows it. And though his future appearance may resemble no earlier one, we shall recognize our terrible and loving-kind Lord.[18]

---

15 *At the Turning*, 57; 'An der Wende', 179.
16 *At the Turning*, 58; 'An der Wende', 179.
17 *At the Turning*, 61; 'An der Wende', 182.
18 *At the Turning*, 182–3; 'An der Wende', 62.

The last of Buber's major works, *Eclipse of God*,[19] is again a short collection of lectures delivered originally in Yale, Princeton, Columbia, Chicago, and elsewhere. Their general message is a continuation of the theme, perceptible in so much of his later writings, that God is not dead as Nietzsche announces, but that the Face of man's supreme *Vis-à-Vis* has become temporarily obscured.

Each historical age is distinguished by the prevailing relationship between religion and reality. Periods when the object of man's 'belief' is independent, with an existence of its own, times when it is a reality with which people feel themselves to be in real relation, even though they may have a most inadequate idea of whoever it is they believe in, alternate with others when the reality formerly believed in is replaced by an *idea* of that reality, an idea that people 'have' and can consequently manipulate.

Such is the age in which we ourselves live. Our unreality makes itself apparent in the way we 'think' religion instead of 'doing' it. It has become a property of the mind instead of the whole person.

Furthermore, by failing to recognize present existence as the medium through which to 'do' the requirements of God, we have admitted a magical element into what passes today for religion. We find it in order to ask, without bothering to listen for what is demanded in return. We try to put pressure on a 'God' who can be used. The magical tendency of today, evident in the attempts of so-called theosophists, and even theologians, to unveil mystery and make it comprehensible, is the result of worshipping the Supreme Being ceremonially without truly communing with him.

For at the heart of the contemporary unreality of religion is an unreality of prayer. Once prayer is infected with the extreme self-consciousness peculiar to modern times, immediacy of man–God relation becomes impossible. Prayer in its precise sense is a plea to God for his Presence to be made known, to become dialogically perceptible. The one prerequisite of genuine prayer is therefore unreserved spontaneity and readiness on the part of the whole man for that Presence. No one who is not himself present can become aware of Presence.

The contribution of philosophy to our religious dilemma is that from having treated the divine as an object of thought, it now ignores God altogether. As the unreality of reigning divine forms has become

[19] *Werke*, i. 505–603; M. Buber, *Eclipse of God*, trans. M. Friedman, Eugene Kamenka, Norbert Guterman, and I. M. Lask (Gollancz, 1953).

reflected in the unreality of the religions that profess their names, philosophers—Buber names more or less the same figures as those mentioned in 'What is Man?' with the addition of Sartre, Hermann Cohen, and the psychologist C. G. Jung—have set out to oppose not only the form but the everlasting *You* itself. To divine forms that have developed a momentum of their own, and grown to be a focus of relation in place of the Formless and Imageless One they were originally intended to represent, philosophy has opposed the 'pure idea', sometimes going so far as to envisage it as the negation of all metaphysical ideas.

Making an abstraction of God does not in itself entail the destruction of the relation essential to religion. One who refuses to limit God to transcendence has a fuller conception of him than someone who does so confine him. On the other hand, the more an idea of God departs from anthropomorphism the more it must be validated by the evidence of concrete experience and completed by immediacy and nearness. For religion to be real, it is not imperative that the divine should be considered a person, but we must be able to enter into relation with it as our supreme *Vis-à-Vis*—and not ours alone.

Such has not happened. Yet this very repudiation of God by philosophy has itself stimulated religious minds to start on a new journey towards a new encounter with him. And as they go on their way, they destroy the forms which in their eyes no longer do him justice.

In our days, Buber ends, returning to the leading topic of relation and irrelation around which *I and You* was written so many years before, irrelation predominates. In the pursuit of so-called security, prosperity, and well-being, the world, our environment, the people among whom we live, even life itself, have come to be regarded merely as sources of potential advantage and disadvantage to the self. The *it*-connection,

swollen to gigantic proportions, has arrogated to itself almost uncontested mastery and command. The *I* of this connection is lord of the hour, an *I* that has all, makes all, succeeds in all, is incapable of saying *you*, of encountering another being. This all-powerful *I*-ness surrounded by *it* cannot by nature acknowledge either God or any true Absolute manifesting itself as of non-human origin. It steps in between and blots out the light of heaven.[20]

But although we may for the time being have done away with the world of transcendence, and earlier principles no longer appear to

[20] *Werke*, i. 598–9; *Eclipse of God*, 166–7.

exist, and although our divine *Vis-à-Vis* may have gone into eclipse, he still endures inviolate on the other side of the obstruction. We may even go so far as to rid ourselves of the word 'God', yet he to whom it applies continues to live in the light of his eternity. He is not dead. It is we who are housed in darkness like a people given over to death. But the eclipse of God's light is not its extinction. 'Already by tomorrow, that which has interposed itself may have retreated.'[21]

Another study to appear in 1952, *Images of Good and Evil*,[22] enters into the problem of the two so-called 'Inclinations' or 'urges' of good and evil, and contrasts the exposition of evil in Bible and Talmud with that of the myths of Zoroastrianism, where they appear as absolutes personified by the constantly warring gods, Ormazd and Ahriman.

First, how did it happen that from having in the beginning pronounced man 'very good', God later saw that 'every imagination of the thoughts of his heart was only evil continually' (Gen. 6: 5)?

The point to which Buber draws attention here is that God does not call man himself wicked but his 'way' (Gen. 6: 12) that fills the earth with deeds of violence, and that this 'way' has its foundation not in an evil soul, but in the evil product of the human imagination.

Later, the rabbis gave to the word *yetzer* ('imagination') a slightly different meaning by discerning in it good and evil impulses, though they taught that both are designed by the Creator to serve man in combination. Evil is the leaven in the dough without which it will not rise. Indeed, it is precisely the presence in man of the evil urge, so they believed, that persuaded God to describe him as 'very good'. Evil is the basis of the good. It is called 'evil' only because it is made so by man when he separates it from its yoke-fellow, the urge towards the good.

The Zoroastrian myths of the spirits of good and evil reflect a later stage of human development. Where the first biblical men slipped and slid into sin, Yima the shepherd-god, into whose charge the supreme god Ormazd placed the world, blessed and praised himself instead of acknowledging the bounties and favours of Ormazd, thereby deliberately placing himself in the no-position of evil. In other words, the Bible sees evil as a failure to decide, but the ancient Persian story expounds it as a decision to do wrong, to be false instead of true, for

---

[21] *Werke*, i. 599; *Eclipse of God*, 167.
[22] *Werke*, i. 607–50; Martin Buber, *Images of Good and Evil*, trans. Michael Bullock (Routledge & Kegan Paul, 1952).

Yima's appropriation to himself of the honour due to Ormazd was a lie against existence.

Buber accepted the traditional Jewish belief. The dimension of the wicked is, he thought, constantly experienced as absence of decision rather than as deliberate choice. Nevertheless, a man will not see his life as consisting of a series of isolated instances of non-decision but as a persistence in indecision, knowledge which he will repress for as long as his instinct of self-preservation predominates over his ability to affirm himself. But as soon as it ceases to do so, the inability of his self-knowledge to permit him to affirm and confirm himself will oblige him to doubt himself instead. The situation will then either become pathological in that his relation with himself will become confused; or he will discover a way out where he least expected it—through a huge effort at self-unification, one that will surprise even him by its power and efficacy, through *teshuvah*.

There is also a third possibility. Everyone needs to be confirmed in his existence by others and also by himself. We can at a pinch dispense with external confirmation if our self-affirmation is such that it needs no supplement. But if self-knowledge brings only rejection, the consolation of our fellows will in no way make up for this. Consequently, if we cannot rectify our self-knowledge by means of *teshuvah*, we must see to it that our self-affirmation is made independent of facts and base it on desiring to be what we actually are. 'This is the human condition to which the myth of Yima's lie corresponds. By praising and blessing himself as the creator of himself, he sins against life. Indeed, he wishes to elevate lying to supreme authority over life, for the truth shall no longer be what he experiences but what he determines it to be.'[23] 'Radical evil' does not exist in the earliest stage of human development. Whatever evil deeds are committed are not so much done as fallen into, happened on. In the second stage, evil is radical because it is willed.

Good, on the other hand, retains its character of directedness all along. Decisions made with the unified soul have but one direction: which can be understood either as directing oneself towards becoming the person one is intended to be, or as directing oneself towards God. But this duality of conception is only one of aspect, 'provided I do not give the name "God" to a projection of myself, or something of that sort, but only to my Creator, the Originator of my uniqueness which is

---

[23] *Werke*, i. 647; *Images of Good and Evil*, 79.

not to be derived from within the world'.[24] Good thought of in this way can be fitted into no ethical system because all those we know came into being by virtue of it. Every ethos has its origin in a revelation, and all revelation relates to participation in the goal of creation, a service in which man is put to the test. 'Without holding his own, and this means, without striking and holding to the One Direction as far as he can, *quantum satis*, he can have what he calls life, a life of the soul, and even a life of the spirit, in all freedom and fruitfulness and in every rank and degree, but existence for him without it, there is none.'[25]

———

In the following year, which was Buber's seventy-fifth, he made his first visit to Germany since the Holocaust to receive the Peace Prize awarded him by the German book trade in Frankfurt. As had happened in 1951, when he was awarded the Hanseatic Goethe Prize in Hamburg, his acceptance of the honour aroused considerable unpopularity and controversy, especially on the part of Jews who had so recently suffered directly or indirectly at the hands of the Nazis, and he was attacked in the Israeli press as well as in that of England and America for what appeared to be his leniency and his forgiveness of the Germans. It is noteworthy that the speech he delivered on this occasion is published in *Nachlese*,[26] which he expressly defines as a collection of what he felt to be most lastingly worthwhile among his writings.

Ten years ago, he told the crowd assembled for the ceremony, 'several thousand' Germans murdered millions of Jews with a ferocity unparalleled in history. These people had put such a huge distance between themselves and true humanity that he could not even hate them. And who was he that he should presume to 'forgive'? There had been Germans who in the days of Auschwitz and Treblinka knew that something terrible was going on and did nothing about it. But he could not judge them, he said. 'My heart, familiar with human weakness, refuses to condemn my neighbour because he was unable to become a martyr.'[27] Remembering the equally well-known human anxiety not to discover a truth which may turn out to be unbearable, he was likewise

[24] *Werke*, i. 647; *Images of Good and Evil*, 81–2.
[25] *Werke*, i. 650; *Images of Good and Evil*, 83.
[26] Martin Buber, 'Das echte Gespräch und die Möglichkeiten des Friedens', *Nachlese* (Lambert Schneider, 1965), 219–30; published in English as 'Genuine Dialogue and the Possibilities of Peace', in *Pointing the Way* (Schocken, 1974).
[27] 'Das echte Gespräch', 220; 'Genuine Dialogue', 233.

unable to condemn the German masses who were ignorant of what was going on but made no attempt to find out what, if anything, lay behind the rumours.

There were however, also those who had refused to obey the commands of their superiors and had suffered death themselves. I see them, Buber said, 'quite near to me, in that special intimacy that sometimes binds us to the dead and to them alone, and there is reverence and love for these German people in my heart'.[28] Apart from a brief mention of the young, who had had nothing to do with the nation's horrendous crime, and whose spirit he felt sure had been made more alert by the recollection of those twelve years of *homo contrahumanus*, the remainder of Buber's address is concerned with the crisis of modern man, which he ascribes primarily to an inability to communicate. We cannot speak to God in prayer. We cannot speak to each other. Nation cannot speak to nation. Why? Because we have lost confidence in each other and in life. We are uncertain whether life has any meaning.

And meanwhile, in the background, waiting to take advantage of *homo humanus* locked in his international divisions and misunderstandings, lurks *homo contrahumanus*—Satan, the Hinderer, the enemy of mankind. Let us not allow this Satanic power to sweep once again through the world, Buber pleads. 'Let us redeem speech from its interdict. Let us have confidence, despite everything.'[29]

As has been said, by the time Franz Rosenzweig died in 1929, he and Buber had reached chapter fifty-three of the Book of Isaiah in their work of Bible translation. Buber then continued on his own until his move to Palestine, planning once he had settled in Jerusalem to carry on with the next very difficult task, the Book of Job. He had already made several attempts to deal with this work but without success. For various reasons the moment was, however, not yet right and the Bible enterprise came to a halt. Then, in 1948, the publisher Salman Schocken let him know that although there was no question of his taking the Scripture translation in its entirety, he would be glad to have Job as soon as it was ready. Two years later, another publishing firm, Hegner, with offices in Switzerland and Germany, made an even better offer by asking for a new and revised edition of all the biblical books already prepared and for the translation of the remaining scrip-

---

[28] 'Das echte Gespräch', 221; 'Genuine Dialogue', 233.
[29] 'Das echte Gespräch', 230; 'Genuine Dialogue', 239.

tural writings to be completed. Buber was delighted and set to work. The Pentateuch was out by 1954, the historical books by 1955, and the prophets by 1958. In the autumn of 1959 Job was finished and by the beginning of 1961 the work of translation was over. The final volume, the Hagiographa, saw the light of day in 1962.

To Buber's immense corpus of writings must therefore be added the rendering into German of the entire Hebrew Bible, partly in cooperation with Rosenzweig, but mostly by himself, for even whilst Rosenzweig was alive the actual work was largely Buber's, as his friend was the first to admit.

One piece of original writing from these last years should perhaps not be allowed to pass unmentioned, if only because it is another example of the extraordinary breadth of Buber's interests and his competence in so many different fields. Given the title by Maurice Friedman of 'Man and his Image-Work',[30] its subject in plain English is artistic creativity. It is an inquiry into the nature of art as an 'essence' (*Wesen*) with its origin in the 'essence' of man. Art, Buber concludes, following a commentary on what is nowadays meant by 'nature'—his point of departure being Dürer's argument that the artist has to 'wrest' art from the nature in which it is embedded—art is

work and witness of relation between *substantia humana* and *substantia rerum*. It is the Between become form. Consequently, we too can say that it is given to a peculiarly special kind of man to wrest art from the nature in which it is embedded. The artist does so, not by seeking to penetrate behind the world of the senses, but by completing its form as a perfected product of the imagination. It is however in the completion that we find the origin.[31]

———

Since no pursuit of the real Buber can be complete until we know what he thought of death, it seems correct to end our search with a short piece which, although he wrote it as long ago as 1927, must still have seemed valid to him in his old age for he includes it in *Nachlese*.

[30] *Werke*, i. 424–41; Martin Buber, 'Man and his Image-Work', in *Knowledge of Man*, trans. M. Friedman (Allen and Unwin 1965), 149–65. 'Image-work' is intended to correspond to the word *Gebild*, which Buber uses in *Images of Good and Evil* for the Hebrew *yetzer*, which in turn signifies both the biblical 'Imagination of the thoughts of the heart' and the 'urge' or 'inclination' of the rabbis. 'Image-work' as an English term is archaic. The *Shorter Oxford English Dictionary* reads: 's.v. imagery: "scenery is nature's image-work" 1647'. But because of its various shades of meaning Buber's *Gebild* is undeniably difficult to translate.

[31] *Werke*, i. 441; 'Man and his Image-Work', 165.

We know nothing about death, nothing but the one fact that we shall die. But what does it mean, to die? We do not know. It is therefore appropriate that we should accept it as the end of everything that we can imagine. To wish to project our imagination beyond death, to anticipate in our minds what death can reveal to us only in existence, appears to me to be disbelief disguised as belief. True belief says: I know nothing about death, but I know that God is eternity, and I know furthermore that he is my God. Whether what we know as time continues beyond our death becomes quite unimportant beside this knowledge that we are God's, who is not 'immortal' but eternal. Instead of imagining our self as being alive although dead, we desire to prepare ourselves for a real death, which is perhaps the end of time, but which, if this is so, is certainly the threshold of eternity.[32]

Buber died in Jerusalem on 13 June 1965, aged eighty-seven. On his tombstone is written a quotation from Psalm 73: 23:

But I am with You always.[33]

---

[32] Martin Buber, 'Nach dem Tod. 1927. Antwort auf eine Rundfrage', *Nachlese*, 259.

[33] I am indebted for this reminder to Roy Oliver, author of *The Wanderer and the Way: The Hebrew Tradition in the Writings of Martin Buber* (East and West Library, 1968).

7

Findings

THE rabbi said, 'Whoever wishes to understand the words of Abaye must first bind his soul to the soul of Abaye.' Where are we to find Buber's soul so that we may bind our souls to his and understand him? In philosophy? He emphatically denied that he was a philosopher, insisting that he was not concerned with ideas *per se* but with communicating his personal experience to his fellow-men. He used the methods and language of philosophy because it was the only way he could convert the unique into the general, express as applicable to all men an insight that had occurred to him individually.[1] In theology? This suggestion he rejected even more vehemently. His name appears in the company of such famous contemporaries as Tillich, Bultmann, Bonhoeffer, to mention but a few, and his opinions are weighed with and against theirs. But he always made it more than clear that he considered himself unentitled to pronounce on the nature of God. He was competent to write only about God in his relation to man, in this present life. He could certainly not forget when explaining the *factum* man that he lives face to face with God, but at no point, he protested,

can I draw God himself into my explanation, any more than I can detach what is to me the undoubted effect of God in history and make it the object of my consideration. Just as I know of no theological world-history, so I know of no theological anthropology in this sense. I know only of a philosophical one. The theological element that has admittedly determined a great part of my study and writing is the basis of my thinking, but not as deriving from something traditional, however important this is to me too, and therefore not as 'theology', but rather as the religious experience to which I am indebted for the independence of my thought.[2]

Whether Buber was a mystic, as is widely held, is not so easy to determine. He undeniably came to believe that mysticism is unreal, in

[1] Martin Buber, *Werke*, 3 vols. (Kösel–Lambert Schneider, 1962–4) i. 1111; P. A. Schilpp and M. Friedman, eds., *The Philosophy of Martin Buber*, Library of Living Philosophers (Open Court, 1967), 689.

[2] *Werke*, i. 1112; Schilpp and Friedman, *The Philosophy of Martin Buber*, 690.

his understanding of the word 'real'. He explicitly refused to accept the notion of union with God, an end and aim of mysticism, and any separation of life into sacred and profane. The mystical experiences to which he had surrendered in his youth played no part in his later life, and he remembered with continuing grief and regret the suicide of a person for whom he had once had no time because he was at that moment engaged in his prayers.

But what is a 'mystic'? Definitions range from 'one initiated into mysteries' to 'one who believes in the spiritual apprehension of truths inaccessible to the understanding', and of course to 'one who seeks by contemplation and self-surrender to obtain union or absorption into the deity'. Buber as a mature man would certainly have been made uneasy by the application to himself of the first qualification and would have totally repudiated the third. He might, with some provisos, have assented to the second: though on reflection, what sort of 'spiritual apprehension' can that be which is distinct from 'the understanding'? Although he had renounced the 'mystical bombast' of which Franz Rosenzweig complained, and also the basic teachings of the masters of mysticism by whom he had been so deeply influenced in his youth, can he have changed so radically that no affinity remained between their outlook and his? The magnet of magnets for Buber, as it was for the Christian, Sufi, and Jewish mystics whom he had earlier admired, was God. But unlike them, he learned to resist any inclination to withdraw from 'real life', life in and for this present world. All the same, there is no denying that now and then we definitely catch an ecstatic inflection in his language which betrays a burning love of God breaking through the controls under which he placed it. Beneath all his intellectuality and erudition and his insistence on earthly realities we become aware of Buber the rapt contemplative.

Another question we may reasonably ask is whether Buber was essentially a teacher. This would seem difficult to contradict, but even so, he wished to make sure that his function should be considered as that of a guide rather than an instructor. 'I merely demonstrate something,' he said. 'I demonstrate reality. I demonstrate something in reality that is no longer seen, or seen too little. I take my listener by the hand and lead him to the window. I push the window open and point outward. I have no doctrine. I conduct a conversation.'[3] He had wanted to indicate the way along which to go, not to explain how to get

---

[3] *Werke*, i. 1114.

there. 'I certainly do not hand a book of principles to someone who accepts my pointer, where he can see how to decide in any given situation. That is not for me. One whose finger is outstretched has one thing to show, not a variety. No, I have in fact no ethical system to offer. Neither do I know of any that is generally applicable and which I should only need to teach.'[4]

Was Buber then a biblical scholar? Here, the comment must be that despite the many years which he spent in the study of Scripture, he is not by and large accepted by present-day biblicists as one of themselves. The reason they give is that whereas a detached analysis of biblical language and sources is called for, and a balanced judgement of its history and structure—an *I–it* approach in effect—Buber believed the prime aim to be an understanding of the text and thought these methods to be by themselves inadequate for such a purpose. He adopted them of course, but for him the Bible was first and foremost the record of a dialogue between heaven and earth, between man and God, a book to be addressed as *you*, a living word which must be allowed to make its own living impact. For him, it was not just a collection of sacred writings dating from different historical periods and transmitted in a variety of ways, but an everlasting voice requiring to be listened to, answered, and obeyed.

In brief, none of these camps holds Buber's soul, so what else do we do to find it? We can study the pattern emerging from the foregoing summary of his written work.

The stress in *At the Turning: Three Addresses on Judaism* is on decision, unification, and *teshuvah*. A renewal of Judaism and a new universalism must go hand in hand.

In *Daniel*, the main themes are the real and realization, meaning and unity.

In *I and You*, two principal threads run through the work. The first is presence, being-with as opposed to being-apart-from. If we so decide, we can be present with the natural world, the world of men and the world of mind and spirit. From being present with them, we can become real and unified. Having become real and unified, we shall be qualified for relation and encounter with the supreme Presence whose Name is HE IS THERE. The second motif is speech. God speaks through his creation and through history. All that happens is his speech. We in return are called on to speak to him via our deeds. If we

---

[4] *Werke*, i. 1117.

have become unaware of Presence we shall no longer hear the Voice. But though the Word may have temporarily disintegrated, there will be a new *teshuvah* on the part of man and a new redemption of the world on the part of God.

Kingship of God advances the earlier justification of the interpretation of the Name YHWH as HE IS THERE.

In 'Question to the Single One' the outstanding topics are response, responsibility, decision, freedom, good, and evil.

The Prophetic Faith enters into the problem of God's changing forms and again expounds the divine Name as revealing what God does. It deals also with *teshuvah* as a return to presence, and speaks of Israel as God's perfected one, made perfect for the coming of the Kingdom.

What is Man? proposes a remedy for the modern alienation of man, whom it defines as one in whose dialogic encounter is realized and recognized.

Moses once more interprets the Name of YHWH. YHWH is he who is with, goes with, and goes before his people. He is a God who appears, speaks, and reveals. He is Israel's *You*, who speaks to her as *I*.

In *Paths in Utopia*, the real community is characterized as one with a Centre, manifest or concealed. It is real because it is a community sprung from necessity and committed to real effort and work.

Two Types of Faith maintains that the call common to all the prophets, including Jesus, was for *teshuvah* and the coming of the Kingdom. For the Jew, there must be a renewal of personal holiness, and for the Christian, a renewal of national holiness, in the service of the eventual unification of the world into the One Kingdom.

In *Eclipse of God* we hear that HE IS THERE is not dead. It is we who have allowed the *I* of irrelation to come between the light of the supreme Presence and ourselves. We have become unreal. There is no reality in us or in our religion, which we think, but do not do. Not being present, we are unconscious of presence and hence of Presence. We must make our *teshuvah*. We must turn back to being there, with our world and with HIM. We must be prepared to suffer the annihilation of despair in order to be renewed.

Lastly, in *Images of Good and Evil* we learn that the evil urge must be re-yoked to its fellow, the good. The undirectedness of evil must be turned into the One Direction of the good. Man must become one and whole.

What in general does all this amount to? The message seems to be as follows.

Make your *teshuvah*.

Imitate the divine attribute of presence by returning to a spirit of responsive and responsible attachment to and for the world and all that exists in it.

Imitate also the divine attribute of unity. Become one and whole and real.

Become perfectly human and thereby play your part in preparing for the coming of God's Kingdom on earth.

This is not philosophy. It is not even philosophical anthropology, where Buber occasionally saw himself as belonging. It is not existentialism, theology, or mysticism. It is not humanism, Hebrew or otherwise. It is religiousness. More specifically, because its God is the God of the Hebrew Bible, and its burden that of the Hebrew prophets, it is biblical religiousness.

Buber was in fact by his own definition a *Schriftsteller*.[5] '*Bekenntnis eines Schriftstellers*', reads the introductory poem in *Nachlese*, that repository of his chosen excerpts: 'A writer's confession of faith'. But a straight translation is no good to us here because *Schriftsteller* is a pun. Buber was a *Schriftsteller*, a writer, and a very expert one. And he was also a *Schrift-Steller*, an exponent of *die Schrift*, Scripture, a writer dedicated to making the Hebrew Bible accessible to the world of today.

Nor is this all, for one more element remains in this complex play on words. In *My Way to Hasidism*, Buber employs the closely related word, '*Schriftstellerei*' (in inverted commas) when referring to the literary compositions of the Hasidim. Therefore, when he identified himself as a *Schrift-Steller*, he will certainly have had in mind his literary work, not only on Scripture, but also on the scriptures of Hasidism.

We may consequently conclude that these two, the Bible and Hasidism, were the twin tabernacles of Buber's soul during his lifetime. It is there that we must look if we are to bind our souls to his.

[5] See H. L. Goldschmidt, *Abschied von Martin Buber* (Hegner, 1966), 7.

PART II
'GOD IS OUR MODEL', SAID THE JEW

8

I Am There

IN the ancient tradition of Jewish religious teaching, Buber looks for the perfection of human nature through the imitation of God. But who or what is this everlasting *You* of which he speaks? Does it really belong, as a concept of the Deity, to the mainstream of Jewish thought? And if so, what more can we learn about its substance and nature from the Bible and Hasidism? Is it possibly part of the succession of divine forms which Buber sees passing through history, changing their shape from age to age, but never their essential character?

A divine form, as Buber describes it, comes into being as the issue, in the idiom of *I and You*, of encounter between *I* and *You*. If it is subsequently accepted by those to whom it is transmitted, it fulfils its function and purpose as a vital fount of energy, in the individual and in the society of which he is part. It acts as a creative stimulus and becomes the focus of all-embracing *I–You* relation. But also, because it corresponds to what is considered at the time to be good and true, it becomes the model to which men turn in regulating their personal and social behaviour. Its effect during this phase of its existence is consequently unitive, every aspect of life coming into its sphere of influence. Inevitably, however, a final period ensues of decline and death. Values alter, knowledge extends or shrinks, horizons widen or diminish, other ideals replace those of earlier periods, and the divine form representing them loses its power to animate, move, and unify. Its dynamism and authority leave it and, to the extent that it is no longer heard to say anything or seen to do anything, it dies.

The crucial stage is the second one, for unless a form of God, besides being accepted as matching the need of the age in which it appears, is quickened and made effective by imitative human action, it will never be anything more than an abstraction. It will never be real. Unless those who worship a God of love do so with loving deeds, he will never be more than a charming idea. Deeds alone can lend him substance, as the Hasidic Rabbi Heschel of Apt (d. 1825) understood when he interpreted a passage from the *Sayings of the Fathers*, 'Know what is above you' (literally, 'above of you').[1]

Know that what is above, is of you. And what is above? Ezekiel tells us, 'And upon the form of the throne a form to be seen resembling a man upon it above' (Ezek. 1: 26). How can this be said of God? For it is written, 'To whom will you compare me that I should resemble him?' (Isa. 40: 25). Yet it is true. The form to be seen resembling a man is of us. It is the form which we shape with the worship of our sincere hearts. With it, we make for our Creator without shape and likeness, for himself, blessed be he and blessed be his Name, a human form. When a man shows mercy and loving-kindness, he shapes God's right hand. And when a man fights the divine war and overcomes evil, he shapes God's left hand. He who is above upon the throne is of you.[2]

But no one can shape God's right hand with works of mercy unless he knows that mercy is the deed of God's right hand. Which is another way of saying that for the form on the throne to ·acquire substance through the imitative acts of those who venerate it, they must know what it does.

What can we say in this respect of the everlasting *You*?

Nothing, because *You* has no identity of its own. And if anyone should suggest that it is everlastingly *You* and that this is what it does, the everlastingness pertains only to its impossibility ever to become an *it*.

You is not a form of God and is impossible to imitate. 'You' is a personal pronoun by which a speaker who knows himself as 'I' addresses another who also knows himself as 'I'. But who is the *I* belonging to the everlasting *You*, the supreme *I* to whom man says *You*? This is what we have to determine if we are to share Buber's vision of the perfect man who lives in imitation of him. It is in this *I* that we shall find the new divine form of which Buber would say, with the Hasidic rabbi known as the Holy Jew, 'God is our model.'[3]

Buber makes clear in his various biblical writings that his notion of God is based in particular on the revelation of himself to Moses as it is

[1] *Pirke Abot*, ii. 11.

[2] Martin Buber, 'Die Erzählungen der Chassidim', *Werke*, 3 vols. (Kösel-Lambert Schneider, 1962–4), iii. 508; *Tales of the Hasidim: Later Masters*, trans. Olga Marx (Schocken, 1948), 117.

[3] Martin Buber, 'Gog und Magog', *Werke*, iii. 1153; see *For the Sake of Heaven*, trans. Ludwig Lewisohn (Meridian Books, 1958), 185.

recorded in the Book of Exodus in the story of the burning bush, so we must try to find the connection between that tremendous event and the divine *I* of the everlasting *You.*

The process of doing so may appear technical and intimidating to anyone unaccustomed to work of this kind, involving as it does not only philological argument, but Hebrew philological argument[4]—though as much as possible of the Hebrew will be eliminated. But if it has not been beyond the writer of this book, who is not a trained biblical scholar, to make the enquiry, it is assuredly within the capacities of her readers to take part in it.

Basically it is a continuation of the detective work that has characterized this study so far, but with a different objective. We enquire into Buber's reasoning concerning God's Name and nature, and supplement his findings with those of his colleague Franz Rosenzweig, and of a contemporary Jewish scholar to whom both men were greatly indebted for their ideas. We next look to see whether the explanations of the divinity advanced by these three are to be found among the ancient rabbinic interpreters known as targumists and midrashists, who composed Aramaic and Hebrew paraphrases and commentaries with a view to expounding, clarifying, and adapting biblical literature. A great deal of this material will be new to many non-Jews.

The third step, since we shall by then find ourselves in the realm of Jewish mystical thought and writings, will be to pursue among the visionary ideas of the mystics the notion of God that has emerged from the investigation so far.

Finally, Christians should find special interest in the fourth development of the search, where the self-same understanding of God is discovered in the New Testament, in the Book of Revelation.

The first step, however, is to re-tell the familiar biblical story in an English as near as possible to the Buber–Rosenzweig German, chiefly to help with the presentation of Buber's argument,[5] but also to give an idea of the literary genre adopted by the translators, with its attention to rhythm in the interest of oral recitation, its reproduction of the use in Hebrew of emphatic repetition, and its forcing of the vocabulary to oblige words to conform as precisely as can be managed to the original. An explanation of the forms HE and HIS applied to God will emerge in due course.

[4] See *Zu einer neuen Verdeutschung der Schrift* (Hegner, 1954), 28 ff.
[5] See Martin Buber, 'Moses', *Werke*, ii. 47–66; *Moses* (East & West Library, 1947), 39–55.

Another very important point to bear in mind is that in Hebrew the one imperfect tense covers the present and the future. Thus the one word can mean 'I am there' and 'I will be there'.

———

Mosheh was herdsman of the sheep of Yitro his father-in-law, priest of
    Midian.
He led the sheep to the far side of the desert.
He came to Horeb the mountain of God.
HIS messenger appeared to him in the blaze of a fire from the midst of the
    thornbush.
He looked;
behold the thornbush burns in the fire yet the thornbush is unconsumed.
Mosheh said,
I will go over
and see this great sight,
why the thornbush is unconsumed.
But when HE saw that he went over to see,
God called him from the midst of the thornbush.
He said,
Mosheh! Mosheh!
And he said,
Here I am!
He said,
Pull off your shoes from your feet,
for the place on which you stand is sanctifying ground.
And said,
I am your father's God,
the God of Abraham,
the God of Yitzhak,
the God of Yaacob.
Mosheh hid his face,
for he was afraid to look at God.
But HE said,
I have seen, seen, the oppression of my people who are in Egypt,
I have heard their cry before their task-masters.
Indeed, I have known their sufferings.
I have come down
to deliver them from the hand of Egypt,
to bring them up from out of that land
to a land good and spacious,
a land flowing with milk and honey,

the place of the Canaanites and the Hittites,
the Amorites and the Perizzites,
the Hivites and the Jebusites.
Now,
behold the cry of the sons of Israel has come to me.
And I have seen also the torment with which the Egyptians torment them.
Now go;
I send you to Pharaoh.
Lead my people, the sons of Israel, out of Egypt!
Mosheh said to God,
Who am I,
that I should go to Pharaoh,
that I should lead the sons of Israel out of Egypt?
But he said,
Surely, I will be there with you.
And this is the sign for you that I myself have sent you:
when you have led the people out of Egypt,
you shall on this mountain serve God. (Exod. 3: 1–12)

Here the first part of the dialogue ends. The voice from the thornbush announces itself as the God of Moses' father and forefathers and charges him with the delivery of the Israelites from their Egyptian slavery. When Moses demurs, he is told, 'Surely, *I will be there* with you' (verse 12). According to Buber, *ehyeh* = 'I will be there', the first person singular of the imperfect tense of the verb *hayah* = 'to be' (not 'to be' in the abstract sense, of which the Bible has as yet no notion, but 'to be' in the sense of 'to become', 'to come to be', 'to become present', 'to be there') is not a simple assurance of God's presence but holds the clue to the divine Name, YHWH.

Mosheh said to God,
I come then to the sons of Israel,
I say to them, The God of your fathers sends me to you.
They will say to me, What is there about his Name?
What shall I then say to them? (Exod. 3: 13)

The peculiarity of the Buber–Rosenzweig version of this passage will be noticed immediately. Instead of anticipating that the Israelites will ask him, 'What is his Name?', Moses foresees that they will enquire *about* God's Name. A fully developed philological argument is advanced in favour of this reading of the Hebrew, but Buber adds as another objection to the usual translation that it is barely conceivable that the Israelites would have been ignorant of the Name of the God of their fathers.

One further consideration apropos of the correct understanding of the question relating to the Name is that the Jews of that time lived in an environment in which magic and the occult were powerful influences. It was believed that to know a person's 'true' name, which might have been his ordinary name pronounced differently or another name altogether, was to have him at one's mercy. Thus, if knowledge of a man's true name made him vulnerable, all the more would this apply to God. The Israelites would have imagined that once in possession of the secret of the divine Name, they would be able to manipulate their God and bend him to their wishes and desires.

————

> God said to Mosheh,
> I will be there such as I will be there.

This statement imputed to God in Exodus 3: 14—in Hebrew, *ehyeh asher ehyeh*—is distinguished by Buber as the revelation of revelations, the sublime centre-point around which the entire story of the burning bush turns. God does not say 'I am who am' or 'I am who I am.' Theological pronouncements of this kind would have been neither understood nor appreciated by the wretched Israelites in need of assistance. Nor would information about God's eternity, or immutability, or whatever else might be inferred by it. The interpretation 'I am who am' is even impossible to justify on the grounds of language, for if the first 'I will be there/I am there' of verse 12 is the correct interpretation of *ehyeh*, the same must be true of the identical word repeated twice in verse 14 (*ehyeh asher ehyeh*), the formula which shows God declining to fix an image of himself for Moses to transmit to the Israelites when they should enquire after him. He will be there with them, he says, not as they anticipate or choose, but as he himself desires and wills to be there. He is not to be coerced, magically or otherwise.

————

> And he said:
> Thus shall you say to the sons of Israel,
> I AM THERE sends me to you. (Exod. 3: 14)

Again, not 'I AM' but 'I AM THERE'. Not 'I EXIST sends me to you', but 'I AM PRESENT sends me to you'. This is God's Name for himself and therefore written in capital letters. It is intended, in combination with the first *ehyeh* of verse 12 and the twice repeated *ehyeh* of verse 14, finally to ensure that the divine revelation is understood. But to make its relevance to the meaning of the mysterious Name YHWH even clearer, one more verse is added.

_____

And God said further to Mosheh:
HE,
the God of your fathers,
the God of Abraham, the God of Yitzhak, the God of Yaacob,
sends me to you.
This is my Name in world-time,
my remembrance for generation after generation. (Exod. 3: 15)

Apart from 'world-time' (*Weltzeit*, a typical forced approximation to the original, '*olam*), the innovation in this passage (and earlier) is of course the substitution, which serves at once as interpretation and reinterpretation, of a pronoun for YHWH.

In regard firstly to the interpretation, it has to accommodate the transposition into German of the element of Presence now seen to be contained in the Name and therefore needing to be conveyed by it. God calls himself I AM THERE to indicate that YHWH means HE IS THERE.

_____

It should be interpolated at this point that no one knows for sure how YHWH was pronounced in pre-Mosaic times. Buber, following a theory favoured by others before him,[6] suggests that the original pronunciation may have been *ya-huwa*, O He!, a sort of Dervish shout—in which case the Name would indeed have been meaningless and the Israelites would understandably have wished to know the 'true' name of their God. After Horeb, however, when YHWH was shown to be related to *ehyeh*, *ya-huwa* may have been altered to *yahweh*, but this again is uncertain since a taboo was eventually placed on its pronouncement aloud by all except the High Priest on the

_____

[6] Buber refers in particular to the German scholar Bernhard Duhm.

Day of Atonement and by the priests when blessing the people in the Temple of Jerusalem. From the early Middle Ages onwards it was even forbidden to add the appropriate vowel signs to the written Tetragram.

Thus the problem confronting Buber and Rosenzweig was how to transfer their reading of YHWH from one language to another without losing anything of the undertones and overtones implicit in the original. For, logical as it would seem to opt for the straightforward HE IS THERE, the translators had to take into account that in 'I will be there such as I will be there', Presence is not the only discernible element. The formula also contains a conspicuous theme of unpredictability and novelty. 'The Eternal' is inadmissible as a rendering of YHWH for the same reason. On the other hand, a paraphrase like 'the LORD', which is used in the Christian Septuagint codices,[7] the Vulgate, and most other translations, and is equivalent to the Jewish custom of reading *adonai* 'my lordship', is unacceptable because it substitutes fiction for fact. YHWH is a name not a title.

To preserve, not conceptually but concretely, all these sentiments as best they could, Buber and Rosenzweig re-interpreted the interpretation HE IS THERE in such a way that the appearance of YHWH in the text is signalled by the appropriate pronoun only. This strange device is explained more fully later in connection with Franz Rosenzweig, who invented it. But for the moment it is sufficient to say that when YHWH speaks, the Name is rendered by I and MY; when he is spoken to, by YOU and YOUR; and when he is spoken about, by HE, HIM, and HIS. Thus 'I am YHWH' (Exod. 6: 3) becomes 'It is *I*'. 'On the day that YHWH God created . . .' (Gen. 2: 4) becomes, 'On the day that HE God created . . .', etc.

Did this insight into the significance of the Name YHWH really penetrate into the heart of biblical Israel? Buber quotes the prophets Hosea and Isaiah in support of his contention that it did. Hosea's understanding of the Name is apparent, he says, in the story of the prophet's marriage to the harlot, in obedience to God's command, as a

[7] Jewish copyists of the Greek Bible have left the divine Name in Hebrew. The English rendering, *Jehovah*, is the result of a medieval misunderstanding by Christians of the custom of marking the consonants YHWH, the Name which is not to be pronounced, with the vowels of its substitute, Adonai.

symbol of Israel's harlotry. Of the third child borne to Hosea by his wife, God says:

> Call his name Lo-ammi,
> Not-My-People
> For you are not my people,
> and I, *I am not there* for you (Hos. 1: 9)[8]

The phrase, 'you are not my people' would seem to demand the customary sequence 'and I, I am not your God', but instead, we have what is meant to be its equivalent: 'and I, I am not there for you'.

An Isaiah passage to which Buber points also couples the mention by God of 'my people' with an identification of himself through the meaning of his Name.

> Therefore shall my people
> know my Name,
> therefore, on that day,
> that I am he who says,
> *Here I am.* (Isa. 52: 6)[9]

———

The thinness of the biblical evidence other than that taken from Exodus 3 which Buber adduces in support of his thesis prompted a further search on the part of the present writer for signs in the Bible of the same understanding. Even a cursory scrutiny soon made it clear that the Name is linked in Scripture over and over again to the notion of benevolent Presence—in particular places, with particular individuals, with the nation, with the world. It would almost seem that the association of the two was so deeply rooted in the minds of the biblical writers that allusion to the one provoked a spontaneous reference to the other. Repeatedly, YHWH is followed by a recollection of past Presence, an assurance of present Presence, or a promise of Presence to come. To support the contention, moreover, that the source of this doctrine is the episode of the burning bush, there are several actual repetitions of the words uttered on Horeb. The following two passages from Joshua are examples.

[8] This is the literal rendering of the Hebrew text, which is not properly reflected in the usual English versions.

[9] In German, *Da bin ich*. Strictly speaking, the *ehyeh* formula is not used here by Isaiah, but *hinneni*, here I am!, the reply given to a call; e.g. when God calls Moses, 'Mosheh! Mosheh!', he answers, *hinneni*! (Exod. 3: 4).

HE said to Jehoshua son of Nun . . .
as *I was with* Mosheh, *I will be there* with you. (Josh. 1: 5)

HE said to Jehoshua:
On this day,
I begin to make you great in the eyes of all Israel;
they shall know
that as *I was with* Mosheh, *I am there* with you. (Josh. 3: 7)

Constantly, YHWH is described as the God who 'walks with', 'dwells with', and 'is with' his people. When Joshua is commanded by Moses to take the Jews across the Jordan to the land which he himself was not destined to see, he tells him to be strong and have courage.

HE *himself goes before you,*
he will himself be with you,
he does not withdraw himself from you,
he does not forsake you.
Fear not!
Waver not! (Deut. 31: 8)

To Moses God says on Mount Sinai:

I give my dwelling in your midst,
my soul does not cast you off.
I walk about in the midst of you
and am your God
and you are my people.
I am your God. (Lev. 26: 11–13)

The prophet Zechariah is another who receives promise of divine Presence.

Many races of the world join ME
on that day;
they become my people
for *I dwell in the midst of you.* (Zech. 2: 11)

Again, at the time when Israel is oppressed by the Midianites, the angel of YHWH appears to Gideon as he is threshing wheat and greets him with:

HE *is with you,* valiant warrior! (Judg. 6: 12)

To which Gideon replies:

Ah lord,
if HE *is truly with us,* why has all this happened to us? (6: 13)

Another explicit interpretation of the Name YHWH in accordance with the revelation on Horeb appears in the Book of Samuel, where the story of Jonathan and David ends with a reminder of the vow of friendship sworn between them in the Name of God.

> What we swore, we two,
> by HIS *Name*,
> saying, HE will be there. (1 Sam. 20: 42)

In effect, on occasions too numerous to recount, man's highest good is seen to consist in God's Presence and his greatest misfortune to rest in God's absence. There is nothing 'mystical' in this teaching, for if on the theological level the divine Presence is believed to be a sign of divine love, on the concrete level it is the people's love of God, proved by their obedience to his Voice and imitation of his 'ways', that makes a reality of that Presence. Likewise, if on the theological level God's withdrawal of Presence is regarded as a signal of his displeasure, on the concrete level it is the people's rejection of his guidance which makes that absence real. It is reality which confirms or denies the truth of theology, not vice versa.

With God at his side, the Jew could hope for success in his undertakings. Without God, nothing could go right. Why do they disobey YHWH, Moses asks the defiant Israelites as they prepare to make war against the Amalekites and Canaanites against God's express command.

> It cannot succeed.
> March not out,
> for HE is no longer among you . . .
> for now you have turned away from following HIM,
> He will not be with you. (Num. 14: 41–3)

Amos also implies that the effect of evil is spiritual death associated with the loss of God's Presence.

> Seek what is good,
> never what is evil,
> that you may continue to live,
> and that HE, the host-encircled God,
> *may be with you*, in the way
> that you are accustomed to say that he is. (Amos 5: 14)

Curiously, Buber overlooked a far more telling passage from the Book of Isaiah than the one he cites. Again, the text does not actually read *ehyeh*, 'I am there/I will be there', but the context remains faithful to its meaning.

> I was to be enquired after
> by those who did not question.
> I was to be found
> by those who did not look for me.
> I said, Here I am! Here I am!
> to a race which did not call on my Name. (Isa. 65: 1)

A final quotation from the Buber–Rosenzweig Bible is added to illustrate the impact made by the very rare use of the straight interpretation of YHWH *before* it is re-interpreted as a pronoun. The prophet Amos rages against Israel for her failure, despite all God's warnings to his people, to make her *teshuvah*. Now God has at last had enough and utters words of menace.

> Therefore,
> thus will I do to you Israel!
> Because
> I will do this to you,
> prepare yourself,
> Israel,
> to confront your God!
> For behold,
> he who shapes the mountains,
> who creates the spirit-wind,
> who announces to man
> his thinking,
> now makes darkness of the dawn,
> and walks along the summits of the earth.
> His Name:
> HE IS THERE, the host-encircled God. (Amos 4: 12–13)

After all this, it comes as a surprise to find that the introduction of the new divine Name was not Buber's responsibility. He himself gives the credit for it to Rosenzweig, assessing his own contribution as mere 'scholarly support'.[10] Rosenzweig, however, in his surviving reflections

---

[10] 'Die Schrift und ihre Verdeutschung', *Werke*, ii. 1178.

on the subject (mainly confined to an article, 'Der Ewige', and to two letters, one written to Buber in January 1926 and the other to Martin Goldner in June 1927), nowhere explicitly claims the novelty for his own. His explanations and observations in these papers are nevertheless most enlightening because they fill some of the gaps left by Buber's on the whole not exhaustive exposition of the problem. Rosenzweig, whose major work *The Star of Redemption* is judged by some to amount to a greater advance in religious thought than anything Buber wrote,[11] no doubt composed the letter to Buber while the two were at work on the translation of Exodus. He tells him that he is particularly troubled by one line in chapter 15, in the so-called Song of Moses sung in praise of God after the safe crossing of the Red Sea: 'YHWH is a man of war; YHWH is his name' (Exod. 15: 3). To word it like this, reproducing YHWH simply as God's Name, results in nonsense, Rosenzweig thought.

He is called YHWH. Is he really! And where does that get me? I am called Marduk, which is a nice name too. A divine Name makes the sentence just as meaningless as a human name would. David is a warrior, David is his name. But here the Name means the title, which in this one Name coincides with the Name. Wilhelm is a warrior hero, Kaiser is his name. In the same way that God himself says, *ani* YHWH (I am YHWH), so, exactly so, man says, YHWH *shĕmo* (YHWH is his Name) . . . Thus, they shall know that: it is HE . . . is my Name. In the Song of Moses, this is not suitable because it would relate back to the man of war. It is necessary here to reach back to the other element of *ehyeh*, the word of presence, and militarise it so that it corresponds to the context. Therefore: HE is a man of war; HE here! his Name.[12]

It will be noticed that whereas Buber argues that YHWH is a name and not a title, Rosenzweig considers it to be both a name and a title. For the rest, there is no allusion to the derivation of HE itself at this point. The matter had obviously already been settled.

The main interest in the second letter, written the following year to Martin Goldner, consists in Rosenzweig's confession of indebtedness to the contemporary German Jewish biblical scholar, Benno Jacob. This has meant that, contrary to expectations, the search for the origin of the new interpretation of the Name of God cannot end with Franz Rosenzweig, but has to continue one step further. Apart from this, the long communication to Goldner runs through the already familiar

---

[11] Translated from the 2nd edn. of 1930 by W. W. Hallo (Routledge & Kegan Paul, 1971).

[12] Franz Rosenzweig, *Briefe* (Schocken, 1935), 554.

argument, adding nothing but presenting Rosenzweig's thought in a slightly different way, with some benefit to lucidity.

Apparently, he and Buber began by rendering YHWH as 'Lord', but this gradually 'became insupportable because it is quite simply incorrect'.[13] When, however, the new idea came to them, they tried it out and it seemed more and more satisfactory, but first they had to get rid of the conviction that the correct vocalization of YHWH is *yahweh*. It may be; but on the other hand, it may not. The important point is that in the text as it is at present, and in the hypothetical sources in which it is thought to be distinguishable, the Tetragram is more than just an eponym. It is also a concept. It has a meaning. This meaning, Rosenzweig explains, is revealed in Exodus 3 but needs to be properly understood. Those who take *ehyeh* to signify 'I am' and hence 'Being', or 'the Being', or 'the Eternal', are philosophizing. The real import of *ehyeh* is more pointed and direct and is expounded briefly by Rashi,[14] by Judah Halevi in his *Kuzari*, iv. 3,[15] and 'in the most wished-for detail in Jacob's magnificent article on Moses and the thornbush'. With the words, 'I will be there such as I will be there', Rosenzweig writes,

God does not name himself as He-who-is, but as He-who-is there, He-who-is-present to you: or rather, as He who comes to you, who helps. For the Hebrew *hayah* is not by nature, like the Indo-Germanic *sein* ('to be'), a copula—static therefore—but a word of coming to be, of happening . . . It is only because this Being becomes present to you if you need him and call on him—'I *will* be there'—that in afterthought, in after thought, he is indeed He who is Ever There, the Absolute, the Eternal, separate from my need and moment, but separable nevertheless only because each future moment could replace my present one. So this Eternity becomes visible only to a Now, my Now; this 'absolute Being' only to my present being-there . . . And how should this be translated? It would be quite incorrect to substitute, for the secondary adjective 'eternal', a primary one, e.g. 'present'. The most important element would then be missing, the co-sounding 'with you'. And 'the Present One' would be no different from 'the Eternal' or 'the Lord'—just a meaning, in effect, and not (which is the essence of the Tetragram) a name pregnant with meaning. A name lives only when it is used as a form of address. The vocative is its one *casus rectus*; even the nominative is already *casus obliquus*.

[13] Rosenzweig, *Briefe*, 599.
[14] Rashi = *R*abbi *Sh*elomo bar *Y*itzhak of Troyes, AD 1040–1105, the most famous of Jewish Bible commentators.
[15] A philosophical work in defence of Judaism by the celebrated Spanish Jewish writer and poet (*c.* 1080–1140).

This becomes very clear in the good origin, the Hebrew substitute *adonai*, of the bad translation, 'LORD'. It does not mean 'the Lord', but is a vocative . . . Because of this, in addition to the vocative passages proper, a stress pointing to the Name *qua* Name enters into the recited text as a whole. It is precisely this that is missing in the rendering of YHWH in western languages by the word LORD.

The relation, reciprocity, contained in the divine Name, first as a name, and then above all through its meaning, must be rendered from the other pole of relation, that of the person using it as a form of address; the being-present-with-you of the original must be reflected in the being-present-with-me of the translation.

Since the vocative is ruled out as too grotesque, there remains only the personal pronoun,

which in its three persons describes precisely the three dimensions of being-present-with-me: that I can speak to another, hear another, and speak about another. Whereby the second person (you) has to come first, since it is the source of the personality of the two others. It is only someone to whom I am prepared to speak who counts for me as an 'I'; and it is only someone to whom I have spoken who counts for me, even when absent, as a person. And from the other standpoint, it is from my being spoken to that my objective and subjective self-awareness derive, my 'he'-awareness and 'I'-awareness—in the psychological singular as well as in the sociological plural. It is only because he is my 'you' that I perceive, from his 'I', him who is present with me and am able to speak about him.[16]

It is difficult not to comment here on the similarity of Rosenzweig's thought, as it is expressed in this final paragraph, to Buber's. Even the language is reminiscent of *I and You*. But altogether, what an extraordinary encounter of ideas this was, so remarkable that at this distance of time it seems presumptuous even to try to separate the strands and assign this contribution to *x* and that to *y*. For whether or not Rosenzweig was solely responsible for introducing the new Name into the translation—and quite apart from Buber's statement to that effect, it appears most likely that he did so—Buber had in fact already conceived of God as the everlasting *You* in *I and You*, and for him it was simply a matter of following on with the remaining pronouns. Moreover, by changing in future editions the version 'I am which I am' of the first to 'I am there such as I am there', he achieved, not a direct correlation (as will be seen later) between the divine Presence of the

[16] Rosenzweig, *Briefe*, no. 502, 23 June 1927.

biblical text and his call for attachment as opposed to detachment, for nearness as opposed to distance, but without doubt a much larger measure of internal consistency.[17]

The article, 'Der Ewige', to which Buber alludes frequently in *Kingship of God*,[18] is a study of the historical evolution of the biblical Name carried out by Rosenzweig to demonstrate the inaccuracy of 'the Eternal', the interpretation selected by the celebrated eighteenth-century German Jewish Bible translator, Moses Mendelssohn (as well as by Calvin). Mendelssohn, finding each of the three chief traditional understandings of the Hebrew correct in its own way, had attempted to devise one formula to cover them all. The first,[19] 'I will be with whom-soever I will be', lays the accent on God's providence. The second[20] understands YHWH to signify 'He who has not passed away and will not pass away because he is the First and the Last'. The third, proposed by Maimonides[21] in his *Guide for the Perplexed*, deduces from the text that God is essentially the Existing One to whom existence is inherent. For these last two, therefore, the content of the Name YHWH is not so much benevolence as eternity and necessary existence. Mendelssohn's attempt to synthesize the three results in the following reading of Exodus 3: 14: 'God said to Moses: I am the Being that is eternal. He said, that is: Thus shall you speak to the children of Israel, the eternal Being who names himself "I am eternal" has sent me to you.'

That Rosenzweig found this version impossible to accept is in itself interesting, since only a decade or so earlier he had evidently endorsed it wholeheartedly, writing in *The Star of Redemption*: 'He is eternal, he alone is eternal, he is the Eternal *per se* . . . In his mouth, "I am" is like "I shall be", and finds explanation in it.'[22] Now he does an about-turn and asserts that the context of the story positively excludes an abstract exegesis. Like Buber, he feels that Moses at that moment needed consolation, not a lecture on God's being; the Israelites desired pri-

---

[17] Compare *Ich und Du* (Insel Verlag, 1923), 129 with *Werke*, I. 154 and *I and Thou*, trans. Ronald Gregor Smith, 2nd edn. (Scribner-T. & T. Clark, 1958), 160.

[18] Franz Rosenzweig, *Kleinere Schriften* (1937), 182–98, cited in *Werke*, ii. 489–723.

[19] That of Onkelos, the presumed author of a fairly literal Aramaic version of the Pentateuch dating from the early centuries of the Christian era.

[20] Presented by Saadia Gaon, a renowned Bible interpreter, philosopher, theologian, and polemicist, AD 892–942.

[21] Moses ben Maimon, AD 1135–1204, the most outstanding of Jewish medieval writers.

[22] Franz Rosenzweig, *The Star of Redemption*, trans. William W. Hallo (Routledge & Kegan Paul for the Littman Library, 1970), 272.

marily to be made aware of his proximity to them, and looked for a promise of help in what had until then been an ancient and obscure divine Name. Therefore, he concludes, 'the only justifiable translation is one that brings to the fore, not an element of eternity, but of presence, of being-there for you and with you'.[23]

It will be noticed that this is not the same as Buber's explication, but the difference is probably more apparent than real. Buber assumes that presence with God and God's Presence with his creation is evinced as 'speech' and inseparable from it, and Rosenzweig, that speech to and by God is a token of, and indivisible from, presence and Presence.

The compression of HE IS THERE into the three dimensions of the personal pronoun he then explains as follows: 'So: he who is present to them, is there with them—HE. He who is present to the I, is there with me—YOU. He who is present to you, is there with you—I.'[24]

Benno Jacob, rabbi and Bible scholar, was born in 1862 in Germany, and died in 1945 in England, where he came to live just before the start of the Second World War. In his middle sixties at the time of his contact with Rosenzweig, Jacob was not a fundamentalist who insisted on the Mosaic authorship of the Bible, but he rejected completely the claims of modern Bible criticism and its search for 'sources'. Scripture's great value and importance lay, so he believed, in the text as it has been handed down. This outlook was therefore similar to that of Buber and Rosenzweig, for whom the question of the origins of the Bible was also not of very great moment. In their opinion it is not so much what the ancient authors had in mind that really matters, but what men and women extract from their reading in their own day and age.

Rosenzweig was in correspondence with Jacob for at least a year prior to the latter's publication of the articles described by Rosenzweig with such enthusiasm as the 'conclusive enquiry' into the subject of the divine Name, 'exemplary in its soberness and circumspection'.[25] Jacob's study is in effect very thorough, so much so that a summary can scarcely do it justice. On the other hand, a proportion of his reasoning, much of it in disagreement with the accepted thought of his time, has already been encountered in the discussion of the views of Buber and Rosenzweig. Indeed, one wonders whether his influence on them may

---

23 Rosenzweig, *Kleinere Schriften*, 188.
24 Ibid. 189.
25 Rosenzweig, 'Der Ewige', *Kleinere Schriften*, 187.

not have been even greater than they themselves realized. Buber, it is true, mentions him in a footnote in *Kingship of God* as an authority to be consulted,[26] with the qualification 'in particular', but despite Rosenzweig's tribute quoted here, neither man can be said to have exactly overemphasized Jacob's impact on his researches. To be fair, though, it should be added that although the process of their analysis may have followed Jacob's, the understanding of the nature of God which resulted from it remains distinctively their own.[27]

In May 1921, Rosenzweig informs Jacob that he has just finished reading, 'with breathless attention', a work of his on source criticism and exegesis, and urges him to embark as his next venture on a complete Torah commentary. Jacob must have immediately sent off his article on Moses by way of reply, for five days later there is another message from Rosenzweig, full of admiration and pressing him even more earnestly to set to work on the proposed commentary. At about the same time, Rosenzweig tells his mother that Jacob is one of the best exegetes he has encountered. 'He knows everything and says it quite simply.'[28] Jacob in any case adopted Rosenzweig's suggestion, and in 1934—he was by that time seventy-two years old—published his major exegetical work, a commentary on Genesis, now available in an abridged edition in English.[29] It was followed by a comprehensive study of Exodus, and another of part of Leviticus.

The aim of Jacob's article, 'Mose am Dornbusch' ('Moses by the thornbush') is to refute the contention of Bible critics that Exodus 3: 15, 'YHWH the God of your fathers', and Exodus 6: 2, '*by my name* YHWH I was not known to them', derive from two different sources. Jacob contends that they misunderstand the latter text, the real meaning of which is that God tells Moses he appeared to Abraham, Isaac, and Jacob as 'El Shadai'—given in the English RSV Bible as 'God Almighty'—and did not reveal to them the significance of 'my name YHWH'.

---

[26] *Werke*, ii. 623, n. 30; Martin Buber, *Kingship of God*, trans. R. Scheiman (Harper & Row–Allen & Unwin, 1967), 191, n. 30. He also draws attention, in *Werke*, ii. 631, n. 11 (*Kingship of God*, 193, n. 11), to another of Jacob's studies, *In Namen Gottes*, written in 1903 and devoted specifically to the divine Name.

[27] Rosenzweig's letters to Jacob mostly have to do with Zionism, to which the latter was opposed, but others are concerned with Bible interpretation, the field in which he was expert.

[28] Rosenzweig, *Briefe*, no. 312, 3 June 1921.

[29] Benno Jacob, *The First Book of the Bible: Genesis*, ed. and trans. Ernest I. Jacob and Walter Jacob (Ktav, 1974).

Examining the story of the burning bush, Jacob analyses the biblical use of the word *shem*, 'name'. A *shem*, he explains, is selected not so much to describe a person as to individualize him and distinguish him from others. As a man's personality develops, and his deeds and experiences make their contribution to the age and environment in which he lives, the name he bears comes to be associated so intimately with a variety of feelings, expectations, judgements, and claims in his regard that these are evoked as soon as it is uttered. His name becomes an expression of what is known, thought, and said of him. It becomes synonymous with his reputation. As he acquires fame, it 'travels' (2 Chr. 26: 8). If he conducts himself shamefully, it 'goes out' (Deut. 22: 14). If he is just and upright, its 'fragrance' spreads afar like oil (S. of S. 1: 3). To possess a 'name' always implies a favourable opinion; 'men of name' in the Bible are men of renown. *Shem* therefore needs no qualification, and *shem tov*, a 'good name', is non-existent in Scripture.

Another characteristic of the biblical understanding of *shem* is that in symbolizing the fame and honour of the person to whom it belongs it becomes identified with the attributes and actions through which the fame is acquired. Thus God's *tehillah* or 'praise' (one of the expressions often used in association with the Name of God) recited on the elementary occasions of harvests, relief from trouble, meals, thanksgiving, and sacrifice, celebrates in each case God's deeds. But these are none other than his Name. God makes for himself a Name by what he does. Men are to seek it and know it. The devout are to utter it, confess it, be joyfully aware of it, exalt it, praise it, sing it, proclaim it as holy. It is to be their banner and war-cry, their weapon and defence. 'Always in the sense that *shem* signifies how God is known and what can be said of him from his wonders in nature and history as Almighty Creator and Saviour. But never is *shem* a word that is venerated superstitiously and idolatrously.'[30]

The greatest of God's deeds for Israel having been the deliverance from Egyptian slavery, the first poetic *tehillah*, the Song of Moses (Exod. 15: 1–18), celebrates the triumphant finale to this act of redemption. In it, God manifested himself in terms of power. It was his mighty deed, the 'inexhaustible theme of every *tehillah*; and the first half of Exodus—indeed the whole history of the Torah—is written for no other purpose than to provide material for this theme.'[31] The divine

[30] Benno Jacob, 'Mose am Dornbusch', *Monatsschrift für Geschichte und Wissenschaft des Judentums*, 1922, 123.
[31] Ibid.

Name is thus inseparable from the notion of power to do great things. Giving his own version of 'YHWH is a man of war; YHWH is his name' (the line from the Song of Moses which, as we have seen, exercises Rosenzweig in his letter to Buber) as 'The Eternal is a man of war, YHWH is his Name', Jacob comments: 'That is to say, this word (YHWH) says everything; hence it often recurs in later prophetic passages as though with it the speaker need say nothing more'.[32]

———

The difference between Jacob's interpretation and that of Buber and Rosenzweig will now be clear. Apart from Jacob's adoption of the pseudonym, 'the Eternal', which Buber and Rosenzweig both refused to accept, where they read YHWH to connote God in his unified, whole, absolute, arbitrary, and benevolent Presence, Jacob sees this same Presence always and necessarily coupled with force, power, might, greatness. Consequently, where *Die Schrift* takes the question concerning God's Name to convey curiosity concerning its significance, Jacob views it as expressing preoccupation on the part of the Israelites over YHWH's ability to act with power on their behalf. They will ask Moses: 'What can you tell us in praise of the effectiveness and might of this God of our fathers?'

The exposition in Jacob's study of the grammatical relation of YHWH to *ehyeh* follows the same course as that of the two other writers but is much more detailed. The Hebrew verb *hayah* to which both words belong means 'to be', and 'to come to be' in a specific sense. That is to say, it does not imply a progressive coming into being, a development, but an immediate, unmediated being-there; a being-there, moreover, totally unconnected with anything that has gone before. 'God said, Let there be light! And light was there' (Gen. 1: 3).

Secondly, *hayah* in biblical language does not signify 'to be' only in the sense of reality as opposed to semblance, but also in the sense of 'being' as opposed to 'being caused to be'. All that comes into existence is 'caused to be' by God. He alone is He-Who-Is, the one Creator All-Mighty, All-Powerful, All-Great, of all things on earth and in heaven.

Both these implications, Jacob insists, are integral to the answers God gives to Moses. 'I will be there with you', he assures him, or 'with your mouth', immediately, in my roles of Creator and Doer of Mighty

Things. 'I will be there with you' with my help and loving-kindness. 'I will be, I will appear (with demonstrations of power) as whoever I will be, as however I will appear (with demonstrations of power), as however I choose to appear. *Fiam talis fiam*.'[33]

To the objection that, interpreted in this way, the statement is too abstract for primitive religion, Benno Jacob—unlike Buber, who distinguishes in the story traces of the magical beliefs current in Egyptian society—retorts that even though Israelite religion may have begun on a primitive level, nothing of this is visible in the Bible. By the time Scripture was compiled, immature elements had been expunged and replaced by true religiousness. Such an interpretation is in any case not primitive. On the contrary, it testifies to a faith in God expressed in a divine Name which grew out of an immediate awareness of 'the presence and effectiveness of a living, creative, helpful, almighty Power different from all other created things'.[34]

YHWH means 'He comes to be', 'He will come to be'. As God's Name, it points to him whose help may be expected with certainty. YHWH is he who lives eternally and manifests himself with power. YHWH is the source of all life, the God of wonders, whose creation is a wonder and whose every wonder is a creation. YHWH is the Rock, and holy, his holiness consisting in his absolute reliability and faithfulness to himself and to his word. YHWH is the Saving God, the Redeemer of the captive and the suffering. 'He is a personality, an I, the I of every I who becomes truly I solely out of him and in him, so that no name can be transformed—as he causes his own to be—from the third person to the self-witness of the first: Yahweh = *ehyeh* (HE IS THERE = I AM THERE). It is with this Name that God consoles and comforts Moses.'[35]

This, then, is the combined lesson on the divine Name and its meaning as the three men taught it. Once it was realized how closely Buber's vision of God resembles that of Franz Rosenzweig and how much they both owe to Benno Jacob, it seemed useful to bring them together. Side by side with Jacob's insistence on the power inherent in the divine nature, the absence of a forceful edge of this kind in Buber's concept of the Deity becomes obvious, whereas it might otherwise have gone unnoticed. Many of the lacunae in Buber's arguments are in addition made good by the other two, singly or together. But also, if it should appear that Buber's originality is diminished by evidence of contemporary religious thought running along lines analogous to his, it is equally possible to argue that, on the contrary, the learned support of

[33] Ibid. 129.   [34] Ibid. 133–4.   [35] Ibid. 135.

such men as Rosenzweig and Jacob provides Buber's unique insights with the much-needed solidity of scholarship supplementary to his own.

Lastly, it will presumably not be overlooked that these other two men, with their observations concerning the 'I' of God, point in the direction of the identity of Buber's everlasting *You*.

9

Presence and Word in Targum and Midrash

ALTHOUGH Buber did at least cast around for a minimum of wider
biblical support for his theory concerning the meaning of the divine
Name, he looked no further afield. Yet it must follow that if, as the
apparent echoes of an identical interpretation in the Bible appear to
confirm, his reading of Exodus 3 is correct, the same notion of
YHWH = God-with-us ought to be perceptible in later post-biblical
Jewish literature and indeed throughout the history of Jewish religious
thought. If we find in Targum and Midrash, and in the further
developments of the mystical schools, an unbroken tradition according
to which I AM THERE is accepted as God's Name for himself, and as
transferring its significance to YHWH, Israel's Name for God, we shall
discover that Buber's everlasting *You*, and the whole teaching of
dialogue and presence that he erected around it, may be regarded
without fear of contradiction to belong to the living body of Jewish
belief and spirituality and to testify furthermore to its continuing
growth and development.

It can be asserted straight away that Buber, Rosenzweig, and Jacob
did not discover in the twentieth century a sense until then overlooked
by all except some of the prophets and sages recorded in the Bible
itself. The ancient paraphrases of the Bible known as the Targums,[1]
and the more elaborate supplementation of the text incorporated into
the body of literature called Midrash,[2] drive home the notion of God

---

[1] These compositions came into being during the period when Aramaic was the
vernacular of Palestinian Jews, i.e. between *c.*500 BC and AD 700. The surviving
targumic versions of the Pentateuch—Onkelos, Pseudo-Jonathan, the Fragmentary
Targum, and Neofiti—date in their substance to the early centuries of the Christian era.

[2] Midrash, literally 'study', is a type of traditional Bible interpretation which includes
all kinds of exegetical works, from commentary verse by verse to sermons based on a
liturgical reading of Scripture. The most important midrashic writings belong to the
period between *c.*AD 200 and AD 500.

as indwelling Presence with persistence. No ambiguity exists here. God present in the world is the theme to which the rabbis turn, line after line and page after page.

It transpires nevertheless from the Targums that matters are no-where near so simple and straightforward as might appear from the arguments of our three contemporary thinkers. Their authors' concept of the Deity leads to far greater depths than might have been antici-pated. They were highly intelligent and articulate men, able to word their thoughts in such a way that they can still, after so many ages, and in such a changed intellectual climate, grip our minds and imagination and move our hearts.

They were also largely logical and consistent. After reading and digesting a biblical passage and determining its import, they re-created it in paraphrase with the help of an imagery that remains more or less constant. Their interpretation, for all its profundity and subtlety, therefore retains an element of limpidity that is absent from the strictly mystical works of later times, yet leaves room for new and still deeper growth and extension.

Two special titles are used in these compositions to replace the Names YHWH, El, and Elohim, and personal pronouns referring to God. Whenever the targumists believe the context warrants it, they substitute for these, or otherwise introduce, one of two Aramaic terms. Shekhinta and Memra.

Shekhinta, 'dwelling', replaces the Name YHWH when God is said to 'dwell' in a place—'in your midst', 'in the Sanctuary', 'in the midst of your camp', etc. He is also alluded to as the Shekhinta when he 'appears', or 'is revealed', when he 'goes up', or 'comes down', when he 'hides' or 'removes' himself, when he 'goes with', 'goes before', or 'goes among' his people, and when there is mention in the Bible of his 'Face'.

YHWH in brief becomes 'the Shekhinta' when he is experienced as fulfilling or refusing to fulfil his function of Presence, and to simplify matters, *Presence* is the term we shall henceforth adopt instead of Shekhinta (although it is not an exact translation).

A few examples set out in parallel columns will illustrate its use.

Bible	Targum
That they may not defile their camp *in the midst of which I dwell* (Num. 5: 3)	That they may not defile their camps for *my Presence dwells among them* (Onkelos)

And YHWH *came down* on Mount Sinai (Exod. 19: 20)	And *the Glory of the Presence of* YHWH *was revealed* on Mount Sinai (Neofiti)
YHWH your God *will himself go over before you* (Deut. 31: 3)	
And *I will surely hide my face* on that day on account of the evils they have done (Deut. 31: 18)	YHWH your God *and his Presence will go over before you* (Pseudo-Jonathan)
	And *I will remove my Presence from them* at that time (Onkelos)

It will be observed that this indwelling Presence is not to be confused with Omnipresence. Nor does it possess any quality of inevitability or permanence. It is a presence that alternates with absence as part of a dialogue of life between God and Israel.

The second of the two titles for God employed in the Targums, Memra (derived from the root *amar*, 'to say'), is an Aramaic term defined (in connection with Num. 11: 20) as 'the Word of YHWH whose Presence dwells among you' (Targum Onkelos). In many ways, it is even more mysterious and rich in implication than the concept of Shekhinah,[3] the more familiar Hebrew equivalent of Shekhinta. The great enigma, still unsolved, is why it became obsolete in late antiquity, never again to return into circulation—unlike Shekhinah, which also disappeared but was restored centuries later. Why too has it been so little studied by biblical scholars? Why is Memra dismissed by authorities of standing as 'an empty, purely formal substitution for the Tetragrammaton',[4] and why is this opinion accepted as valid even to the present day by large numbers of scholars? Whatever the reason for its subsequent neglect—it has been suggested that its prompt exclusion from Jewish religious writings was due originally to the incorporation of the Word doctrine into Christianity via the Hellenistic–Jewish *Logos* speculation—it would seem to clamour for attention. For the Word, 'the Word of YHWH', 'my Word', what YHWH 'says', is as it seems *ehyeh* itself, I AM THERE.

By *ehyeh*, the targumists, obeying the same reasoning as that followed by Buber, Rosenzweig, and Jacob, understood like them that God was communicating to Moses the knowledge he has of himself. But they

---

[3] A post-biblical Hebrew word related to nouns meaning 'tent', 'dwelling-place' (*mishkan*), and 'neighbour', 'one who lives nearby', 'one who is present with one' (*shakhen*).

[4] P. Billerbeck, *Kommentar zum Neuen Testament aus Talmud und Midrash*, ii (Munich, 1956), 302–33. See also V. Hamp, *Der Begriff 'Wort' in der aramäischen Bibelübersetzungen* (Munich, 1938). For a recent and very welcome exception, see C. T. R. Hayward, *Divine Name and Presence: The Memra* (Allanheld, Osmun, 1981).

were faced with the problem of how to transmit the complexities of meaning not included in the concept Shekhinta, yet recognized by them as belonging to the biblical doctrine of God. Thus, how were they to extend the notions of presence, and of the absolute freedom, authority, independence, and power implicit in 'I will be there such as I will be there', so that God is simultaneously represented as ever-living Creator of all that exists?

In part, they do this by stressing wherever possible the association of 'I am there/I will be there' with other tenses and forms, particularly the jussive and imperative of the verb 'to be'. YHWH is not only he who is and will be present; room is made for the past tense. He was always there. He is the Everlasting One. And it was he who, with his commands 'Be there!' and 'Let it be there!' called the universe into existence and presence.

Yet even with all this, the insight of the Targums into the significance of YHWH in the light of *ehyeh* was still not exhausted. One more aspect of its intricate and genial understanding of the Godhead needed to be formulated: i.e. that the medium through which God works and exists is speech.

Hence the inspired replacement of *ehyeh* in the Bible by Word, or Memra. YHWH is he who says of himself, I AM THERE. 'I am there' is the *Word* of the Presence of YHWH. The verb *amar*, 'to say', goes with its derivatives to join those of the verb 'to be', and the combination of presence, speech, and creation is rounded off and made perfect. God is the supreme, ever-living, never-silent Speaker. He is the Speaker of his own Presence, and of the presence of the whole of creation. YHWH's Word is his Voice. And even more frequently, YHWH's Word is his Heart, 'heart' in Hebrew parlance being the seat of thought. 'YHWH said in his heart' (Gen. 8: 21) is given in the Targums of Onkelos and Pseudo-Jonathan as 'YHWH said in his Word'.

To sum up, the Aramaic equivalent of Presence is used of God in his role of co-Dweller, co-Traveller, whose nearness to his creatures is manifested and hidden, granted and withdrawn, according to his pleasure or displeasure with them. It is the equivalent of Israel's Name for him: YHWH/HE IS THERE.

Word, by contrast, represents God's Name for him: I AM THERE. It is as close as the targumists allow themselves to approach to God's 'I' and is employed in such situations as those in which God encounters, speaks with, makes a covenant with, and above all 'is with' an individual, a group, a nation. Repeatedly, the phrase 'YHWH was with . . .' is rendered 'The Word of YHWH was with . . .'; or, accommodating the quality of benevolence and protection inseparable from the Presence of God: 'The Word of YHWH was his Helper.'

The pattern is not infrangible. There are exceptions. But it is so constant that one is led to wonder whether expert study might reveal reasons for the variations.

Turning at last to the targumic version of the story of the burning bush, the Exodus text according to which Moses brings his father-in-law's sheep to 'Horeb the mountain of God [Elohim]' (Exod. 3: 1), the allusion to Horeb is judged not sufficiently explicit and Targum Neofiti paraphrases it: 'Mount Horeb above which the Glory of the Presence was revealed'.

Similarly, when the heavenly Voice announces itself as the God of the forefathers and Moses hides his face because he is afraid to look at God (Exod. 3: 6), Neofiti writes: 'for he was afraid to look on the Glory of the Presence of YHWH'.

With the *ehyeh* of verse 12 comes the first radical departure from the biblical text. Moses, shrinking from the responsibility laid on him, is comforted by God with the words ordinarily translated, 'But I will be there with you.' This is not how the Targums understand the phrase. Two of them, Onkelos and Pseudo-Jonathan, offer the seemingly extraordinary interpretation: 'Because my Word will be your Helper.'

Targum Neofiti, by retaining 'I will be there' and combining it with 'my Word', is even more precise: 'But my Word will be there with you.'[5]

Such an understanding is quite different from the conventional one, with its allocation of central importance to God's 'I am/I will be there such as I am/I will be there', and an ancillary function to the preceding and subsequent occurrences of 'I am/I will be there.' For the targumists, with their eye on the summing up of the episode on Horeb in verse 15— '. . . I AM THERE sends me to you . . . YHWH the God of your fathers . . . sends me to you . . . This is my Name for ever . . .'—it is I AM THERE that is the climax of the revelation, and the other saying that serves as the gloss.

---

[5] In the main text, a literal translation, 'I will be there with you', is supplemented by a gloss, 'my Word' being inserted between 'I will be there' and 'with you'. The implication is that 'my Word' = 'I will be there.'

Moses, still reluctant, asks what he is to say to the Israelites when they question him about the Name of the God of their fathers.[6] Again the Targums depart from the biblical text, but this time they offer a paraphrase in terms of the imagery already devised for *ehyeh* itself, that of the *Word*. Hence Pseudo-Jonathan rewrites God's mysterious reply: 'And YHWH said to Mosheh, he who spoke and the world was there, who spoke and all things were there . . .'

Having substituted YHWH for Elohim ('Elohim said to Moses'), and having given himself in this way the opportunity of covering the themes of speech and creation integral to YHWH, the targumist goes straight on to identify, without circumlocution, the 'I am there' of the following 'I AM THERE sends me to you' as God's 'I', and by expressly mentioning the two meanings contained in the imperfect tense, is able also to interpret that 'I' as eternal. His version of the rest of this Exodus passage therefore runs: 'And he said, Say this to the people of Israel: I [*ana*] who is and will be there, sends me to you.'

The Fragmentary Targum and Neofiti are too similar to require analysis, Neofiti reading: 'And YHWH said to Mosheh, *ehyeh asher ehyeh* . . . He who said to the world, Be there! and the world was there from the beginning, and who will say again, Be there! and it will be there.'[7] A Neofiti variant strikes another note, however: 'And YHWH said to Mosheh, I was there before the world was created. I am he who was your Helper in the Egyptian captivity, and I am he who will be your Helper in every generation.' Apart from the added reference to God's eternity, this interpretation reverts directly to the paraphrase provided by Onkelos and Pseudo-Jonathan for verse 12: 'Because my Word will be your Helper.' According to its teaching, YHWH says of himself: Before the world was there, I am there. At the time of your distress in Egypt, I am there with you. I am there with every generation to come. I will be there such as I will be there, with my loving-kindness, for your succour.

For the targumists, as for Buber and his colleagues, to know YHWH was to know YHWH's Name. Pharaoh asks Moses: 'Who is YHWH that I

[6] There is none of the worry shown by Buber, Rosenzweig, and Jacob on the score of this famous question, which is translated into Aramaic as it is, without explanation or elaboration.

[7] Ancient interpreters were persuaded that every word of the Bible has meaning, therefore repetitions—a common stylistic feature in biblical Hebrew—must signify more than may appear. Hence the convention evolved whereby in forms of speech such as *ehyeh asher ehyeh*, the first mention of the repeated word is understood to refer to this world, and the second to the world to come.

should listen to his voice and let Israel go? I do not know YHWH' (Exod. 5: 2). Onkelos renders this: 'The Name of YHWH is not known to me that I should listen to his voice. The Name of YHWH is not revealed to me.'[8]

Pharaoh must necessarily have known the deity of the thousands of Jews inhabiting his kingdom, but like the Israelites themselves, who would ask Moses about his Name, he did not know their God inasmuch as he did not know its meaning either. Like them, he was without the key to it: I AM THERE.

In case the argument is still unclear, it should be helpful to follow the targumic treatment of another event in the Book of Exodus (chapters 33 and 34). The Israelites have sinned by worshipping the golden calf and God is angry. He commands Moses to go on towards the Promised Land but tells him that he himself—'My Presence', 'the Glory of my Presence', according to the targumists—will not accompany his people. Moses pleads with God and he eventually relents. Moses then has the temerity to ask: 'Show me I pray your Glory' (33: 18). To which God answers:

I will cause all my Goodness to pass before you and will proclaim my Name YHWH before you, that I am gracious to whomsoever I am gracious and show mercy to whomsoever I show mercy. But he said, You cannot see my Face, for no man sees me and lives. And YHWH said, Behold there is a place by me where you shall stand upon the rock, and while my Glory passes by, I will put you in a cleft of the rock, and I will cover you with my Palm until I have passed by. Then I will take away my Palm and you shall see my Back. But my Face shall not be seen. (Exod. 33: 19–23)

This reply of God falls into two parts, a general summary and a detailed programme. In the first, Moses is told that he cannot see God's Glory, identified also as God's Face, and remain alive, but that he will instead be made aware of God's Goodness, and God's Name will be proclaimed. The programme however is set out as follows:

---

[8] Pseudo-Jonathan gives a parallel interpretation: 'The Name of YHWH is not revealed to me . . . for I have not found the Name of YHWH in the *Book of the Angels*.' This work was probably a composition containing magical formulae attributed to the rebellious angels who descended from heaven to marry the daughters of men. A full story of this sort appears in the First Book of Enoch.

1. God will stand Moses beside him in a cleft of rock and will cover him with his Palm until his Glory has passed by.

2. He will cause all his Glory to pass by Moses.

3. God will remove his Palm and Moses will see his Back.

But what actually happens in the event as it is described in Exodus 34?

1. And YHWH descended in the cloud and stood with him there, and he proclaimed the Name of YHWH.

2. YHWH passed before him.

3. And he proclaimed YHWH, YHWH God, merciful and gracious . . . (Exod. 34: 5–9).

There seems at first sight to be only the most tenuous connection between the programme and the event. Indeed, since several of the moves announced by God do not in fact occur, one might be forgiven for failing to perceive any coherence between the two even at second sight. Yet the targumists assume without hesitation that the two must belong together and to demonstrate that this is so, they supplement the text where they feel it to be necessary and emend apparent inconsistencies.[9]

Each point of the programme in Exodus 33 will now be examined in conjunction with the corresponding stage of the event according to Exodus 34.

In the first item of the programme, God tells Moses that he will stand him beside him in a cleft of rock and will cover him with his Palm while his Glory passes by. In the first item of the event, YHWH descends in a cloud, stands with Moses, and proclaims the Name YHWH.

The two discrepancies here are the *Palm*, mentioned in the programme but dropped from the event, with which God is to cover Moses from the sight of his Face or Glory, and the cloud, not anticipated in the programme but featuring in the event, in which YHWH descends. Furthermore, the proclamation of the Name, although appearing in the summary of the revelation promised by God, is missing from the detailed programme. These problems are reconciled by Onkelos in the follow manner:

[9] The structure of Jewish Bible exegesis is analysed in detail in G. Vermes, *Scripture and Tradition in Judaism* (Leiden, 1961; 2nd edn. 1973).

Programme	*Event*
And YHWH said, Behold there is a place prepared before me and you shall stand on a rock. And it shall be that when my Glory passes by, I will place you in a cave of the rock and my Word shall overshadow you until I have passed.	And YHWH was revealed in the cloud and stood with him there and proclaimed the Name of YHWH.

Just as Pseudo-Jonathan converts 'I am your shield' (Gen. 15: 1), God's comfort to Abraham, to 'My Word is your shield', so here the protective Palm of God is also envisaged as his Word. The unheralded cloud and the proclamation of the divine Name can then be made to tally with the programme: Moses becomes aware of the simultaneously hidden and revealed *ehyeh*/I AM THERE, and calls out his Name, YHWH, HE IS THERE.

Targum Onkelos conveys by innuendo the understanding made explicit in the Pseudo-Jonathan version. The Name of YHWH proclaimed by Moses even becomes 'the Name of the Word of YHWH,' as it does also in Neofiti.

Programme	*Event*
And YHWH said, Behold a place is prepared before me and you shall stand on a rock. And it shall be that when the Glory of my Presence passes before you, I will place you in a cave of the rock and will overshadow you with my Word until I have passed by.	And YHWH revealed himself in the cloud of the Glory of his Presence and Moses stood with him there.[10] And Moses proclaimed the Name of the Word of YHWH.

Neofiti and the Fragmentary Targum do not paraphrase 'my *Palm*' in the programme, but leave it as it is. Neofiti's novel contribution here is to identify God's Goodness which Moses is to see with the *angelic hosts* represented as a celestial train following the passage of the divine Glory.[11]

---

[10] It will be noticed that Pseudo-Jonathan adjusts his event at this point to make it consistent with his programme, which is not the case in the biblical text. He also openly specifies in the following sentence that *Moses* proclaims the Name, whereas the Bible leaves the subject of the verb undefined.

[11] For a similar image in the Dead Sea Scrolls, see 'The Divine Throne-Chariot', in Geza Vermes, *The Dead Sea Scrolls in English*, 2nd edn. (Penguin, 1975), 212.

Programme	Event
And YHWH said, Behold there is a place set aside before me and you shall stand prepared on the rock. And when the Glory of my presence passes by, I will spread over you the Palm of my Hand until the hosts of angels, which you will see, pass by.	And the Glory of the Presence of YHWH was revealed in the cloud and stood beside him there, and he prayed in the Name of the Word of YHWH.

As a second item of the biblical programme, God tells Moses he will cause his Glory to pass by him. The second item of the event records simply that YHWH passed before him.

Onkelos in his interpretation remains as usual close to the Bible.

Programme	Event
And I will cause the parade of my Glory to pass by.	And YHWH caused his Presence to pass before his face.

The Targum thus regards YHWH's Glory and Presence as identical.

Pseudo-Jonathan, the Fragmentary Targum, and Neofiti, on the other hand, adopt the metaphor already used by Neofiti and equate God's invisible Glory with the hosts of ministering angels. The understanding here is that the heavenly procession does not follow YHWH but precedes him (that 'minister before me').

Programme	Event
And I will cause the hosts of angels to pass by that stand and minister before me. (Pseudo-Jonathan, Fragmentary Targum, Neofiti)	And YHWH caused his Presence to pass before his face. (Pseudo-Jonathan)
	And the Glory of the Presence of YHWH passed by before him. (Fragmentary Targum, Neofiti)

The climax of the episode is now reached. As third point of the biblical programme, Moses is told that God will remove his Palm and Moses will then see his Back. As third point in the event, the Name of God is invoked and this is followed by a panegyric enlarging on the significance of YHWH in the light of 'I will be there such as I will be there', that he is gracious to whomsoever he is gracious and merciful to whomsoever he is merciful, etc.

The Targums throw no extra light on the event. Apart from minor variations in the eulogy, they repeat the text fairly literally. On the other hand, differences become evident at this juncture of the programme in connection with the crucial 'my Back', where a paraphrase has to be found that will explain its correspondence to the panegyric on the Name. Again, Onkelos shows no great originality, writing merely: 'You shall see what is behind me.'

In parenthesis, the same tradition is reflected, in an earthier and more specific fashion, in a rabbinic commentary on a passage from the Book of Numbers. On the text 'He shall behold the form of YHWH' (Num. 12: 8), the comment is: 'This concerns the vision of the buttocks . . . Scripture says, "And I will remove my Palm and you shall see what is behind me" (Exod. 33: 23).'[12] Onkelos, in any case, makes no greater effort than does the biblical writer himself to relate the foreseen vision of God's Back to the actual recitation of 'YHWH, YHWH God . . .'

The other interpreters do make such an attempt. Pseudo-Jonathan's is one of the most elaborate. Moses will see, he explains, 'the knot of the word [not Word] of the phylactery of my Presence'.

This could be a conflation. It is possible that two versions, one reading 'the knot of the phylactery' and the other 'the word of the phylactery', were later combined into 'the knot of the word of the phylactery' etc. Nevertheless, bearing in mind that the interpreter's work was to forge a reasonable link between God's Back and his Name, the Pseudo-Jonathan rendering is also acceptable as it stands.[13] His meaning could therefore be that as God removes his Palm, Moses will see on it the knot of the straps holding the arm phylactery in place. An identical tradition is preserved in the name of a first or second century AD rabbi, Simeon the Hasid. ' "And I will remove my Palm and you will see my Back." This teaches that the Holy One, blessed be he, showed Moses the knot of the phylactery.'[14]

The key, however, to Pseudo-Jonathan's interpretation rests in the 'word' of God's glorious Presence contained in the phylactery: YHWH.

Again, the problem is explained more easily by quoting another

[12] *Sifre on Num.* 12: 8, 103, ed. H. S. Horovitz, 102.
[13] A phylactery is a small box-like receptacle worn by observant Jews on the forehead and left arm and containing certain biblical texts, chief among them the classic prayer, 'Hear O Israel, YHWH our God, YHWH is one' (Deut. 6: 4).
[14] *BT Berakhot*, 7a.

haggadah,[15] since it actually alludes to 'the Name of YHWH named above you', i.e. on the forehead.

Rabbi Abin ben Rabbi Ada said in the name of Rabbi Isaac: How is it that the Holy One, blessed be he, dons phylacteries? For it is written, 'YHWH has sworn by his right hand and by his mighty arm' (Isa. 62: 8). 'His right hand', this means the Law, as it is written, 'At my right hand is a fire of the Law for them' (Deut. 33: 2). 'And by his mighty arm', this means the phylacteries, as it is written, 'YHWH will give might to his people' (Ps. 29: 11). For it is written, 'And all the nations of the earth shall see that the Name of YHWH is named above you and they shall fear you . . .' (Deut. 28: 10).[16]

The Fragmentary Targum and Neofiti follow a course of reasoning parallel to that of Pseudo-Jonathan but employ a different terminology and do not exercise their imaginations to the same extent. Their versions read, respectively: 'And I will cause you to see the saying [*dibbura*]'; 'And you shall see the saying [*dibbura*] of the Glory of my Presence'. The conclusion arrived at here is that of Pseudo-Jonathan: the vision which Moses will be permitted to see, referred to in the Bible as God's Back, will be one of the saying or word of the Glory itself. And this saying or word is the recitation 'YHWH, YHWH God . . .'

An ancient commentary on Numbers confirms this deduction. Concerning the text 'With him I will speak mouth to mouth, clearly, and not in riddles' (Num. 2: 8), it observes: ' "Clearly", this is the vision of the word (*dibbur*).' A questioner objects: 'You say that this is the clear vision of the word. Is it not rather the clear vision of the Presence?' To which the answer is: 'Scripture says, "And he said, You cannot see my Face, for man cannot see my Face and live." '[17]

———

Little by little, the significance of this other dialogue between Moses and God falls into shape. Moses desired to see God's Glory, or Face, but was refused because as a human creature he would have found the vision intolerable. Instead, he was offered the protection of God's Word, I AM THERE, and a vision, from within that protection, of God's Goodness or Back.

And what was that Back?

God's Name, YHWH.

Moses learned the true meaning of YHWH from the revelation in the

[15] *Haggadah* is an exegetical form applied to historical, doctrinal and moral (but not legal) passages of Scriptures.   [16] *BT Berakhot*, 6a.

[17] Exod. 33: 20; *Sifre on Num.* 12: 8, 103, ed. H. S. Horovitz, 101.

burning bush when God said of himself, 'I am there', and further, 'I am/I will be there such as I am/I will be there'. On this other occasion, he is permitted to see 'clearly', and no longer in 'riddles', the Goodness, that is to say the deeds, associated with YHWH's Name. He discovers too that these effects of God's Presence in the world are not the whole of God, but only his Back, the activities of that part of God which 'is there' with his creation.

YHWH, YHWH God, gracious and merciful, patient, far removed from anger and near of mercy and bounteous to do grace and truth; keeping grace and goodness unto thousands and procuring forgiveness of sins, but by no means leaving sins unpunished. On the day of the great judgment he will remember the sins of the wicked fathers on the sons, and on the sons of rebellious sons to the third and to the fourth generation.[18] And Moses hurried and bowed down to the ground and praised and glorified. (Neofiti)

MIDRASH

The purpose of the great body of literature known as Midrash is homiletic as well as interpretative. Where the Targums proceed from one biblical verse to the next, paraphrasing, expounding, or simplifying when this seems required, midrashic commentary assembles passages from various parts of the Bible with a view to clarifying one in the light of another, or to driving home certain homiletic points.

Whether or not as a result of this more concrete and practical approach, the doctrine of the Presence loses in Midrash a small measure of the purity of meaning attached to it in the Targums. It is for instance YHWH = God-with-us, but at times it is also YHWH = God-in-heaven, where Moses 'ascends' in order to speak with him, and where angels feed on his 'radiance'. Eventually, Jewish mystical thought will locate the Presence entirely in heaven, seated on his glorious Throne-Chariot. Again, although in Midrash the Presence is YHWH himself and not yet the distinct 'personality' of later speculation, already it shows signs of moving off towards a separate identity equipped with mouth, feet, wings, face, and even garments.

One other characteristic of Midrash which should be noted is that the twin concept of the Word is no longer found side by side with that of the Presence. The delicate nuances of meaning found in the Targums are in consequence absent from these writings.

[18] It is interesting to observe how the Targums temper the severity of the biblical text by describing the fathers as 'wicked' and the children as 'rebellious'.

A midrashic comment on a passage from the story of Balaam introduces a typical example of its many allusions to the mouth of the
Presence. When Balaam told the servant of Balak that even if Balak
were to give him a house full of silver and gold, 'I could not transgress
against the mouth of YHWH my God' (Num. 24: 13), the midrashist
explains: 'He prophesied that he could not remove the blessings with
which the fathers were blessed by the mouth of the Presence.'[19]

Unlike the Targums, therefore, which employ the title Presence
only in particular circumstances and situations, and which in the
context of the mouth of YHWH select Word instead, in Midrash
Presence is a straight rendering of YHWH.

Elsewhere, the dead Moses is portrayed as supported by the wings
of the Presence. 'Scripture teaches (that) when Moses died, he lay on
the wings of the Presence.'[20]

Another haggadah explains the biblical mention of Aaron being
divested of his priestly robes as a preliminary to being robed in the
garments of the Presence in the world to come. 'Rabbi Simai said: It is
written, "Moses stripped Aaron of his garments and put them on
Eleazar his son" (Num. 20: 28). Scripture teaches here that he
divested him of his priestly garments until he should find himself
clothed in the garments of the Presence.'[21]

A powerful theme found in Midrash but not in the Targums is
the idea, later expanded by medieval Jewish mystics to first-rank
importance, that the Presence 'contracted' so that it might fit into
the world. A teaching from the mid-third century AD develops this
notion.

Rabbi Judah ben Simon in the name of Rabbi Yohanan: Three sayings were
heard by Moses from the mouth of the Almighty so that he was afraid and
shrank back. In the hour that he said, 'You shall make for me a Sanctuary'
(Exod. 25: 8), Moses said before the Holy One, blessed be he, Lord of worlds,
'heaven and heaven's heaven cannot contain you' (1 Kgs. 8: 27), and you say,
'You shall make for me a Sanctuary!' The Holy One, blessed be he, said to
him, Moses, not as you think, but twenty boards in the north, and twenty to the
south, and eight in the west, then I will descend and contract my Presence
under and between them. For it is written, 'I will assemble with you there.'
(Exod. 25: 22)[22]

---

[19] *Tanhuma*, Buber iv. 137.   [20] *PT Sota*, 1: 10 (17c).

[21] *Sifre Zutta*, 27 § 13, ed. H. S. Horovitz, 319.

[22] *Pesikta Rabbati*, 16: 7. The Hebrew verb translated 'I will assemble' is taken to
mean 'I will come together', 'I will shrink into a smaller size.'

Another peculiarity of Midrash compared with the Targums is that the indwelling Presence is often represented as radiance or light, and also as food. Indeed, the three frequently appear together, as in the following interpretation. According to the biblical story, Moses fasted for forty days and forty nights whilst he 'was there' with YHWH on Mount Sinai (Exod. 34: 28), yet when he came down with the tables of testimony, 'his face shone because he has been talking with God' (Exod. 34: 29). How was it that although he had eaten nothing for so long, Moses's face still shone? The rabbis felt this called for an explanation. ' "Bread ate he not" (Exod. 34: 28). But what did he eat? He was nourished by the radiance of the Presence'.[23]

From this, a homily develops concerning the elders of Israel who 'beheld God and ate and drank' (Exod. 24: 11).

Our teachers say, For they nourished their eyes on the Presence. They said, Did not Moses do the same, that he ascended into heaven and beheld the Presence and needed neither food nor drink? We too, when we behold the Presence, will need neither food nor drink. And nevertheless, 'they beheld God' and needed food and drink. For it is written, 'And they ate and drank.'[24]

In a second *haggadah*, the radiance of the Presence is conceived of as the nourishment of the whole of life, of all living things in their entirety, and not only of the chosen few.

Rabbi Isaac said: It is written 'My offering, my food' (Num. 28: 2). Is there, then, eating and drinking before the Name, blessed be he? But if you wish to say there is, learn from his angels and servants which are flaming fire. For it is written, 'His servants are flaming fire' (Ps. 104: 4). And by what are they nourished? Rabbi Yudan said in the name of Rabbi Isaac: They nourish themselves on the radiance of the Presence. For it is written, 'In the light of the king's countenance is life' (Prov. 16: 15). And Rabbi Haggai said in the name of Rabbi Isaac: It is written, 'And you give life to them all' (Neh. 9: 6). You are the sustenance of all things.[25]

Scholars largely insist that as in the Targums, the Presence in Midrash is not understood as Omnipresence but is always seen to rest in the confines of a specific space, in accordance with the divine mood of the moment. It is however difficult to avoid concluding that the tendency towards universalism, apparent in Rabbi Haggai's teaching that the radiance of the Presence is the food of all life, also made itself

---

[23] *Ex. Rabbah*, 47: 5.   [24] *Tanhuma*, Buber iii. 67–8.
[25] *Pesikta Rabbati*, 16: 2.

felt from time to time in regard to the Presence as such. Two sayings from the first half of the third century AD certainly seem to bear this out. In the first, 'Rabbi Joshua ben Levi said: Man is forbidden to walk upright for four yards, for it is written, "The whole earth is full of his glory" (Isa. 6: 3). Rabbi Huna son of Rabbi Joshua did not walk four yards with his head uncovered, for he said, The Presence is over my head.'[26] The same belief seems to underlie the teaching of Rabban Gamaliel, who flourished in about AD 100. A Gentile once asked him why God revealed himself to Moses in a thornbush. 'He said to him: If he had revealed himself from a carob-tree or a fig-tree, you would ask the same question. To send you away empty is impossible. To teach you (therefore) that no place on earth is free of the Presence, God spoke to Moses even from the thornbush.'[27] To this spatial extension of the dominion of the Presence is added a temporal enlargement, some of the sages teaching that although in this world it is perceived by individual men and women, in the world to come it will be seen by all men. 'Rabbi Pinhas said: Like a king who showed himself to his household by means of his image. For in this world, the Presence reveals itself only to individuals, but in the world to come, the "glory of YHWH will reveal itself and all flesh will see it together. Indeed, the mouth of YHWH has so spoken" (Isa. 40: 5).'[28]

In general, however, Midrash associates the Presence with the same activities as do the Targums: descents, ascents, appearances and revelations, accompaniments and withdrawals. Ten 'descents' are counted, but the various collections do not exactly tally, as is apparent from the following two.

The Presence came down into the world in ten descents. Once in the garden of Eden, as it is written, 'And they heard the sound of YHWH God walking in the garden' (Gen. 3: 8). Once in the generation of the tower, as it is written, 'And YHWH came down to see the city and the tower' (Gen. 11: 5). Once in Sodom, as it is written, 'I will go down and see whether it is in accordance with the cry of complaint which has come to me' (Gen. 18: 21). Once in Egypt, as it is written, 'I came down to deliver them out of the hand of Egypt' (Exod. 3: 8). Once at the Sea, as it is written, 'He bowed the heavens, he came down' (2 Sam. 22: 10). Once on Sinai, as it is written, 'Then YHWH came down on Mount Sinai' (Exod. 19: 20). Once in the pillar of cloud, as it is written, 'YHWH came down into the cloud' (Num. 11: 25). Once in the sanctuary, as it is written, 'This gate shall remain shut. It shall not be opened and no man shall enter by it. For YHWH God of Israel has entered by it' (Ezek. 44: 2). And once

[26] BT Kiddushin, 31a.   [27] Num. Rabbah, 12: 4.
[28] Lev. Rabbah, 1: 14, ed. M. Margulies, 32.

in the time to come in the days of Gog and Magog, for it is written, 'On that day, his feet shall stand on the Mount of Olives' (Zech. 14: 4).[29]

The other list reads:

Once in the garden of Eden. Once in the generation of the division. Once in Sodom. Once in the thornbush. Once on Sinai. Twice at the cleaving of the rock. Twice in the Tent of Presence. And once in the time to come.[30]

One interesting feature of these lists is that they seem to be independent of targumic interpretations relating to the same texts. Without comparing all ten, no Presence imagery is applied in the Targums to 'the sound of YHWH God walking in the garden' (Gen. 3: 8), though Onkelos renders it 'the voice of the Word of YHWH God walking'. Again, only Neofiti adopts the Presence metaphor for 'And YHWH came down to see . . .' (Gen. 11: 5), which is given by Onkelos and Pseudo-Jonathan respectively as 'And YHWH was revealed to punish', and 'And the Word of YHWH was revealed against . . .'. As for 'I will go down and see . . .' (Gen. 18: 21), all the Targums repeat this text literally and without paraphrase.

In regard to the revelations and appearances of the Presence—though strictly speaking the descents are also revelations—Midrash teaches not only that they occur, but also how and where in the religious life God's indwelling Presence is to be detected. Rabbi Ishmael, for example, is concerned to emphasize that to eat with one's companions 'before God' is to be aware of their presence and hence of the supreme Presence itself. 'Rabbi Ishmael taught: "Aaron came" (with all the elders of Israel to eat bread with Moses' father-in-law before God (Exod. 18: 12). Did they then eat before God? But it transpires from this that whoever sees the face of his companion, it is as though he sees the Face of the Presence.'[31] Rabbi Judah applies the same moral to the prescribed attitude towards spiritual 'elders'. 'Rabbi Judah taught: It is not written, "All who sought Moses," but "all who sought YHWH" ("would go out to the Tent of Meeting which was outside the camp" (Exod. 33: 7). This teaches that whoever sees the face of an elder, it is as though he sees the Face of the Presence.'[32] Rabbi Halafta of Sepphoris, speaking in terms that recall the words of Jesus in the New Testament, points out that God is with those who

[29] *Aboth de-Rabbi Nathan*, A, ch. 34, ed. Schechter, 102. These amount to nine descents, not ten!

[30] *Pirke de-Rabbi Eliezer*, ch. 14.

[31] *PT Erubin*, 5: 1.

[32] *Midrash on Psalms*, 25: 6.

come together to speak and think 'on his Name'. 'Rabbi Halafta of Sepphoris said: Wherever two or three sit in the market-place and words of the Torah are with them, the Presence is revealed over them. For it is written, "Then those who feared YHWH spoke with one another. YHWH heeded them and heard them, and a book of remembrance was written before him of those who feared YHWH and thought on his Name" (Mal. 3: 16).'[33]

Another typical short sermon turns on the favourite problem, one that has already figured here, of why God chose the common thorn or scrub for his revelation on Mount Horeb.

Rabbi Eleazar ben Arakh said: Why did the Holy One, blessed be he, reveal himself to Moses from highest heaven down to the thornbush? Should he not have revealed himself from the cedars of Lebanon, and from the peaks of the mountains, and from the summits of the hills? But the Holy One, blessed be he, humbled his Presence and made its way in accordance with the way of the earth [derekh eretz] so that the nations of the world might not say, Because he is a God and Lord of his world, his way is not according to the law.[34]

Undeniably, the texture of the Presence imagery in Midrash gains from being related to everyday life. At the same time, it is in another sense poorer because of the absence of the Word motif and the limitless avenues of thought to which it leads. Yet basically, the doctrine which it is intended to propagate remains the same. YHWH is he who was there, who is there, and who will be there, in whatever form he chooses to be there.

I am he who was in Egypt and I am he who was at the Sea. I am he who was at Sinai. I am he who was in the past and I am he who will be in the future. I am he who is in this world and I am he who will be in the world to come. As it is said, 'See now that I, even I, am he.' (Deut. 32: 39)[35]

But perhaps this final midrashic text is the most meaningful of all.

'Ehyeh asher ehyeh.' The Holy One, blessed be he, said to Moses, Go and say to the Israelites, I was there with you in the servitude of the kingdoms. But he said to him, Lord of the world, the present distress is enough. Whereat the Holy One, blessed be he, answered and said, Go and say to them, 'I AM THERE has sent me to you.'[36]

---

[33] *Aboth de-Rabbi Nathan*, B, ch. 34, ed. Schechter, 74.

[34] *Mekhilta d'Rabbi Simon b. Jochai*, ed. J. N. Epstein and E. Z. Melamed, 2.

[35] *Mekhilta on Ex. 20: 22*, ed. J. Z. Lauterbach II, 231.

[36] *BT Berakhot*, 9*b*.

IO

The Likeness of the Glory
of YHWH

BUBER rejected mysticism. He does not disguise his early attraction to it, but as he makes plain not only in *I and You*[1] but elsewhere, at a certain stage of his development he came to the conclusion that the practices of mysticism are in conflict with the fulfilment of true human personality, and its aims in any case impossible to attain. He found quite simply that the way of the mystic is not the right way to live.

The tradition to which Buber belongs is nevertheless the Jewish mystical tradition. Tracing it backward in time, his immediate source was Polish–Russian Hasidism, which inherited Lurianic kabbalah, which in turn evolved from kabbalah proper, which was preceded by *merkavah* or Throne-Chariot mysticism and the parallel (though part of a very different stream) works of rabbinical literature. Medieval German Hasidism, which like kabbalah adopted the vision of the Throne-Chariot as its main theme, also forms part of the descent.

Reversing the process and following, very roughly, its path forward from past to present, the speculations of the Throne-Chariot visionaries turned mainly, as we shall see, on a text from Ezekiel. The German Hasidim and the kabbalists, taking over these ideas, generated a new body of thought by incorporating into them notions current in their own times and religious climate. In the sixteenth century, Isaac Luria Ashkenazi pioneered modifications to kabbalistic thought. Later still, his teachings were absorbed and re-formulated by the Baal Shem Tov, the founder of eighteenth-century Hasidism. Finally, Martin Buber re-interpreted the doctrines of the Baal Shem and his followers with the intention of making them comprehensible and accessible to the larger, not exclusively Jewish, modern world.

In other words, in the written works representing this age-long evolution of the Jewish religious mind, a thread is detectable reaching

[1] Martin Buber, *Werke*, 3 vols. (Kösel–Lambert Schneider, 1962–4), i. 134–42; *I and Thou*, trans. R. Gregor Smith, 2nd edn. (Scribner–T. & T. Clark, 1958), 83–95.

right through from the rabbinic doctrine of God to the concept of the Deity expressed in Buber's teachings as the everlasting *You*.

———

For approximately eleven hundred years, from the first century BC to the tenth century AD, the Jewish mystical imagination was obsessed by two main topics: the story of the creation, and a vision of Ezekiel. The word of YHWH came to him, the prophet relates, and the hand of YHWH was on him, and he looked and saw the 'likeness' of four living creatures, each with four faces and four wings, and each accompanied by a wheel. And when the living creatures moved, the wheels moved with them, 'for the spirit of the living creatures was in the wheels' (Ezek. 1: 21).

And above the firmament over their heads there was the likeness of a Throne, in appearance like sapphire; and seated above the likeness of a Throne was a likeness as it were of a human form.

And upward from what had the appearance of his loins I saw as it were gleaming bronze, like the appearance of fire enclosed round about; and downward from what had the appearance of his loins I saw as it were the appearance of fire, and there was brightness round about him.

Like the appearance of the bow that is in the cloud on the day of rain, so was the appearance of the brightnesss round about.

Such was the appearance of the likeness of the Glory of YHWH. (Ezek. 1: 26–8)

This conception of the 'likeness of a Throne' bearing above it 'the appearance of the likeness of the Glory of YHWH' stimulated compositions totally unlike any considered hitherto, a body of literature *sui generis*, infused with dread and awe in face of the terrible splendour of the Godhead. Throne-Chariot literature contains, as a foremost scholar in the field of Jewish mysticism emphasizes, almost no sign of the love of God, and the idea of divine immanence 'plays practically no part' in it.[2] On the contrary, the Deity is invested with such infinite grandeur and remoteness that he is separated from his creatures by a gulf impossible to bridge even when they are caught in the grip of ecstasy. For the élite contemplating the Majesty on the Throne, God is the very reverse of Presence; he is the Furthest of the Far. Yet because of the traditional association of glory and light with the Shekhinah, Presence is nevertheless the title which the Throne-Chariot mystics give to the transcendent Godhead whom they place at such a point of remoteness from themselves and hope only to see as their final reward.

[2] G. Scholem, *Major Trends in Jewish Mysticism* (Thames & Hudson, 1955), 55.

Furthermore, although they allot to the divine Presence a different situation and a changed role, it is still an aspect of God and not distinct from him. Little by little, however, this doctrine alters and the tendency to divide God from his indwelling Presence, already noticeable in Midrash,[3] becomes more and more pronounced, until in the end, moving into an identity of its own, the Presence acquires substance in the shape of a body, a personality, and later even a sex (female). Whereas formerly the notion of the Presence served to illumine and interpret the divine Name, it becomes itself subject in time to a gradual process of interpretation which eventually places it so far from God himself that the great tenth-century scholar Saadia is able to define it as a created light, God's first creation. The symbol of light, it will be noted, is still perpetuated.

———

German Hasidism of the Middle Ages continued the Throne-Chariot initiative, but from the fourteenth century onwards this gradually lost ground, due to the influence of Spanish kabbalah, to a new religious mood, a sense of divine immanence so vigorous and so far-reaching as almost to amount to pantheism. It was undoubtedly accompanied by a love of God. God was to be seen in all things, and all things were to be seen in God. He was in all things when they were created, and also before they were created. The Hasidim of this period even went so far as to wonder why they should address their prayers to heaven when God is present here on earth. Yet they did not look for him actually to manifest himself through the natural world of what is ordinary and usual, but only through the extraordinary wonders and miracles effected by his Glory or Presence in heaven.

———

In the movement known as kabbalah,[4] literally, 'tradition', the divine Glory and its powers was once more the principal object of contemplation. Emerging on the scene of history in southern France in the twelfth century—though kabbalism came into being long before, in the Talmudic era—these mystics and ecstatics flourished in Spain until the expulsion of the Jews from that country in 1492. Following this enormous shock to Judaism, kabbalah was transformed. Where it had

[3] Most prominently in *Midrash on Prov.* 22: 29, ed. M. Buber, 47*a*, 'The Presence stood before the Holy One, blessed be he, and said . . .'.

[4] For kabbalah see esp. G. Scholem, *Kabbalah* (Keter, 1974). Cf. also *Encyclopaedia Judaica*, x, under the same heading.

previously been directed towards plumbing the mysteries concealed in the Godhead and towards reaching back, not only to the hidden meanings of the scriptural text but even to the secrets supposed to have been revealed to Adam at the beginning of time, it now concerned itself more with human redemption. Where kabbalists had viewed themselves as the guardians of mystical knowledge, and as an élite set apart from the masses to concentrate with single-minded absorption on complex and esoteric theories relating to the divine nature and, most conspicuously, the divine Name and Names,[5] they now sought to enter into touch with the community.

One of the fundamental tenets of kabbalah is that only part of God, the part accessible to the mind via the created world, should correctly be called 'God'. The rest must be forever *deus absconditus*, totally beyond the reach of thought. This theory, based on the words addressed to Moses that he might see God's Back but never his Face (Exod. 33: 23), was developed by Isaac Ibn Latif, a thirteenth-century kabbalist, who argued that God's Back is as far as even the keenest religious understanding is able to stretch, though he allowed that a person may at that point be granted a vision of the image of the divine Face during ecstasy. Another Isaac, Isaac the Blind, who lived in Provence a little earlier than the Spanish Jew, Ibn Latif, gave to this Face of God turned away from the world, and sharply distinguished from God the Creator, the title of *Ein-Sof,* Without-End. It was specifically stipulated that *Ein-Sof* is not to be regarded as the proper name of this hidden Godhead, but, as a later kabbalist explained, 'a word meaning his complete concealment, and our sacred tongue has no word like these two to signify his concealment. And it is not right to say "*Ein-Sof,* blessed be He", or "May He be blessed", because He cannot be blessed by our lips.'[6]

Compared with such extreme diffidence in face of the Mystery of Mysteries, the search of the kabbalists for God revealed was bold and persistent. So intense was their preoccupation with his being and activities that, not content with watching for them to become evident in creation, they pressed back into the obscure recesses of God's presumed pre-creative existence where he begins to emerge from his hiddenness and to move towards his creative role. For God does not, according to this school of mystical thought, suddenly become the

[5] It was the belief of kabbalists that the entire Torah is a commentary on the Name of God.

[6] Barukh Kosover, *c.*1770. See Scholem, *Kabbalah,* 90.

Creator of the universe. He 'emanates' from his self-concealment in a series of ten stages or *sefirot*. From the first, called Supreme Crown, he proceeds to Wisdom, from Wisdom to Intelligence, from Intelligence to Love, from Love to Power or Judgement, from Power to Compassion, from Compassion to Endurance, from Endurance to Majesty, from Majesty to Foundation, and from Foundation to the last of his emanations, Sovereignty or Presence.

These spheres, which represent intermediary states or attributes lying between God and all that exists apart from him, also serve as a progressive revelation of the various divine Names. Thus the first stage, Supreme Crown, is associated with the Name I AM THERE; and the last, Sovereignty, is linked to the Name Shekhinah, Presence. Other Names of God appearing between these two are Yah, El (Deity), Elohim (God), YHWH, YHWH of hosts, Elohim of hosts, El Shaddai (Almighty Deity) and Adonai (Lord). In the present context, only the first and the last emanations concern us, since they show that in kabbalah I AM THERE is interpreted to signify not only God's will to be present with his creation, but also his will for creation's presence. As he starts to move towards his creative work, his Name for himself conveys both his own intended Presence as well as the intended present existence of the world. Secondly, they show that as he arrives at the point of readiness for the world to be summoned into being, his Name Presence conveys at one and the same time the world's 'being there' and his own 'being there' with it.

Another theory founded on the concept of the progressive emergence of God out of himself has to do with the divine personality as such. According to this, in his first emanation God is simply HE. So near is he at this level to his dense self-concealment that he has no name at all. In the next stage of the unfolding of his being, when he becomes perceptible and therefore capable of being expressed and addressed, he is YOU. But in his final individuation, God is I. It is at this point, in his aspect of Presence, that man becomes aware of him. From knowledge of God's I, so kabbalism teaches, he can go on to knowledge of God's YOU, and of his HE, and from thence proceed to the depths of Nothingness. As Gershom Scholem writes:

To gauge the degree of paradox implied by these remarkable and very influential thoughts one must remember that in general, the mystics, in speaking of God's immanence in creation, are inclined to depersonalize him: the immanent God only too easily becomes an impersonal God-head. In fact, this tendency has always been one of the main pitfalls of pantheism. All the more remarkable is the fact that the Kabbalists, and even those among them who are inclined to pantheism, managed to avoid it, for as we have seen the Zohar[7] identifies the highest development of God's personality with precisely that stage of His unfolding which is nearest to human experience, indeed which is immanent and mysteriously present in every one of us.[8]

Isaac Luria, the sixteenth-century holy man and exponent of kabbalah, rebelled against kabbalist élitism and exclusivism. Convinced that all men can be united with God, he set out to repair the breach that had for so long gaped between mystical religious thought and the everyday life of ordinary Jews.

One of his most notable contributions in this respect was founded on the ancient myth of *tzimtzum*, the 'contraction' of God's Presence, which kabbalah understood not as a process in which the greater squeezed itself together to fit into the smaller, but as its retreat into itself—to make space for what was not itself. 'How did He produce and create the world? As a man who draws in and contracts his breath so that the smaller can contain the larger, so He contracted his Light into a hand's breadth according to his own measure and the world was left in darkness. And in that darkness he cut boulders and hewed rocks.'[9] Thus whereas God's saying (Exod. 25: 22) 'I will assemble with you there' is paraphrased in Midrash as 'I will descend and contract my Presence',[10] i.e. I will compress my Presence so that its dimensions will conform to that of the Sanctuary, kabbalah sees God withdrawing his light, one of the synonyms of Presence, into himself so as to create space for what is not himself.

As Luria expounded the creation, before the world began nothing existed apart from *Ein-Sof. Ein-Sof* was everywhere and everywhere was *Ein-Sof*. To make room for his creative work, *Ein-Sof* had therefore to retreat into himself. He then called into being *Adam kadmon*, Primordial Man.

Adam kadmon was not *homo sapiens*. He was a configuration of the light which flowed from *Ein-Sof*, and the light of *Ein-Sof* streamed from the eyes, ears, mouth, and nose of *Adam kadmon*.

To catch the light of *Ein-Sof* streaming from *Adam kadmon*, vessels had been made ready; but not all of them were adequate. Those assigned to the first divine emanation, Supreme Crown, and to the

---

[7] The great classic of Spanish kabbalah, written some time after 1275 by an unknown author, possibly Moses de Leon.
[8] Scholem, *Major Trends*, 216.   [9] Scholem, *Kabbalah*, 129.   [10] See above, p. 114.

second and third, Wisdom and Intelligence, held firm, and though the vessel allotted to the tenth emanation of Sovereignty (= Presence) cracked, it too did not break. The others shattered into countless millions of fragments, and sparks of the light of *Ein-Sof* flew out into every corner of creation. Each one became embedded in the world, imprisoned in its own husk or 'shell'.

When man proper, the First Man, Adam of Genesis, was created, his sin reactivated the drama of the broken vessels. Nor was this all, for his own soul also dispersed in millions of sparks, like the light of *Ein-Sof*. The light of the First Man fell and went into exile with the light of *Ein-Sof*.

The task required of the descendants of the First Man is 'mending'. They have to 'mend' the damage caused by the breaking of the vessels. They must redeem the sparks of the indwelling Presence from their banishment and re-unite them with God; and they must redeem their own soul-sparks.

In plain words, Luria's vision sees the redemption of the world taking place through the redemption of God by the world. The perfection of God, the re-unification of God within himself, depends on man. As a Hasidic teacher later observed, man's duty is not to save his soul but to 'elevate' heaven', the implication being that the latter also accomplishes the former, for the release of God's hidden and fragmented Presence in the world demands man's own unified presence with it.

With God and his Presence re-joined, and man re-joined within himself, all of God's creation will be re-joined into the unity of a life lived in the one Presence.

Where, it may be asked at this point, is the announced link between the earliest and latest concepts of God in the one stream of Jewish mystical tradition?

It is admittedly not to be found on the level of the changing forms of God themselves. The *I* of Buber's everlasting *You* is really not recognizable in, for instance, the likeness on the Throne, however hard one looks. On the other hand, it is undeniable that every insight into the nature of God leads back ultimately to the one source. Buber derived his ideas concerning God in part from his predecessors, as they did from theirs, but this handing down of modified traditions from one aeon to another is a secondary legacy. The prime and essential inheritance has been the root from which each divine form has sprung: the belief that God and his Name are one. From time to time, it seems as though the channels along which the revelation of revelations flows have grown muddy and choked. One concept does not always lead smoothly and surely to the next, as in the perfectly articulated schemes characteristic of the Targums. Not only do the indivisible pair, YHWH and his Presence, fall apart, but even the inseparable notions of 'indwelling' and Presence do the same, with the result that in place of the one image of God in his function of loving Presence in the world we have a variety of permutations on the subjects of God, his Presence, his 'dwelling' on earth, his 'dwelling' in heaven, and so on.

The reason for this peripheral disintegration must be that after the Babylonian exile (i.e. some time after 500 BC), the divine Name was no longer uttered aloud by Jews in general. In fact, since the written symbols YHWH immediately evoked in the reader—and still do—the interpretation Adonai, 'my Lord', it would not be inexact to say that it had long since ceased even to be read silently. YHWH as a sound conveying to the Hebrew speaker a relationship to the verb 'to be there', and provoking in consequence certain other thought-associations connected with the notion of presence, fell very many ages ago into its profound silence.

The marvel is not so much the negative one that the traditional idea of God did not in the circumstances break loose from its attachment to the Name, as that the Name, although never spoken and never heard, has continued throughout history to act as the hub about which all thought concerning God has inevitably turned. Always it has been intrinsic to Jewish belief that—as far as God in his relation with man is concerned—it is in his aspect of Presence, with all that that entails, that his essential activity *vis-à-vis* the world resides; indeed, even when the understanding of the Name is not apparently identified with the conviction that God is Presence, the latter notion still presses to the forefront of the Jewish religious mind. The twelfth-century Spanish-Jewish philosopher Maimonides explains *ehyeh asher ehyeh* to mean that God thereby describes himself as 'the existing Being which is the existing Being'. He therefore clearly sees no implication of Presence in the Name, but only of absolute existence—a familiar notion in Aristotelian thought. At the same time, he argues the derivation of Shekhinah from the verb meaning 'to dwell', expounds it as alluding to God's Presence or 'Providence', identifies it with 'the *Glory* of YHWH' and with 'light', and even with 'him that dwelt in the bush' (Deut. 33:

16). Most importantly, although he explicitly rejects the identification of the Presence with God, Maimonides winds up his great work in such a manner as to make it quite obvious that despite all he has written, God in his view is YHWH = HE IS THERE. Notwithstanding his development of the Name in austere and abstract terms of 'eternal existence', God's nature as he describes it is essentially marked by the attribute of benevolent Presence which he has deliberately discarded. His closing message to his readers is: 'God is near to all who call him if they call him in truth and turn to him. He is found by each man who seeks him if he always goes towards him and never goes astray. Amen.'[11]

And what of the Throne-Chariot visionaries, for whom God was glorious and terrifying, and above all remote? How can they have arrived at a conclusion so contrary from an identical biblical point of departure?

For all the distance that they felt obliged to lay between God and man, and for all the seemingly rare and chilly climate of their religious imagination, in their case too, the sum of all they hoped for was the Presence of God. Nowhere is this more clearly expressed than in one of the most outstanding works of this genre of mysticism, so far unmentioned because its dedication to 'the revelation of Jesus Christ' (Rev. 1: 1) precludes it from the Jewish stream proper.[12]

In the New Testament Book of Revelation, usually dated to the closing years of the first century AD, the Name of God resounds majestically throughout all the dream sequences filled with angels, lamps, two-edged swords, lightnings, thunder, plagues, spirits of God, the Lamb, the Throne, and 'him who was seated on it.'

I am the Alpha and the Omega, says the Lord God, who is and who was and who is to come, the Almighty. (1: 8)

... who lives for ever and ever, who created heaven and what is in it, the earth and what is in it, and the sea and what is in it. (10: 6)

Holy, holy, holy, the Lord God Almighty, who was and is and is to come. (4: 8)

I am the Alpha and the Omega, the beginning and the end. (21: 6)

[11] Maimonides, *The Guide to the Perplexed* (Routledge, 1942), 397.
[12] Another reason for the omission of Revelation is that the introduction of one part of the corpus of Christian mysticism into that of Judaism would inevitably lead to others, with a probable increase of confusion all around.

All these references to God are in line with the targumic paraphrases of 'I am/I will be there such as I am/I will be there' which present God as the Everlasting Being, the Creator, who said to the world, Be there! and it was there. Moreover, still greater stress is laid on this significance by the application of a 'blasphemous name' (13: 1) to the Beast, the personification of evil, the anti-God, and by the attribution to it of qualities which form an anti-Name. 'The Beast that you saw was and is not and is to ascend . . . and go to perdition . . . because it was and is not and is to come' (17: 8).

Yet although the Occupant of the Throne in this Christian work is distinguished during the greater part of the narrative by his eternity and creation, it becomes evident with the approach of its climax that, as in Maimonides' *Guide to the Perplexed*, the overriding understanding of God lying at its heart is again that of his indwelling Presence. A hint of this appears already in chapter 13, where the Beast is said to have 'opened its mouth to utter blasphemies against God, blaspheming his Name and his dwelling' (13: 6).

His 'dwelling'?

'Dwelling' in Greek is *skene*, which recalls a similar expression in the Prologue of the Gospel of John, 'And the Word became flesh and dwelt [eskenosen] among us' (1: 14). It seems not unreasonable to conclude that the author of Revelation, like the Fourth Evangelist, deliberately chose terms which would not only reproduce the import, but even imitate the sound of the Hebrew Shekhinah, the indwelling Presence of God.

———

Since the Word has found its own way into the discussion, it will not be out of place to remark that plenty of room for thought still remains concerning what is meant by it, not only in the Prologue, but also in Revelation, where we read: 'He is clad in a robe dipped in blood and the name by which he is known is The Word of God' (Rev. 19: 3). If the apocalyptic vision is essentially one of the eventual triumph of God's indwelling Presence over his exile from the world, it is more than possible that underlying the Greek *Logos* used in both contexts is Memra, the Word of YHWH, which is 'I am there'. The correspondence of *Logos* to Memra is of course not a new suggestion, nor is the similarity between the Greek *skene* and the Hebrew Shekhinah a novel discovery. The difference is that whereas Memra was formerly be-lieved to be an empty formula meaning little or nothing, it is now suggested that the very opposite is the case. Is it possible that New Testament writers deliberately applied Word and Presence imagery to Jesus?[13]

———

Returning to the theme of Presence in Revelation, a further clue appears in the use of one of its synonyms, 'the Glory of God' (15: 8), but the real point at which the concept begins to take fire is in the final vision of chapter 21. 'Then I saw a new heaven and a new earth . . . and I heard the great voice from the Throne saying: Behold the dwelling of God is with man. He will dwell with them and they shall be his people and God himself shall be there with them.' (21: 1–3).[14] He who sits on the Throne then proclaims: 'Behold I make all things new' (21: 5), and the Bride of the Lamb, the New Jerusalem, is seen descending from heaven, 'having the Glory of God, its radiance like a most rare jewel' (21: 11). The twelve gates in its high walls are inscribed with the names of the twelve tribes of Israel and its twelve foundations are called after the twelve apostles of the Lamb. In this city is no Temple, 'for its Temple is the Lord God the Almighty and the Lamb. And the city has no need of sun or moon, for the Glory of God is its light, and its lamp is the Lamb' (21: 22–3). Through the middle of the holy city flows the river of the water of life from the Throne of God and the Lamb, irrigating the Tree of Life whose leaves are 'for the healing of the nations'. Nothing accursed exists there, 'but the Throne of God and of the Lamb shall be in it, and his servants shall worship him. And they shall see his Face and his Name shall be written on their foreheads. And night shall be no more. They need no light of lamp or sun, for the Lord God will be their light and they shall reign for ever and ever' (22: 3–5).

Thus the author of Revelation also preserves the two disparate traditions, the notions of indwelling Presence, and of the Alpha and Omega who is, who was, and who is to come, Creator of the world and all it contains. But what in the final resort is this vision about, with its imagery of God and the Lamb, and so many of the appurtenances of Jewish Throne-Chariot mysticism? It looks forward to a perfect age

[13] The words 'and they shall be his people and God himself shall be there with them' are the exact reverse of God's saying to Hosea 'For you are not my people and I am not there for you' (Hos. 1: 9).

[14] Not to be forgotten either, in this connection, is 'And his name shall be called Emmanuel (which means God with us)' (Matt. 1: 23).

when the light of the Presence will be a lamp by night to the created world, and a sun by day; when God will dwell in no Temple because the Presence itself will be a Sanctuary. It foretells a perfect time when God's Face will at last be seen, and his Name, HE IS THERE, be everywhere known and remembered.

———

And what of the New Jerusalem of the prophet Ezekiel himself, upon whose vision the author of Revelation founded his own, and who has been the inspiration of mystics from time immemorial?

One conspicuous difference between the two heavenly establishments is that the Presence actually dwells in Ezekiel's Temple and there is no question in the prophet's mind of the Sanctuary becoming obsolete. On the contrary, verse after verse enumerates its measurements and describes its furniture and cult. Apart from this, Ezekiel's city also has water flowing through it, with banks on which grow trees whose leaves are for healing. Ezekiel's city also has twelve gates inscribed after the twelve tribes of Israel. And the name of Ezekiel's city? 'And the name of the city henceforth shall be: YHWH is there' (Ezek. 48: 35).

I I

This I *and* You *is Enough for the World*

THERE has been controversy in the upper echelons of the study of Hasidism about the reliability of Buber's presentation of the movement's teaching. It should consequently be made clear from the outset that no responsibility is accepted here for any distortion resulting from his rendition of Hasidic ideas. Buber reiterated publicly, and more than once, that he considered himself an interpreter and not a historian of Hasidism, and it is with his interpretation that the Buber student is concerned. Those looking for a disinterested approach will turn to other sources.

This is in no way to imply that Buber put into the mouths of the *zaddikim*, the Hasidic teachers and leaders, sayings that are implausible, or that he falsified anything; but, as he himself admitted, he selected from Hasidic doctrine only what he and (as he thought) the world needed, and simply ignored whatever failed to measure up to his own high standards of intelligence and true religiousness. (He applied the same test to Scripture.) In particular, he omitted from his synthesis any elements of Hasidism which appeared to conflict with the biblical vision of God because tinged with magic, superstition, and bigotry. By the same token, he accentuated and brought into sharpest relief doctrines which seemed to elucidate and confirm it.

In short, Buber has merely followed the example of all who find themselves at the crossroads of thought and strike out in a new direction. The founder of Hasidism did the same before him. When he returned to public life after years spent in the study of Lurianic kabbalah,[1] it was not just Isaac Luria's opinions that he passed on, but his own understanding of them, an adaptation suited to the greatly differing pressures and exigencies of his own times and situation. Luria, meditating and teaching over a century earlier in the far-off Levant, had greatly enriched Jewish religious thought and made an

[1] For kabbalah, see esp. G. Scholem's relevant entry in *Encyclopaedia Judaica*, x, also published separately as *Kabbalah* (Keter, 1974).

important contribution towards popularizing ideas until then inaccessible to the ordinary man. The Baal Shem's talent was that he was able to carry this improvement further and give religious direction and purpose, not only to people with the time and education to read and cogitate, but to the poor hard-working peasants, artisans, shopkeepers, publicans, etc. of the Jewish communities of eastern Europe. For his guidance to prove acceptable, comprehensible, and helpful to them, it had to remain close to simplicity and reality, which meant that he was obliged to allow a fair proportion of the more abstract notions of kabbalah to fall by the way: though it should be added in parenthesis that in all probability a greater measure of the movement's mystical tenets persisted in Hasidism than Buber perhaps wished to grant once he had himself become critical of mysticism's aims and effects.

The intention of the Baal Shem was to relate religious maxims and truths to the actualities of earthly life and the 'inmost heart'. As far, therefore, as Hasidic teaching on God is concerned, allusions to the divine nature are expressly and repeatedly made to correspond to characteristics of human nature, in the belief that, as Luria taught, whatever is in God exists in embryo in man and is intended to grow and develop in him. Rabbi Mosheh of Kobryn (d. 1858) could assert that he was able to discern God in his attribute of unity through his unifying impact on himself. Commenting on part of the Passover *haggadah*, the riddle, 'One, who knows it? One, I know it,' he explains:

One, who knows it? Who can discern the Only One? The seraphim themselves ask, 'Where is the place of his Glory?' Nevertheless, One, I know it. For as the sage [the medieval poet–philosopher Judah Halevi] says, 'Where do I find Thee, and where do I not find Thee?' And the seraphim answer, 'The whole earth is full of his Glory' (Isa. 6: 3). I can discern the Only One in what he does in me.[2]

Underlying this tale is the doctrine of the Presence once more and the myth of the 'sparks' inherited from Luria, but its essentially Hasidic slant resides in the way the theological element is made to match an inner human condition. The unity and uniqueness of God are amenable to man's perception. Or rather, the unity and uniqueness of God are perceptible by those who have themselves attained to a measure of

[2] Martin Buber, *Werke*, 3 vols. (Kösel–Lambert Schneider, 1962–4), iii. 559; *Tales of the Hasidim: Later Masters*, trans. Olga Marx (Schocken, 1948), 169.

wholeness and integration. In their own unified self they see God's. As Buber says, Hasidism is kabbalah become ethos.

———

But how did the teachers of Hasidism think of God?

Rabbi Shneur Zalman, who died in 1813 after founding a Lithuanian branch of Hasidism called Habad (which, incongruous though it may seem in the light of the following anecdote, laid more emphasis on the place of reason and intellect than did Hasidism in general), made his confession of faith consciously or unconsciously in conformity with the revelation on Horeb. According to this story, he asked a student who had come into his room:

'Mosheh, what is this—"God"?'

The student was silent.

The Rav asked a second and a third time, 'Why don't you say something?'

'Because I don't know.'

'Do I know then?' asked the Rav. 'Yet I *must* say, for it is thus that I must say it. He is plainly there and apart from him nothing is plainly there, and *that* is what he is.'[3]

In explanation of the Rav's statement, 'apart from him nothing is there,' it should be remarked that Hasidism taught a variant of the *tzimtzum* myth. Objecting that if God 'contracted' himself, retreated into himself, to leave room for the presence of creation, this would result in a limitation of God himself and a division between him and the world, it interpreted the creative process as entailing a gradual shading of God's light so that his creatures might enjoy a sense of independent existence. It believed the universe to have emerged out of him like a snail extruding from a shell formed out of its own substance, and that in that sense nothing exists that is apart from him. A Hasidic interpretation of a passage from Deuteronomy illustrates this. The text, 'Know this day and lay it to your heart that YHWH is God in heaven above and on the earth beneath. There is none else' (Deut. 4: 39), is intended to mean that YHWH is the one and only God. The Hasid, however, was instructed to understand 'There is *none* else' as 'There is *nothing* else'.

God created the world because he wished to be known, loved, and desired. From having been one and alone, he longed for something

———

[3] *Werke*, iii. 390; *Tales of the Hasidim: Early Masters*, trans. Olga Marx (Schocken, 1947), 269.

besides himself. He therefore radiated from out of himself what are
categorized as 'the spheres of separation, of creation, of formation, of
production; the worlds of ideas, of forces, of forms, of matter; the
realms of genius, of spirit, of soul, of life'.[4]

In these was built the universe whose place God is, and whose
nucleus he is. According to this concept, he has, so to speak, wrapped
up his destiny in layers and coverings, only the outermost of which has
to do with the human world. But that is where his indwelling Presence
is banished. That point of its furthest remove from the Godhead is
where it calls out to be returned, back through all the realms, worlds,
and spheres, to its 'root'.

In addition, then, to the usual idea of upper and lower worlds with
its verticality of movement up and down, of ascents and descents, the
vision of God to which Hasidism subscribed sees a quite different
divine motion proceeding from inside outward and back again—a
process outward towards indwelling Presence, and back towards
reunification. Of the created world and God within it, the kabbalist
offers the following image: 'The world of production is the one that
appears to our material eyes. But explore it more deeply and you
unwrap its materiality, and this is the world of formation. And unwrap
it further, it is the world of creation. And explore its nature more
deeply still, and it is the world of separation; until you come to the
Boundless One, blessed be he.' According to this synthesis, therefore,
God is transcendent, far above and far beyond the whole, and simultaneously, in the form of his indwelling Presence, at the heart of the
whole, and at the heart of every single part of the whole. And it is here
that he is to be sought, here that he is to be listened for.

God 'spoke' the creation of the universe. Creation issued out of
his 'mouth'. Consequently, with the dispersion of his Glory in the
'breaking of the vessels', countless millions of new mouths came
into being, all of them able to 'speak' new words. This myth played a
most influential role in Hasidic thought on God. He is the Speaker,
the Lord of the Voice, unceasingly uttering through unexpected
'mouths' his love, commands, guidance, anger, consolation. The entire
universe is no more than a word spoken by him, but nothing in it is so
unworthy that he will not reveal himself from out of it to those who
seek him and listen for him. As Rabbi Isaac Meir of Ger (d. 1866)
explained:

---

[4] *Werke*, iii. 806; *Hasidism* (Philosophical Library, 1948), 65.

Scripture's account of the Voice over Sinai, that it 'added no more' (Deut. 5: 22), is understood by the Targums to mean that it continued without interruption. And indeed, the Voice speaks today as it did long ago. But to hear it, it is necessary, as it was then, to be prepared. As it is written, 'And now, if you will listen, listen, to my Voice' (Exod. 19: 5). The Now is this: when we listen to it.[5]

The belief in the ubiquity of God, and also the characteristic Hasidic custom of bringing all religious speculation back to man himself, makes its appearance in a saying of Rabbi Pinhas of Korets, an eighteenth-century rabbi and a pupil of the Baal Shem. He was asked why God is given the name 'The Place' in rabbinical literature. God is of course the Place of the world, but why not call him this, instead of simply 'The Place'. Because, the rabbi replied, man 'should enter into God so that God encompasses him and becomes his Place'.[6]

This all-pervading consciousness of the divine Presence was not to be merely a pleasant continuing warmth in which the Hasidim were encouraged to bask. The Baal Shem desired above all to eliminate such passivity. No, their awareness of the 'sparks' of the indwelling Presence was to be real and acute and to act as a vital and dynamic call to action on the part of his followers. They were to hear the Shekhinah crying for release from every cook-pot and every cart-horse, every house-wall and every field of corn, from every task performed or requiring to be done, from everything that happened to them. Nothing, in the estimation of this teaching, is too humble to contain a 'spark', nothing animate or inanimate too unworthy to serve as a mouth for the heavenly Voice. Because of God's Presence in them, all things must be present to his servants. By means of their presence, they would be able to distinguish and satisfy the needs of all things, and in doing so, would do the same for the needs of God and his Presence. In the language of religion, Hasidism was to be a sanctification of the whole of life.

In the Baal Shem's approach to an understanding of God, reliance was placed not so much on traditional Jewish religious learning and study—a change which, as has been said, Shneur Zalman regretted and against which he and his school reacted—as on the conviction that life is itself the arena in which the destiny of man and God, inextricably involved with one another, is to be decided. God's destiny and work depend on man's. Human destiny and achievement were from the beginning intended to complement God's. About God, however, as a Being to be explored and known, most Hasidic teachings as Buber

[5] *Werke*, iii. 806; *Hasidism*, 65.   [6] *Werke*, iii. 242; *Hasidism*, 124.

presents them have little to say. On the contrary, the tendency is to
reinforce the kabbalistic thesis of an ultimate total divine concealment
beyond which is Nothingness, and even to make a positive cult of the
religious agnosticism common at a certain level to all types of mysticism and expressed by, for example, the anonymous Christian author of
The Cloud of Unknowing when he wrote of God: 'By love may he be
gotten and holden, but by thought neither.'[7]

An illustration of Hasidism's own attitude in this respect is described
in an anecdote relating to the *zaddik* Jacob Isaac of Pzhysha, the Holy
Jew.

The Jew was once asked to test the thirteen-year-old Enoch, the future Rabbi
of Alexander, in the Gemara.[8] The boy was obliged to reflect for an hour on
the passage given him before he could explain it. Afterwards, the *zaddik* laid
his hand on Enoch's cheek and said: 'When I was thirteen, passages more
difficult than this became instantly clear to me, and when I was eighteen I
counted as a master of Torah. But I came to see that a man cannot reach
perfection by learning alone. I understood what has been said of our father
Abraham, that he searched the sun, the moon and the stars, and nowhere
found God, and how the Presence of God was revealed to him in not-finding.
Then I searched until I too arrived at the truth of not-finding.'[9]

It should not be assumed from this that what Hasidism recommended
was a supine acceptance of ignorance concerning God. On the contrary, the Baal Shem warned against this in his spiritual counsel.
Unknowledge of God is to be embraced positively, he taught. 'Would
that they had forsaken me, says God, and kept my Teaching.'[10]

This is to be interpreted in the following way:

The final meaning of knowledge is that we cannot know. But there are two
kinds of inability to know. The first is immediate; a person does not even begin
to enquire or understand just because it is impossible to know. Another
enquires and searches until he understands that one cannot know. And the
difference between them? To whom shall we compare them? To two who wish
to know the king. The first sets foot in all the king's apartments; he takes
delight in the king's treasures and halls of state; and thereupon he realizes that

[7] *The Cloud of Unknowing* by an English mystic of the fourteenth century, 6th edn.
(Burns & Oates, 1952), 14.
[8] The Gemara is part of the Talmud supplementing and expounding the Mishnah.
[9] *Werke*, iii. 610–11; *Tales of the Hasidim: Later Masters*, 224–5.
[10] *Midrash Ekhah Rabbati*, Proem 2. 'Teaching' is a literal translation of Torah, the
Hebrew name for the Pentateuch.

he cannot get to know the king. The other says to himself: Since it is impossible to know the king, we won't even go in but will resign ourselves to not knowing him.

This is how we should understand the meaning of those words of God. They have forsaken me: that is, they have given up knowing me because it is impossible. But would that they have forsaken me out of enquiry and under-standing by keeping my Teaching![11]

If only, the Baal Shem regrets, they had not apathetically concluded that because God cannot be known there is no point in enquiring after him. If only they had arrived at a true knowledge of God by way of a knowledge of Scripture.

———

And now how does Buber's attitude to the knowledge of God compare with the approach distinctive of the religious movement from which he inherited it?

In the book of personal reminiscences from which various passages are quoted in Part I of this study, he records that he was once asked if he believed in God. After a slight hesitation, he reassured his ques-tioner that yes, he did believe in God. Later, he wondered if he had been truthful. Did he in fact purely and simply believe in God? The answer he gives to his own question is of great importance to a correct assessment of his position *vis-à-vis* faith in God. If, he says, 'belief in God means being able to speak *of* him in the third person, I do not believe in God. If belief in him means being able to speak *to* him, I do believe in God.'[12]

Thus he refuses to recognize a God 'believed in'. He acknowledges instead a God 'lived with'. A God with believed desires, qualities, plans, likes, and dislikes is for him an *it*-God, a subject of speculation but never the *Vis-à-Vis* to whom man says *You*.

The same careful rejection of every temptation to consider God as an object is conspicuous in *I and You*, where Buber writes of him as 'that Being which confronts us immediately, momentarily and lastingly face to face, that which can rightly only be addressed, not expressed'.[13]

[11] *Werke*, iii. 51.
[12] 'Frage und Antwort' in *Begegnung: Autobiographische Fragmente*, 2nd edn. (Kohl-hammer, 1961), 33–35; *Meetings*, ed. Maurice Friedman (Open Court, 1973), 42–4. Also, 'Autobiographical Fragments', in *The Philosophy of Martin Buber*, ed. P. A. Schilpp and M. Friedman (Open Court, 1967), 23–5.
[13] *Werke*, i. 132; *I and Thou*, trans. R. Gregor Smith, 2nd edn. (Scribner–T. & T. Clark, 1958), 80–1.

Or again, as 'that before which, within which, out of which and into which we live, the Mystery . . .'[14]

Another interesting feature of Buber's approach to the Godhead is that, as a concept, the everlasting *You* preserves the many meanings and shades of meaning integral to belief in the undefinability and inscrutability of God, yet at the same time keeps intact, and even enhances, the traditional doctrine of close and intimate contact with him. It would be the greatest mistake to place the everlasting *You* in a theological category similar to say, 'the everlasting God'; 'everlasting' here reflects no knowledge of God's eternity, but only the impossibility of ever being other than *You. You* must by nature be everlastingly *You.* We may experience its absence as well as its presence, but that absence can never take on the remoteness of an *it.*

If it is not immediately evident that the everlasting *You,* as well as being solely and unequivocally a religious concept, is one that stems from Judaism, this may be because Buber deliberately transposes it from religion to a religiousness which he tries to keep independent of religion. Hasidism, although it scandalized orthodoxy, never moved beyond the confines of the Jewish religion in thought, word, or deed. It was a manifestation of Jewish religiousness within the Jewish religion and was directed exclusively to Jews. Buber by contrast, wishing to reach the ear of a larger world, felt obliged to convey to it what he in any case believed, namely that the religiousness which he advocated, the religious way of life, is not a speciality of any religion, but within reach of every human heart, in religion or out of it.

Over the course of time, Buber commentators, experts in one branch of learning or another, have tended to analyse his subtle notions of God almost to the point of extinction. The *Vis-à-Vis,* never to be an object of thought, has none the less been categorized, weighed up, and compared. Its delicate vagueness has almost been lost sight of under the heavy load of thought piled on top of it. What a keen pleasure, then, suddenly to come across a passage, written by no *Buberkenner* (so far as one knows), expressing precisely what one may be sure was Buber's own meaning by 'the everlasting *You*'! This is what Dom Moraes has to say about God:

I came eventually, by the time I was fifteen, to disbelieve in God. But at noon, the solitary hawk still hung at the meridian; the gold and marble shone still in the church I did not visit. The parts were still there—what was the whole?

---

[14] *Werke,* i. 153; *I and Thou,* 111.

Ever since childhood, I have been subject to a curious experience of, I suppose, the spirit. There were certain times when I became numb and unconscious of what happened around me . . . At these instants, an intense sensation both of illumination and of terror swept over me . . . If there was a God, I thought, he was this immense loneliness.

I was fifteen then, and am now nearly thirty . . . But my dialogue with the humped invisible presence of which I am continually conscious has come to no conclusion. His name is often on my lips, but only as an exclamation of surprise or dismay. Yet in the middle of famines or wars, in remote corners of the world, I have heard the starved, the wounded and the sorrowful call upon that name. You brought us this catastrophe, the wronged mothlike voices seemed to whisper, and if you will you can take it away . . .

The starved Indian mother with a dead child in her arms, the Israeli soldier with his leg shot away, do not call on the God of their priests, though they may use his name because it is the only one they know. They call upon some enormous presence beyond and outside themselves, as a child calls upon its parents, because if that presence did not exist, there would be neither alleviation nor purpose for their suffering.[15]

Here is Buber's everlasting *You*. This 'humped invisible presence,' this 'enormous presence' beyond and outside the children of this world, this *You* who brings disaster and can if he wishes take it away, to whom the injured and the suffering cry for aid and reassurance, whose name, which is not a name, they use because it is the only one they know; this is the Mystery, the Being 'before which, out of which and into which we live'.

————

The everlasting *You*, in accord with the tradition from which it springs, is not merely the Listener to a human monologue. In the reciprocity of *I–You* relation it 'utters' a response. At the sound of calls of distress it 'comes down' and 'is there'. It wipes 'every tear from their eyes' (Rev. 21: 3–4). It hears, and it also 'speaks'.[16]

Again, Buber cannot in the circumstances develop theologically his idea of the everlasting *You* as the divine Speaker. He cannot elaborate within his setting of *I–You* relation on the Voice whose Word created the world. The reality of Buber's Speaker consists in his really being heard; indeed, the reality in general of the everlasting *You* consists in the wrath really being feared, the love really experienced, the guidance

[15] Dom Moraes, *Nova*, October 1967.
[16] Hans Kohn, *Martin Buber: sein Werk und Seine Zeit*, 3rd edn. (Melzer, 1961), 240.

really acknowledged, the comfort really felt. God's part in the dialogue
we can only know from the human part.

One small concession to theological thinking, and one that could be
seen as slightly weakening the defences erected around the inviolable
You, may be detected in Buber's argument that although God cannot
be defined as a Person, he must at least be thought of as also a Person.
In his own words:

> The designation of God as a Person is indispensable for those who mean by
> 'God', as I do, no principle—though mystics such as Eckhart sometimes
> identify him with 'Being', and who mean by 'God', as I do, no idea—though
> philosophers such as Plato have at times been able to maintain that he is, but
> who mean by 'God', as I do, him who, whatever else he may be, enters by
> means of creative, revelatory, and redemptive acts into immediate relation with
> us men and thereby makes it possible for us to enter into immediate relation
> with him. This ground and meaning of our life constitutes a reciprocity such as
> can only exist between persons. The concept of personality is, of course,
> wholly inadequate to describe God's essential being, but it is licit and necessary
> to say that God is *also* a Person.[17]

When Buber emerged from the five years of absorption in Hasidism to
which he retired after his first overwhelming encounter with the *Testament of Rabbi Israel Baal-Shem*, his mind was deeply stamped by the
teachings of the movement's founder and its leading personalities, and
his greatest desire was to pass on what he had learned from them. But
whereas, as has been said, the Besht addressed himself to circles
exclusively Jewish, and largely (in present-day terms) ignorant, the
world for which Buber wrote and spoke was of educated, intellectually
sophisticated, and not necessarily religious—let alone Jewish—people
to whom much that was taken for granted by the pious Hasidim would
have seemed alien if not repugnant. It was to this sort of milieu, and in
its own language, that he wished to communicate the central truths of
Hasidism as firmly, concisely, and comprehensively as possible, without however compromising any of the tenuousness and uncertainty
integral to a position in which it is accepted that no statement relating
to God can be 'proved'. A theologian unworried about his suitability to
act as his Maker's mouthpiece, or his ability to see and comprehend
matters by nature invisible and incomprehensible, can define his messages with matching clarity, but where this assumption is renounced

[17] *Werke*, i. 169; *I and Thou*, 135.

for the sober realization that all 'knowledge' of God is questionable, and even—horrid thought!—that there may be no God to know, room must be left for this extra inflection of diffidence and insecurity.

Thus the God with whom the Hasidim lived in devoted faith and obedience, never for a second doubting his everlasting love and authority, and certainly not questioning his actual existence, becomes enveloped under Buber's treatment in a 'cloud of the Presence' far thicker than they themselves would have understood or tolerated. Certainly, the Baal Shem counselled unknowledge as the end to which all knowledge must lead, but he also accepted without demur the sacrosanctity and discipline of the Jewish faith. Buber, although he acknowledged the possible helpfulness of institutional religion and respected those who genuinely adhere to it, saw it largely as a threat to the immediate relation which should exist between man and God. He faced with equanimity, and clearly thought others could do the same, the prospect of living unsupported by the assurances and promises of religion.

For Hasidism, God comes first. His love and Presence give meaning to all earthly love and presence; his requirements are met in the fulfilment of all others. It is by serving God that man serves and redeems the world. The way leads from heaven downward. When the Rabbi of Radoshitz, Issachar Dov Baer (d. 1814), was asked the meaning of the saying, 'My son, I and You are enough for the world,' he showed by his reply that he thought that the whole of life's consequence could be summed up in a right relation between man and God. The words mean, he explained, 'that the essential significance of the creation of the world is that they say, "You are our God," and the Holy one, blessed be he, says, "I am the Lord your God." This I and You is enough for the world.'[18]

The way of Buber's neo-Hasidism is directed from earth upward. True and loving relation comes first, genuine presence with the many *you*s of everyday life. It teaches us and prepares us for encounter and relation with the everlasting *You*. Where in Hasidism God is the point of departure, for Buber, he is one of arrival: though as we shall see, there is no straightforward end or beginning to either path.

———

Do we after all this see anything more of the *I* to whom the *You* of Buber's dialogical life is addressed, its supreme exemplar, its 'God'? I

[18] *Werke*, iii. 591; *Tales of the Hasidim: Later Masters*, 205.

believe we do. But strangely enough, it is not the divine form which Buber himself offers us, the august, unpredictable and elusive Majesty of 'I am there such as I am there'. This is *the* 'word of revelation', he tells us in *I and You*,[19] *the* clue to the significance of the divine Name and hence of the nature of the Godhead. But something, we would suggest, is slightly out of alignment in his identification of the divine Partner in contemporary man–God dialogue. Such a Being is not adapted to the role he assigns to the everlasting *You*. The truth is that the primary revelation does not spring from the first half of Exodus 3:14, from God's allusion to his changing modes of presence, but, as Franz Rosenzweig argued so forcibly,[20] from the second half of the verse, where the Deity actually designates himself as he who is there with his people. 'Thus shall you say to the sons of Israel: I AM THERE sends me to you.' This is the divine *I*, we think, to whom Buber's *You* is said. This is the 'Word' which the targumists say 'shall be your Helper'. This is the Presence in which benevolence is implicit. This is he of whom the Holy Jew observed: 'God is our Model.'

And where shall we discover what this Model does? Buber's answer is: in the lives of the Hasidim.

[19] *Werke*, i. 154; *I and Thou*, 112.
[20] Franz Rosenzweig, *Briefe* (Schocken, 1935), 554.

PART III
I PERCEIVED THE IDEA OF THE PERFECT MAN

12

Imitatio dei

'PERFECT' in Buber's terms is not intended to mean 'without fault'. When he wrote apropos of his first encounter with *The Testament of Rabbi Israel Baal-Shem* that through it he had 'perceived the idea of the perfect man',[1] he was not implying that he had found in Hasidism and its holy men the sinlessness of virtuous paragons, perfectly good, perfectly humble, perfectly charitable, and so on. Far from it: on this point, as on many others, Buber agreed with Jesus that only God is 'good'. The ideal discerned by Buber at that time was of living in a certain way, turned in a certain direction, and of being able by this means to achieve the integrity and wholeness a man needs to become perfectly himself, or rather, perfectly what he is destined to be. The *zaddik* did so, in Buber's estimation, by devoting himself within the discipline of the Hasidic life to the imitation of God as Judaism practises it. He is not projected by Buber as the perfect man for today, any more than Hasidism is proposed as the religion for the present moment, yet to grasp the real human likeness corresponding to Buber's new divine form we have to come closer to both the *zaddik* and his religious principles. We have to know something of the piety within Hasidism to share Buber's insight into piety *per se*, and we have to realize what is entailed by the imitation of God within Judaism if we wish to understand what is required by Buber's own *imitatio* of the God he addressed as *You*.

The Christian church has from the beginning approached the following of God primarily as an imitation of the Imitator *par excellence*. In the opening years of the second century, Ignatius of Antioch was advising the Philadelphians: 'Be imitators of Jesus Christ as he was imitator of his Father' (Phil. 7: 2). Paul had already done the same before him, though less directly, counselling the Ephesians: 'Be imitators of God as beloved children and walk in love as Christ loved us' (Eph. 5: 1–2).

---

[1] Martin Buber, *Werke*, 3 vols. (Kösel–Lambert Schneider, 1962–4), iii: 967–8; *Hasidism and Modern Man*, trans. M. Friedman (Horizon, 1958), 59.

The Christian imitative process does not, moreover, stop with the imitation of Jesus. From imitation of the Imitator, it moves on to imitation of imitators of the Imitator, to one further removed from the imitation of God himself. Again, Paul led the way. Addressing himself on this occasion to the people of Corinth, he told them: 'Be imitators of me as I am of Christ' (1 Cor. 11: 1).

Since those early times, the band of holy exemplars (first among them the mother of Jesus, who in certain sectors of Christianity has become a celestial model in her own right) has so swelled to fill the Christian calendar that the *imitator Christi* has, if he feels so inclined, a big selection of intermediaries, some ancient, some new, from which to choose should the immediate following of the Master seem too difficult or his figure too remote. But whatever path he takes, it is guided by the memory of a life lived on earth, by the recollection handed down from generation to generation of a human lifetime. That this tradition has become 'mythologized' takes away nothing from its function as the axis of the Christian imitation of God.

The person responsible for the crowded Christian spiritual scene was of course not Jesus. His was the Jewish pursuit of holiness which enjoins not so much the imitation of holy men (though it does this also) as of the Holy One 'whose Name is Holy' (Isa. 57: 15). 'Become holy for *I* am holy' (Lev. 19: 2) is the biblical command. Jesus, assuming the status of son *vis-à-vis* the Father, necessarily gave to his *imitatio* a filial character, practising and promulgating it uniquely in terms of that relationship. Truly, truly, he said, 'the son can do nothing of his own accord, but only what he sees the Father doing. For whatever he does, that the son does likewise' (John 5: 19).

But where does the son look to see what the Father is doing? He attends to the attributes contained in the divine Name and he looks to see how God manifested them to the forefathers. 'It is written (Deut. 11: 22), "To love YHWH your God, to walk in all his ways." Which are God's ways? Those which he himself called out before Moses (Exod. 34: 6): "Godhead, merciful, gracious, long-suffering, rich in benevolence and faithfulness." '[2]

Another rabbinic commentary develops the theme of the imitation of God's attributes more thoroughly.

'To walk in his ways.' These are the ways of The Place: 'YHWH, YHWH God, merciful and gracious, slow to anger and abounding in steadfast love and

---

[2] *Sifre on Deut.* 11: 22, ed. L. Finkelstein, 49.

faithfulness, keeping steadfast love for thousands, forgiving iniquity and sin, and clearing.'[3]

And it is said, 'And all who are called by the Name of YHWH shall be saved.'[4] How is it possible for man to be called by the Name of The Place? As The Place is called 'merciful', so shall you be 'merciful'. The Holy One, blessed be he, is called 'gracious', so shall you be gracious, as it is written, 'merciful and gracious YHWH' etc. (Ps. 145: 8) and make gifts freely. The Place is called 'righteous', as it is written, 'For YHWH is righteous and he loves righteous deeds' (Ps. 11: 7), so shall you be righteous. The Place is called 'ever-loving', as it is written, 'For I am ever-loving, oracle of YHWH' (Jer. 3: 12), so shall you be ever-loving. Therefore it is written, 'And all who are called by the Name of YHWH shall be saved' (Joel 2: 32). And it is written, 'All who are called by my Name, whom I created for my glory, whom I formed and made' (Isa. 43: 7). And it is written, 'All that YHWH has done is for his own sake' (Prov. 6: 4).[5]

It should be added that not all of God's qualities are to be imitated by man. The rabbis exclude jealousy ('For YHWH whose Name is Jealousy is a jealous God' [Exod. 34: 14]); revenge ('YHWH thou God of vengeance, thou God of vengeance, shine forth!' [Ps. 94: 1]); pride ('Sing to YHWH for he has triumphed proudly!' [Exod. 15: 21]); and acting in devious ways.[6] These are characteristics reserved to the Deity alone.

In case, however, any uncertainty should still remain about *how* God's ways are to be followed, the rabbis cite the examples recorded in Scripture of how God justified his own divine nature in deeds of mercy, grace and love.

It is written (Deut. 13: 5), 'Follow after YHWH your God.' How can man walk in the footsteps of Majesty? Is it not written (Deut. 4: 24), 'YHWH your God is a consuming fire'? But it is meant thus. Follow the *midot*, the 'attributes', the ways in which God's works were manifested to man. As he clothed the first men when they were naked, as he visited the sick Abraham at the oaks of

[3] In a variant. On this Leon Roth comments: 'By an instructive tour de force of exegesis, the list of the divine attributes is made to stop at the affirmative, which is inserted by a common Hebrew idiom, to give emphasis to the following negative. The text itself, when the negative is included, reads, "And who will *by no means* clear (the guilty)."' See *Judaism: A Portrait* (Faber, 1960), 84.

[4] Because of the absence of vowel pointing, this reading is just as possible as 'And all who call *on* the Name of YHWH . . .'

[5] *Sifre on Deut.* 11: 22, ed. L. Finkelstein, 49.

[6] See S. Schechter, *Some Aspects of Rabbinic Theology* (Black, 1909), 204; A. Marmorstein, *Studies in Jewish Theology* (Oxford University Press, 1950), 106–21; Louis Jacobs, *A Jewish Theology* (Darton Longman & Todd, 1973), 233–42.

Mamre (according to tradition, Abraham was at that time suffering from circumcision), as he comforted Isaac with blessings after Abraham's death, to the last of God's deeds in the Pentateuch, when he himself buried Moses: these are the *midot* made perceptible to the senses, a model visible to man, and the *mitzvot*, the 'commandments', are the *midot* humanized. 'The work of my hands', the Midrash gives God to say to Abraham, 'is to do good. You have taken up the work of my hands' (*Gen. Rabbah* on Gen. 23: 19).[7]

The goal aimed at in the imitation of God is not to become like him but to realize and perfect the likeness to him impressed on man at the creation of the world. Rabbi Aha, a fourth-century Palestinian master, interprets the saying in the psalm, 'YHWH is God, he has made us and we are his' (Ps. 100: 3), as meaning that YHWH made us and we perfect or complete our souls 'to him'—this being the literal reading of the Hebrew word 'his'.[8]

We perfect our souls to God. This 'being like' God is therefore not something unconnected with our earthly life. It is our life's goal—if indeed our life is a perfection of our souls to God . . . We perfect our souls to God. The meaning of this is that each one who does so, perfects *his* likeness, his *yehidah*, his 'singularity', his uniqueness *as* the image of God.[9]

———

A few words need to be added as it were in parenthesis to this sketch of the Jewish imitation of God, for it is taught also that although man cannot truly resemble God in this life, by perfecting his soul he prepares for the enjoyment of God's own perfect being in the world to come, where he will resemble him indeed. To Buber, this doctrine was very congenial. He draws particular attention to it in his treatment of the *imitatio* and quotes an ancient source to support it.

Moses' saying, 'Now you are today like the stars of heaven in multitude' (Deut. 1: 10), is interpreted in the Midrash—by means of a punning exegesis which reads 'lord' (*rab*) insted of 'multitude,' *rob*—'Today you are like the stars, but in the existence to come you are destined to resemble your Lord' (Deut. Rabbah on Deut. 1: 10). And another text from the same book (4: 4) is completed by the Midrash more forcefully still. It interprets, 'But you, cleaving to YHWH your God, are living all of you this day,' as: 'In this world Israel cleaves to God, but in the existence to come they will exist and resemble.'[10]

---

[7] *Werke*, ii. 1064. [8] See *Gen. Rabbah* 49: 29. [9] *Werke*, ii. 1061.
[10] *Pesikta Rabbati*, 11: 7, ed. Friedmann, 46*b*; *Werke*, ii. 1050.

13

The True Helper

IT is uncanny how faithful Buber has been to Jewish tradition in his
identification of the *zaddik*, the follower of YHWH and prototype of his
own 'perfect man', as 'the helper'. The coincidence is the more
astonishing in that, as has been said, he appears not to have been aware
of the targumic equation I AM THERE = 'the Helper'. He does not, in
any case, appeal to these sources, which he surely would have done
had he known of them. It reminds us of the saying of one of the
followers of the Baal Shem that when a Hasid binds his soul to that of
his teacher, and to that of his teacher's teacher, 'link joins link, and the
Teaching (Torah) flows from Moses to Joshua, from Joshua to the
elders, and so on to his teacher, and from his teacher to him'.[1]

A *zaddik*, before the word acquired its Hasidic connotation, was
simply the good man, the just man, the Jew at his best, living according
to a pattern of harmony, balance, and order. *Hasid*, on the other hand,
means 'devout', 'pious', and was originally applied to the enthusiast,
the innovator, the inspired nonconformist, the extremist even, one
whose religious life possessed a dimension of intensity and depth not
shared by the *zaddik*. Some of the ancient rabbis belonged to the
category of *hasid*. So did Jesus.

A third type was the *hakham*, the 'sage', the talmudical scholar
absorbed in his books and prayers. The celebrated Gaon of Vilna,
Elijah ben Solomon Zalman (1720–97), whose fierce opposition to the
movement founded by the Baal Shem Tov led him to excommunicate
its members and destroy their writings, was a characteristic *hakham*.

With the coming of Hasidism, the significance attached to *zaddik*
and *hasid* somewhat confusingly exchanged places. A *hasid* who took
over the religious leadership of a Jewish community in Poland or the
Ukraine became known as a *zaddik*, and the *zaddikim* who attached
themselves to him were given the title Hasidim.

[1] Martin Buber, *Werke*, 3 vols. (Kösel–Lambert Schneider, 1962–4), iii. 541; *Tales of
the Hasidim: Later Masters* (Schocken, 1948), 153. This is a free rendering of the opening
lines of the *Sayings of the Fathers*, a tractate of the Mishnah.

The *zaddik* was the indispensable pivot of his congregation. He was the holy man close to God, and close also to the world and its problems big and small. He was mediator between heaven and earth, not as one standing between man and God, but as one whose task it was to help each individual to develop his own personal relation with God and to give it greater reality and immediacy. He was the spiritual director to whom the people brought their troubles grave and petty. He was a healer of the soul and the body, expert in the effects of the one on the other. He was the teacher to whom young men flocked from far and wide, frequently leaving their women and children to fend for themselves, sometimes for years. Yet it would be true to say that it was his actual presence among them rather than his teachings, the example he set them of an integrated and holy life, that influenced the people most deeply. He did not merely preach Torah. He became Torah. One *zaddik* described the ideal at which he aimed thus:

A man should pay heed that all his actions are Torah, and that he himself becomes a Torah, until one learns from his habits and movements and motionless 'cleaving', and he becomes like the heavens of which it is said, 'No utterance at all, no speech, their voice is inaudible, yet their sound goes out over all the earth, their message to the end of the world' (Ps. 19: 4).[2]

Likewise, another *zaddik* said of his teacher: 'I learnt Torah from all my teacher's members.'[3]

Each of the *zaddikim* of the classical period of Hasidism was distinguished by some special gift. Some were men of immense and powerful magnetism, like Israel ben Eliezer, the Baal Shem Tov, himself. Some were ecstatics. Some were strict ascetics, like Abraham the Angel (d. 1776), who fathered two sons and afterwards lived in strict celibacy. In parenthesis, it should be added that his abjuration of sex was evidently not regarded with much favour. We hear in one of the Hasidic tales that after Rabbi Abraham died, his wife dreamt that she saw him enter a hall in which the great were sitting on their thrones. He confessed to them that his wife had a grievance against him because he had stayed apart from her on earth and that he would have to ask her forgiveness for this. 'I forgive you with all my heart,' she called out to him in her dream. A very distinctive Hasidic touch is given to the end of this story. Instead of the expected pardoning of Rabbi Abraham and the award to

---

[2] *Werke*, iii. 287; *Tales of the Hasidim: Early Masters* (Schocken, 1947), 169.
[3] *Werke*, iii. 84; *Tales of the Hasidim: Early Masters*, 6.

him of a throne of his own, we hear that *his wife* 'awoke comforted'.[4]

Some *zaddikim*, like Shelomo of Karlin (d. 1792), were famous for the burning ardour of their prayer. When a friend once asked Rabbi Shelomo to promise to visit him the next day, he reacted as though the request were preposterous.

How can you ask me to promise! This evening I must pray and recite the *Shema*, and when I do that, my soul will be on the brink of life. Then comes the darkness of sleep. And in the early morning, there is the great Morning Prayer, which is a striding through all the worlds. And finally, there is the falling on one's face, when the soul leans over life's brink. It may be that this time, too, I shall not die. But how can I promise, now, to do something after I have prayed?[5]

Rabbi Uri of Strelisk, nicknamed the Seraph, who died some thirty years after Shelomo, was another prayerful man. His devotions were so overwhelming and ecstatic that before going off to pray in the mornings he would set his house in order and say farewell to his wife and children.

Other *zaddikim* were noted for their love of the whole created world. The rabbi of Zbarazh, Ze'ev Wolf (d. *c.*1800–20), is said to have explained to a coachman that no horse ever needs to be whipped once one has learnt to speak to it. Another great lover was Mosheh Leib of Sasov (d. 1807). A person one day expressed astonishment at the intensity with which Mosheh made the sufferings of others his own, and suffered with them. He was amazed. 'What do you mean, "suffer with"? It is after all my own suffering, so what else can I do but suffer it?'[6] A personality of the greatest weight in the Hasidic movement, the rabbi of Bratslav, Nahman ben Simhah (d. 1810) combined a profound sympathy with nature with a belief that every living creature has a language of its own. He was not unique in this respect; a number of anecdotes are attributed to other *zaddikim* to the effect that birds, beasts, and even frogs can 'talk'. Nahman regretted that people are deaf to the songs which even the vegetable world sings to God, exclaiming on one occasion: 'How lovely and sweet it is to hear them singing! And therefore it is good to worship God among them, in lonely wandering in the countryside among the plants of the earth, and to pour out one's words to God in sincerity. All the words of the

[4] *Werke*, iii. 235; *Tales of the Hasidim: Early Masters*, 117.
[5] *Werke*, iii. 396–7; *Tales of the Hasidim: Early Masters*, 275–6.
[6] *Werke*, iii. 478; *Tales of the Hasidim: Later Masters*, 86.

countryside then enter into your own, and increase their strength.'[7]
Speech of every kind fascinated Rabbi Nahman. The 'word' was for
him a precious mystery, and the act of teaching, in which the 'word'
travels to and fro, from teacher to pupil and back again, affecting them
both and arousing new thoughts and ideas in both, was for him a sort
of miracle.

Very many *zaddikim* were conspicuous for their intense love of God.
Aaron of Karlin (d. 1772) was considered to be such a living fount of
divine love that all who heard him pray were infected by it. It was
nevertheless a love accompanied by fear. Without fear, he maintained,
we merely love a pleasant idol, not the great and terrible Lord.

Another passionate lover of God was Elimelekh of Lizhensk (d.
1786), who was overcome by such raptures when he prayed that he had
to keep his eye on his watch in case he should 'fly away for
blessedness'.[8]

Some *zaddikim*, like Shmelke of Nikolsburg (d. 1778), were famous
preachers. Others were notable for their humility. Meshullam Zusya of
Hanipol (d. 1800) belonged to the company of the humble known as
'God's fools'.[9] In a discussion with his brother on how to gain some
idea of God's greatness, he gave it as his opinion that the first step is to
acknowledge one's own lowliness. Not so, said the brother; humility is
the *result* of contemplating divine Majesty. Their teacher decided that
both were right, but that (and again we perceive the distinctive Hasidic
realism) 'the inner grace is with one who begins with himself and not
with the Creator'.[10]

Another of Hasidism's eminent figures, Jacob Isaac of Lublin (d.
1815), was named 'the Seer' because of his exceptional powers of
intuition. He needed only to glance at his visitors' foreheads, we are
told, or to read the written petitions which they handed to him, and he
was able to see not only into their natures and the course of their
present lives, but even into the progress made by their souls in their

---

[7] *Werke*, iii. 898; Martin Buber, *The Tales of Rabbi Nachman*, trans. M. Friedman
(Souvenir, 1974), 24–5.

[8] *Werke*, iii. 374; *Tales of the Hasidim: Early Masters*, 253.

[9] Buber has also been assigned to their ranks by Arthur Cohen, who writes: 'I do not
think he would object to being called, with considerable qualification, a holy fool;
indeed, the holy fool in western tradition is one mistaken for a fool, because the presence
of God is so profoundly internalized as to become one with the life of the body, the
intellect, and the spirit' (*Martin Buber*, Bowes and Bowes, 1957, 10). The logic of the
statement is not altogether easy to follow.

[10] *Werke*, iii. 363; *Tales of the Hasidim: Early Masters*, 243.

transmigration from world to world in search of perfection. According to Buber, countless numbers came to the Seer so that their souls might be penetrated and illuminated by the light of his eyes.[11]

As for bodily cures, the Baal Shem was himself a healer. So was Issachar Dov Baer of Radoshitz (d. 1843), whose latent gift is said to have been recognized and released when he was quite young by the saint known simply as the Jew, Jacob Isaac of Pzhysha (d. 1813). His child was once very sick, and on seeing Issachar passing the house the Jew called him inside and laid the baby in his arms. 'Take him,' the father begged, 'and I know that you will give him back to us cured.' Issachar was dismayed. Nothing like this had happened to him before, and he had no idea that he possessed healing powers; but he took the child, laid him back in the cradle, and rocked him. 'And as he rocked him, he poured out his soul imploringly to God. After one hour, the boy was out of danger.'[12]

The fame of some of these men of God was based not so much on their personal qualities as on the main theme of their teaching. That of Abraham of Stretyn (d. 1865), for example, was founded on his preoccupation with unity. Although a guiding principle to Judaism in general, to him it was of overriding importance. The Jew, he maintained, should become so unified within himself that each of his five senses can take over the functions of the remaining four. By contrast, a favourite topic of Menahem Mendel of Kotzk (d. 1859) was truth. But even so, he conceded that truth takes second place after unity, because it is not until a man is unified that he can become true. 'Truth does not exist until the whole man has become unified and one in his service, and a truth from beginning to end of the letters of Scripture.'[13] Other *zaddikim* were adepts of silence. Mendel of Vorki (d. 1859), who lived during the period when the movement was falling into decline, and was one of the last of the memorable Hasidic figures, regarded silence not as a rite, and not as an ascetic exercise, but as his way of worshipping God.

Shneur Zalman, the Rav, whom we have met earlier in connection with the Hasidic doctrine of God,[14] was rather different from all these others. As has been said, he broke away from Hasidism proper and founded his own Lithuanian school known as Habad,[15] which by

[11] *Werke*, iii. 110.   [12] *Werke*, iii. 588; *Tales of the Hasidim: Later Masters*, 202.
[13] *Werke*, iii. 144.   [14] See p. 133 above.
[15] From the initial letters of the first three divine emanations according to kabbalah: *hokhmah* (wisdom), *binah* (intelligence), *da'at* (knowledge).

laying emphasis on the place of the intellect in the religious life, weakened the Hasidic concept of the unification of the self. He also undermined it by his insistence that the ordinary man—as opposed to the more spiritually advanced—should positively reject 'foreign thoughts' that enter his mind instead of redirecting them to God as taught by Hasidism itself. Furthermore, by regarding it as of paramount importance that the individual should employ his own reasoning powers, the Rav at one stroke deprived the *zaddik* of his central function in the Hasidic community: that of a cosmic mediator.

There is little evidence in Hasidism of the category *talmid hakham*, but some of these withdrawn and scholarly types were without doubt to be found. They were clearly looked on with as little approval as the *zaddik* who abstained from sexual intercourse, for Israel of Rizhyn (d. 1850), interprets as follows the verse, 'Heaven is heaven of YHWH: the earth he gave to the children of men' (Ps. 115: 16):

There are two kinds of *zaddikim*. The first kind learn and pray all day long and consider themselves free of all lower things so that they can attain to holiness. But the others do not think of themselves, but only of raising the holy sparks that are sunk in all things, and they occupy themselves with all lower things. Those who are forever preparing themselves for heaven are called 'heaven' in the verse, and have set themselves apart for God. But the others are the 'earth' which has been given to the children of men.[16]

None of these Hasidic leaders was selected by Buber as a specific pattern of perfection, and none of their specific virtues, teachings, or talents. It was the *zaddik* in his role at the centre of his community whom he postulated as the perfect man, the *zaddik* as an elevating and sanctifying force, in touch with above and below, bringing together man and man, man and God, and man and his own self. It was the *zaddik* as a reflection, in his own person and example, of God the ever-present Helper. It was the *zaddik* leading and guiding his people, and assisting each to persevere in his own *imitatio dei*.

Buber maintains that although by the time he made contact with Hasidism as a child it had lost its purity and vitality, and the power and influence placed in the hands of the *zaddik* had come to be misused and misconstrued, he had noticed even then with how much awe and reverence the *rebbe* was regarded. Although still so young, he apparently

[16] *Werke*, iii. 446; *Tales of the Hasidim: Later Masters*, 53.

felt that this was what the world was about—the perfect man—and that the perfect man is none other than the true helper.[17]

He once had the rather embarrassing experience of being taken for a *zaddik* himself. One day, he was talking with a group of young people in a café when a middle-aged man of fairly prosperous and bourgeois appearance introduced himself as a rather distant connection of his father. Buber asked him to join them, and this he did, listening with the greatest show of attention, though obviously not understanding much of what was going on. Every now and then, Buber would break off to ask this Mr X whether there was something he wished to speak to him about, but each time Mr X demurred and begged Buber to go on with his discussion. When the meeting at last came to an end, it transpired that Mr X needed Buber's advice. With great diffidence and respect, he disclosed that he had a daughter, and that he had found her a possible husband. The young man was a lawyer. What he wanted to hear from Buber was whether the potential son-in-law was a good and decent fellow. Buber was taken aback and pointed out that he had so far not met the person in question. Nothing daunted, Mr X put other questions to him, asking whether the man had a good head on his shoulders, etc. Bewildered, Buber could only hedge. He repeated as kindly and tactfully as he could that it was really not possible for him to say. But Mr X did not believe this for a moment. Thanking Buber, he took his leave, murmuring with a sad and deprecating smile: '*Herr Doktor*, you don't *want* to say.'[18]

In this rather absurd encounter, Buber was introduced at first hand to the role of the *zaddik*, and discovered the sort of help the latter was expected to give, and the kind of insight he was believed to possess.

I who am no *zaddik*, not secure in God but in peril before God, a man struggling ever anew for God's light and ever anew vanishing into God's abysses, nevertheless, when asked after the trivial and responding with the trivial, experienced from within, for the first time, the true *zaddik*, who is asked after revelation and responds with revelation. I experienced him in his soul's fundamental relation to the world: in his responsibility.[19]

Although he admits that since the decline of Hasidism, the demands made on the *zaddik* have fallen to the level illustrated by this story, Buber still insists that the authority wielded by the *rebbe* remains

---

[17] Martin Buber, *Begegnung: Autobiographische Fragmente*, 2nd edn. (Kohlhammer, 1961), 29; *Meetings* (Open Court, 1973), 38.

[18] *Begegnung*, 29–31; *Meetings*, 39–41.   [19] *Begegnung*, 31–2; *Meetings*, 41.

legitimate. He even argues that the power of the helper over those who cry out for help is *the* one legitimate power. Indeed, he goes further: looking into the future, he wonders if the office of *rebbe* does not hold the germ of 'future orders'. The *zaddik* may have slipped from the high place he once occupied. He may seem to have lost something of his wisdom and spirituality and to have learned to profit in more ways than one from the credulousness and superstition of his people. Nevertheless, 'is he not possibly what he was once thought and appointed to be: helper in the spirit, teacher of the world's meaning, guide to the divine sparks?'[20]

Helper. Teacher. Guide. The qualifications are not chosen at random. They are taken verbatim from *My Way to Hasidism*, written over forty years earlier in 1917:

He speaks: and he knows that what he says is destiny. He does not have to decide over countries and nations, but ever again only over the course, small and great, of an individual life, so finite and yet so limitless. People come to him, and each requires him to say something, requires his help. And though the needs they bring him may be material and semi-material, in his world-view there is nothing material that cannot be elevated to spirit. And what he does for all of them is this: *he elevates their need before he appeases it.* He is thus helper in the spirit, teacher of the world's meaning, guide to the divine sparks. It is he, the perfect man, the true helper, who matters to the world. It is he for whom the world waits, for whom it waits ever anew.[21]

---

[20] *Begegnung*, 29; *Meetings*, 52.
[21] *Werke*, iii. 973; *Hasidism and Modern Man* (Philosophical Library, 1948), 68–9.

14

Religion as Presence[1]

THE *zaddik* was for Buber an ideal, but he was not proposing that people of the present time should become latter-day *zaddikim*. Bearing in mind the sophistication of modern man, educated, travelled, sceptical, the very suggestion is absurd. But he believed that, circumscribed though they were (in his eyes) by the formalities and observances of religion, the Hasidim taught a way of life which allowed them to fulfil and satisfy innate needs and aspirations and to develop their personalities to the full. Concerned to lift the barrier behind which the God of our days is hidden, and to re-establish true relation between man and the world in which he dwells, between man and man, and between man and God, Buber points to the attributes and teachings of the *zaddikim* as evidence of the beneficial effects of living in such a condition of relation hour by hour and day by day.

He was none the less no more anxious to persuade contemporary society to shoulder the 'yoke' of religion which the *zaddik* took on himself than he was to reproduce exact copies of this holy type of human being. He was, as we have seen, averse to religion, and endeavoured to point away from its externals towards its essence, which is religiousness. This can of course also be found in a setting of organized rites, beliefs, and observances, but exists more easily, so he thought, apart from them.

In Buber's account of the Hasidic religious life we see the outline within which he plotted his own idea of the life of dialogue. The Hasidic principles, ideals, and virtues on which he lays stress, and which he develops and explains, are contained in his own thought, though in other proportions and other forms. Indeed, one of the great advantages of becoming familiar with Hasidic teaching is that its language of 'cleaving', 'sparks', 'shells', 'intention', and the rest, allows Buber's own *I–you/I–it* jargon, with its 'presence', 'remoteness',

[1] 'Religion as Presence' was the title of a lecture course given by Buber at the Freies Jüdisches Lehrhaus in 1922. See p. 25 above.

'attachment', 'relation', 'irrelation', and so on, to make a very different impact that it can otherwise do.

This is of great importance. His ideas have certainly reached, on a broad front, the restricted circles of the intelligentia and the professionally religious, though it is doubtful whether they have penetrated even here to any very great depth. But he did not write merely for the benefit of clever middle-class men and women with 'spiritual' leanings. Clever 'spiritual' middle-class Jew though he was himself, he meant his ideas also for 'the people', for what tradition calls the *'am ha'aretz*. Is it too much to hope that when his intellectual approach, the only one natural to him, is seen for what it really is, namely the reformulation in a contemporary mode of ancient, simple, and authentically religious things, the gist of what he is saying will gradually spread more widely and enter the heart of what is condescendingly regarded as the 'ordinary' man? When his philosophical–anthropological terminology is seen to relate to real circumstances and real situations lived in real life, may it not eventually make sense on a larger scale than at present?

We must hope so, for in the last resort, what Buber wanted was not a stimulating upsurge of speculation on 'spirituality' and the like, but a plain, straightforward renascence of holiness *as he understood it*, of the personal holiness characterized by Christianity and the corporate holiness distinctive of Judaism. He looked for the sanctification of humanity, of that 'great unholy body destined to become holy'.[2]

On the smaller and exclusive scene of the Baal Shem Tov's operations, this aim was achieved largely with the help of the myths of the divine 'sparks' and of the 'speaking' of creation by God. The notion of the 'sparks' deeply influenced, in a real and effective way, all that his followers said and did. With each and every thing believed to be a 'shell' holding its own exiled particle of God's indwelling Presence, every homely object and common event becomes unique and precious. Every act, even the most prosaic, performed with the intention of redeeming the Presence from its banishment in a 'shell', and of re-unifying it with its source in God, is a contribution to the redemption of the world. Each man can, so it was thought,

at every time, and through every one of his most ordinary actions, discover and redeem those sparks if only he performs it in purity, wholly directed towards, and gathered into, God. It is a matter, therefore, not of worshipping God at

[2] Martin Buber, *Werke*, 3 vols. (Kösel–Lambert Schneider, 1962–4, iii. 802; *Hasidism*, trans. Carlyle and Mary Witton-Davies (Philosophical Library, 1948), 59.

isolated times alone, nor with particular words and gestures, but with one's whole life, one's whole everyday, one's whole worldliness.[3]

With their tendency to reason from heaven downward, the *zaddikim* would not agree that man's prime obligation is to perfect his soul. His primary duty, indeed the very reason for his existence, is to promote the destiny of God in the world. God thus becomes (in part) as dependent on his creatures as they are on him. Isaiah may have spoken of Abraham as God's friend ('The offspring of Abraham my friend', Isa. 41: 8), but in the eyes of the Hasidim, God needs all men for his friends. A passage from the psalm, 'I am a visitor on earth, hide not your commandments from me,' is interpreted: 'You are a visitor on earth as I am, and have no resting-place for your indwelling. Do not abandon me therefore, but disclose your commandments to me so that I may be your friend.'[4] Another master, Yehiel Mikhael of Zloczov (d. 1786), reading the biblical text literally, gives to the injunction 'Become holy for I am holy' (Lev. 8: 2) the meaning 'Become holy that I am holy,' become holy *in order that* God may be holy. He says: 'You must understand it like this. My holiness which is above the world derives from your holiness. As you sanctify my Name below, so is it sanctified in the heights of heaven. For it is written, "Give God strength" (Ps. 68: 35).'[5]

The Baal Shem was sure that holiness is within the reach of all men, but he was not so unreasonable as to suppose that all his people were endowed with the same aptitude for it. He therefore counselled the more spiritually advanced to worship God with love, but without mortification. The rest, with no great talent for loving worship, were advised to limit themselves to remembering constantly that nothing exists in which there is not life; that everything receives the form in which it is seen from the life that is in it; and that this life is God's life.

———

The Hasidic way turned on six major counsels of perfection: cleaving (the literal meaning of the Hebrew word *devekut*), humility, holy intention, worship, ardour, and joy.

[3] *Werke*, iii. 962; Martin Buber, *Hasidism and Modern Man*, trans. M. Friedman (Horizon, 1958).
[4] *Werke*, iii. 943; *Hasidism and Modern Man*, 36.
[5] *Werke*, iii. 268; Martin Buber, *Tales of the Hasidim: Early Masters*, trans. Olga Marx (Schocken, 1947), 149.

1. *Cleaving*   The commandment to cleave to God appears repeatedly in the Bible. Constantly, the injunction to love God is followed by another to adhere to him. Thus Joshua, when he summons the tribes of Reuben and Gad, and the half-tribe of Manasseh, orders them to obey the law of Moses and reminds them that this is 'to love YHWH your God and to walk in all his ways and to cleave to him and to serve him with all your heart and with all your soul' (Josh. 22: 5). This cleaving to God, which is part of the demonstration of love for God, together with imitating him and serving him with the entire self, was understood by the earliest kabbalists to demand detachment from everything other than God. Such is the advice of Moses ben Nahman, or Nahmanides, the eminent thirteenth-century Spanish kabbalist, who taught that the commandment to walk after God and cleave to him

warns him not to worship God and another beside him; he is to worship God alone in his heart and in his actions. And it is plausible that the meaning of 'cleaving' is to remember God and His love constantly, not to divert your thought from Him in all your earthly doings. Such a man may be talking to other people, but his heart is not with them since he is in the presence of God. And it is further plausible that those who have attained to this rung do, even in their earthly life, partake of eternal life, because they have made themselves a dwelling-place of the *Shekhinah*.[6]

To have mastered the feat of cleaving was, in the estimation of the Jewish mystics of that time, to have reached the uppermost rung of the ladder of holiness. Nine hours out of twenty-four were to be set aside for the contemplation of *devekut*, and specific spiritual and intellectual exercises were prescribed for those still struggling to achieve it. 'I set YHWH ever before me' (Ps. 16: 8) the psalmist says, this being expounded by another Spanish Jew, Abraham, Ibn Ezra: 'Intellectual activity and moral discipline have led him (the psalmist) to set the Name before him, day and night, and behold his soul is attached to his Creator before ever it is separated from his body.'[7]

As a way to holiness, the idea of cleaving underwent a radical transformation in the teaching of the Baal Shem Tov. Although it admittedly retained a certain amount of the emphasis laid on its

[6] Cited by Gershom Scholem, *The Messianic Idea in Judaism* (Allen and Unwin, 1971), 205.

[7] Cf. Georges Vajda, *L'amour de Dieu dans la théologie juive du moyen âge* (Vrin, 1957), 112.

relation to prayer and Torah study, the Besht proposed that when the Hasidim read the Bible, they should not concentrate, as before, on the external shapes of the letters, but should aim at cleaving by focusing on their inner spiritual significance. His boldest move, however, was to reverse the progress towards sanctity by up-ending the ladder of holiness so that instead of forming its top rung, reached after much endeavour only by a few, cleaving became the first and bottom rung, the *sine qua non* incumbent on all of his followers. Whereas it had been an intellectual and spiritual exercise, and a binding of the self to God by means of an unbinding from what is not God, the Baal Shem brought cleaving within the range of every Jew. To be conscious of God's Presence in his daily life, the first step to holiness, is itself a cleaving to God. 'God pervades everything,' Gershom Scholem writes in his own explanation of cleaving: 'Therefore, to be aware of this real omnipresence and immanence of God is already the realization of the state of *devekuth*.'[8]

That some anxiety existed over how to maintain a positive and on-going sense of divine Presence is clear from some of the tales told of the *zaddikim*. Rabbi Yehiel Mikhael, for one, pointed out to his people that they must expect a sense of distance from God to alternate with feelings of nearness.

We read in the psalm, 'Who may ascend the mountain of YHWH and who may stand in the place of his holiness?' (Ps. 24: 3). This is to be compared to a man who travels up a mountain in his cart, and when half way up, his horses are tired and he has to stop so that they can get their breath. Now a person without discernment will roll down at that point. But the discerning takes a stone and wedges it under the cart whilst it is stationary. He can thus reach the top of the mountain. Whoever does not fall when he has to interrupt his worship, but knows how to remain standing, he will ascend the mountain of the Lord.[9]

Almost the same problem had been put to the Baal Shem himself. He was asked why it is that one who cleaves to God sometimes feels far from him. A father, he answered, teaching his little child to walk, stands in front of him in case he should stumble. The child walks between his father's outstretched hands. But as he advances the father steps backward and holds his hands wider apart.[10]

The two lessons of the parable are that the more intense the

---

[8] Scholem, *The Messianic Idea in Judaism*, 209.

[9] *Werke*, iii. 271; *Tales of the Hasidim: Early Masters*, 147.

[10] *Werke*, iii. 281; *Tales of the Hasidim: Early Masters*, 65.

experience of God's nearness, the more likely it is that an opposite remoteness will be felt at times; and in this relation between man and God, his withdrawal into distance is as much a part of his love, care, and instruction, as his nearness.

For a glimpse of what cleaving meant to a 'man of the spirit', it is enough to mention a remark attributed to the *zaddik* known as 'the Seraph', Rabbi Uri of Strelisk (d. 1826). To visitors who had travelled to his town to speak to him he once said: 'You travel to see me. And where do I travel? I travel and travel continuously to where I may cleave to God.'[11]

In its several and varying degrees, from the level of the passionate lovers of God like Rabbi Uri to that of 'the rest' referred to earlier, cleaving was the beginning of the spiritual life in Hasidism, though of course also its end. It involved, again in Scholem's words, 'a constant being-with-God',[12] an unceasing effort to be present with him whose essential nature it is to be present with his creatures. The Baal Shem said:

Consider the person who day in and day out rushes about on his business in the market through the streets. He almost forgets that there is a Creator of the world. Not until it is time to pray *Minhah* [the afternoon prayer] does it occur to him, 'I must pray.' But then he sighs from the bottom of his heart because his day has been spent in such futility, and he runs into a side street and stands and prays. He is held dear, very dear, before God, and his prayer pierces the heavens.[13]

2. *Humility*   *Shiflut* is not what is generally understood by humility. Humility as preached in particular by the Christian church is an end in itself and intrinsic to the *imitatio Christi*. In the literature of Christian mysticism, it is an abasement, and in the final resort even a nullifica-tion, of the human in the God–man relationship. To perfect their humility, Christian saints have gone to extreme and terrible lengths, inviting vilification and abuse and rejoicing in every sort of ridicule and obloquy. The cultivation of poverty (holy poverty) has been part of the same exercise. Its purpose has been to separate a person from all possessions, to render him totally poor (like Jesus), with the aim of detaching him from all things material and immaterial which might

---

[11] *Werke*, iii. 535; *Tales of the Hasidim: Later Masters*, trans. Olga Marx (Schocken, 1948), 147.

[12] Scholem, *The Messianic Idea in Judaism*, 204.

[13] *Werke*, iii. 185; *Tales of the Hasidism: Early Masters*: 69.

come between him and his ultimate Good. (Indeed, one is reminded in this respect of the detachment from the world demanded by kabbalistic *devekut*).

The potential damage of such maltreatment of the self is considerable. It is possible that mystics, by diminishing themselves in this way, may improve their enjoyment of intercourse with what they believe to be heaven, but as far as 'the rest' are concerned, such tactics can have deleterious effects; a certain measure of self-esteem, self-regard, and even self-love is essential to health and stability. Where men and women—usually the professional religious, since in the ordinary course of events, the world being what it is, the so-called layman can only pay lip-service to this 'evangelical' virtue—subject themselves to a systematic destruction of their 'pride', the result is only too often to be seen in an all-round impoverishment of their personal development. Exerting themselves to become 'like little children', they risk falling into a condition of puerility. Alternatively, where the natural instinct of self-preservation is strong, humiliation may not be genuine, but assumed, and result in a compromise of the person's integrity. But even when 'pride' appears to have been successfully crushed, it is liable to make itself felt on some other front. The voluntary embrace of extreme humility in accordance with the recommendations of the church can only too easily lead to another kind of *hubris* associated with the cloth, the habit, or ecclesiastical office.

All this is said with a view to contrasting 'humility' with *shiflut*. The humility represented by *shiflut* is quite different. Alive to the psychological necessity to love and honour the self, the Jewish teaching on humility not only does nothing to lessen a person's self-esteem; it positively encourages it by blessing and 'elevating' it. The Hasid is reminded constantly that the gravest sin he can commit is to forget that he is a son of the King. He is not to be proud; pride is one of the divine attributes which he must not imitate. Rabbi Dov Baer of Mezritch (d. 1772) when consulted on how pride is to be broken, said: 'The attribute of pride belongs to God, as it is written "The Lord is king, he has clothed himself in pride" (Ps. 93: 1). There is therefore no advice on how to break this attribute. We must wrestle with it every day of our lives.'[14] Pride, inherent to man made in the likeness of God, must be fought and mastered but not destroyed. It must be countered by the practice of *shiflut*, with its basic teaching that although the son of the King, each is one man among other men. Each is a part and not the

[14] *Werke*, iii. 217; *Tales of the Hasidim: Early Masters*, 100.

whole. In Buber's words: 'The individual looks on God and embraces him. The individual redeems the fallen worlds. And yet the individual is not a whole but a part. And the purer and more perfect he is, the more genuinely he knows that he is a part, and the more keenly the community of living beings stirs in him. This is the mystery of humility.'[15]

A second distinctive mark of Hasidic humility is that it is regarded not so much as an end in itself as a step towards fulfilling the far greater obligation of love. The love of God that inspires it is inseparable from a love of God's creation. Humility is encouraged to flow into daily life, in combination with a pride mastered and controlled, as a sense of belonging to the world and of participating in its work, its guilt, its suffering, and its redemption. *Shiflut* does not look for an abasement of the human person so that God should be correspondingly glorified. On the contrary, it confirms by means of man's own presence 'in the depths' that the Presence of God is also there. Lowering themselves to the level of the least and the humblest in order to be with them, the lovers of God find that that is where God is also. To quote Rabbi Uri once more:

We read in the psalm, 'If I climb to heaven, you are there, If I make my bed in the realm of the tombs, there you are' (Ps. 139: 8). If I imagine myself to be great and to move in heaven, I find that God is a faraway 'there', and the higher I reach, the further away he is. But if I make my bed in the depths and humble myself to the lowest world, there he is, with me.[16]

Similarly the Baal Shem:

I permit sinners to approach me if they are not proud. I keep learned men and the sinless at a distance if they are proud. For the sinner who knows that he is so, and therefore has a low opinion of himself—God is with him who 'dwells with them in the midst of their stain' (Lev. 16: 16). But whoever prides himself on having no burden of sin to bear, of him God says, as it is written in the Gemara, 'I and he have no room in the world.'[17]

The central aim of humility in the Hasidic setting is to perfect a love for the created world similar to that demonstrated by the divine Helper himself, who assists those whom he loves by being present with them. The earthly helper is to do likewise. He is to help, not from feelings of com-passion but from a deep and true awareness of co-existence: 'not,

[15] *Werke*, iii. 40; *Hasidism and Modern Man*, 112.
[16] *Werke*, iii. 534; *Tales of the Hasidim: Later Masters*, 146.
[17] *Werke*, iii. 188; *Tales of the Hasidim: Early Masters*, 172.

that is to say, out of a sharp quick pain which one wishes to banish, but out of love, out of living-with the other [*Mitleben*] . . . He who lives-with the other in this way realizes, by means of what he does, the truth that all souls are one because each is a spark from the Primordial Soul and it is whole within them all.'[18]

Many of the Hasidic tales illustrate the themes of love and humility more movingly because more directly. There is the story of the sad peasant who asked Rabbi Mosheh Loeb if he loved him. The rabbi assured him that yes, he did love him. The peasant was still unsure. If the rabbi loved him, he countered, he would know what was wrong with him. And Rabbi Loeb understood suddenly that the real meaning of love is that it leads a person to perceive the needs of others and to carry their burdens. 'Thus lives the humble man, who is righteous and loving and a helper: mingling with all, yet untouched by all, devoted to the many yet collected within his own singleness, fulfilling on the rocky summits of solitude a covenant with the Infinite, and in the valley of life, a covenant with those on earth.'[19]

3. *Holy intention* The concept of *kavvanah* appears to have followed much the same career as that of cleaving. Originally, it was total devotion to God, an integration of the whole man so that his outer attitudes matched his inner convictions. Isaiah is alluding to an absence of intention on the part of Israel when he gives God to say: 'Inasmuch as this nation draws near with its mouth alone, and honours me with its lips alone, whereas its heart is far from me' (Isa. 29: 13–14). The remoteness of the 'heart' from God does not, incidentally, imply an absence of love. For the biblical writers, the heart is the seat of thought, not the emotions (though the innermost thoughts are located in the kidneys, e.g. 'who tries the hearts and the kidneys', Ps. 7: 7). The emotions in this scheme of things have their place in the bowels, e.g. 'the bowels of compassion', etc. The '*kavvanah* of the heart', as it is later sometimes called, is consequently a turning of the *mind* to God, and Isaiah is rebuking Israel because the people's *mind* is not properly in touch with God while they pay outward respect to him. It is into the heart = mind that God looks and the heart = mind that he requires. As the Talmud teaches: 'Man looks on the outward appearance, but YHWH looks on the heart (1 Sam. 16: 7). The Holy One, blessed be he, demands the heart.'[20]

[18] *Werke*, iii. 45; *Hasidism and Modern Man*, 121.
[19] Ibid.   [20] *Sanh.*, 106*b*.

The earliest significance, then, of holy intention was integrity and sincerity. The Talmudic injunction and others like it—'It matters not whether a man does much or little, provided that he directs his heart to heaven'[21]—can only be that God asks for external obeisance to be accompanied by a devotion to him of the whole self.

The wider field in which intention was expected to operate shrank fairly quickly to the smaller one of prayer and ritual observances. Moving away from the idea of the unified person turned towards God, it developed into what might be termed a mental exercise in which the mind was trained to concentrate on what was being said and done during the performance of religious duties. Maimonides was recommending this type of intention in the twelfth century when he prescribed that the worshipper should 'empty his mind of all other thoughts and regard himself as standing before the very Presence of God'.[22]

Among kabbalists, the deepening and narrowing of the understanding of intention gained still further ground, and by the sixteenth century Isaac Luria had evolved a doctrine which prescribed that concentration on the simple meaning of the written word was to give place to a system of special mystical and esoteric thoughts, most of them centred on the divine Name or names, and often totally divorced from the actual significance of the text studied. It is worth noting that Gershom Scholem employs the word 'magic' more than once in this connection. 'Luria's doctrine of mystical prayer stands directly on the border-line between mysticism and magic, where the one only too easily passes into the other.'[23]

The earlier Hasidim did not respond to these particular teachings, and in their eyes *kavvanah* became a matter of the emotions rather than of the intellect, and so close to cleaving as to be almost indistinguishable from it.[24] However, this shift of emphasis provoked others, and on the one hand Luria's esotericism returned to favour, while on the other holy intention was again understood as absorption in the written and spoken word. The following story illustrates the effect expected from the latter type. 'A *zaddik* said: "If a person says, 'The Lord is my God,' meaning that he is mine and I am his, how does his soul not leave his

---

[21] *M. Men.*, 13: 11; *Ber.*, 5b, 17a. [22] *Hilkhoth tefillah*, iv. 16.

[23] Gershom Scholem, *Major Trends in Jewish Mysticism* (Thames and Hudson, 1955), 277.

[24] See J. G. Weiss, 'The Kavvanoth of Prayer in Early Hasidism', *Journal of Jewish Studies*, 9 (1958), 163–92.

body?" As soon as he said this, he fell into deep unconsciousness.'[25]

On the whole, Buber's representation of intention in Hasidism corresponds to the saying of Rabbi Dov Baer of Mezritch (d. 1772), who observed of God: 'All He desires is the single *kavvanah* in which man binds his soul to His true essence, blessed be He, alone.'[26] He distinguishes, however, between the two traditional aspects of intention-cum-cleaving and intention associated with the world, classifying them respectively as 'intention of receiving' and 'intention of giving'.

Intention of receiving, as Buber explains it, operates in the familiar field of the redemption of the divine sparks contained in all things. By accepting life as coming from the hands of God, and by carefully tending and using everything with which he comes into contact, the Hasid is able to break open the 'shells' which imprison the indwelling Presence and bring about its reunion with God. 'The significance and destiny of *kavvanah* is this: that it is given to men to raise the fallen and liberate the captive. Not merely to wait, not merely to watch. Man is able actively to bring about the redemption of the world. And this in fact is *kavvanah*: the mystery of the soul directed towards the redemption of the world.'[27]

To lend even more weight to the mythical imagery of the Presence, Hasidism goes so far as to envisage the imprisoned sparks of God as having human shape. 'The spark in a rock or plant or another creature is, as it were, a complete form sitting in the middle of the thing like a block, unable to stretch out its hands and feet and with its head lying on its knees. But he who is able to raise the holy spark, leads it into freedom; and no freeing of captives is greater than this one.'[28] Intention of receiving was believed to affect not only material objects but the human soul. The spirits of the living and the dead were regarded as seats of the indwelling Presence. As far as the dead were concerned, Hasidism inherited from kabbalah the idea of metempsychosis and taught that the souls of those who die without reaching perfection wander through the world searching for opportunities to mend the damage caused in former lives and thereby unify their spiritual structure. Before God's Kingdom can come, God himself must be unified; but in addition, these soul-sparks, which all have their 'root' in the soul

---

[25] *Werke*, iii. 34–5; *Hasidism and Modern Man*, 101–2.

[26] Quoted from Dov Baer's *Imre Binah* in Louis Jacobs, *Hasidic Prayer* (Routledge & Kegan Paul for the Littman Library, 1972), 91.

[27] *Werke*, iii. 34–5; *Hasidism and Modern Man*, 101.

[28] *Werke*, iii. 36; *Hasidism and Modern Man*, 104.

of Adam and were scattered at the time of Adam's sin, must also be re-unified with that First Soul. As one Hasidic parable expounds it, the prince will not permit the Meal to start until the last of the guests has entered the Banquet Chamber. 'But this is the way of redemption: that all the souls and soul-sparks which have sprung from the Primal Soul, and which in the primal darkening of the world or through the guilt of the ages have sunk and become scattered in all created things, should end their wandering and return home purified.'[29]

Buber's interpretation of 'intention of giving' in the form of concentration and meditation on the written word is not too easy to follow, chiefly because he does not deal fully enough with the Hasidic sources which he cites.[30] Language, in the view of kabbalah, and specifically the Hebrew language, the language of the Bible, is full of mystery. This mystery, furthermore, is attached not simply to the content of whatever is expressed, but to the words that comprise it, and even to the individual letters from which the words are formed. Buber bothers only very loosely with this exclusive and highly complex aspect of the kabbalistic mysticism of language, preferring to dwell on what he discerns as an emphasis on the written and spoken word which allows the divine Voice continuously to speak new and unexpected messages. The holy intention of absorption in the word is explained as follows with the help of a Hasidic text. 'One should utter words as though the heavens were opened in them. And as though it were not that you take the word into your mouth but as though you enter into the word.'[31] He then goes on to assert that one who makes himself familiar with the 'song' which conveys what is within to what is without, and with the 'holy dance' which juxtaposes individual words so that they merge into the 'song of distances', becomes filled with divine power, 'and it is as though he recreates heaven and earth and all the world'.[32] A person, that is to say, who 'enters into' a passage which he has read or heard recited and, having discerned its meaning, is able to re-communicate it in a *new* literary or spoken form, such a man is equipped to re-create for the benefit of the world 'without' the discovery he has made

[29] *Werke*, iii. 34; *Hasidism and Modern Man*, 101.

[30] Whether Buber's understanding of this type of *kavvanah* coincides with Hasidism's own is once more another question. The present writer is not qualified to judge, and readers needing a historical analysis must take into account the conclusions of the specialists. See in particular Scholem, *The Messianic Idea in Judaism*, 249.

[31] *Werke*, iii. 37; *Hasidism and Modern Man*, 106–7.

[32] *Werke*, iii. 37; *Hasidism and Modern Man*, 107.

'within'. He may not be of any use to the wandering soul-sparks, but
he makes his contribution to the redemption of the world. 'For in each
letter are the Three: world, soul and Godhead. They ascend and
adhere and unite with one another; and subsequently the letters unite
and the word comes into being; and the words unite in God in true
union, for a man has enclosed his soul in them; and all the words unite
and ascend and the great ecstasy is born.'[33]

This sort of text calls for an explanation, but Buber passes it over as
though its meaning were self-evident. It is safe to say, however, that
when he writes about the '*kavvanah* of giving', what he has in mind is
the single-minded attention to the written and spoken word which
results in the genesis of new ideas and new insights, and in their
communication to others. Such a bald summary does not of course do
justice to the passage cited, which obviously contains various other
significances.

To become a creator and a giver of this kind, man must himself
become a new creation. But to become a new creation he must first be
un-created. Like the egg which must break so that the chick may
emerge, and like the seed which must perish for the flower to bloom,
he must come as near as possible to Nothing before he can arrive at
Something. 'And this is what is known as wisdom: a thought which
has no revelation. And thus if man wishes a new creation to come
from out of him, he must attain as far as he is able to the attribute
of Nothingness. And then God creates a new creation in him, and he is
as a source which does not run dry, and as a stream which does not
fail.'[34]

Remarkable though this idea of the intention of giving may seem, it
ought not to surprise those who remember the story with which this
study opens, the tale of the daemonic book, *Ar Vif*, the pages of which
are red, and the black letters of which remain invisible until the book
has been fought and overcome. Nor should it strike as strange those
who have noticed the allusion which appears throughout Buber's
works to the mystery and sanctity of language. His veneration of the
word underlies and even underpins his whole view of God and man.
Hans Kohn draws attention to this characteristic repeatedly, actually
defining Buber's outlook at its mature stage as a 'philosophy of
language' and reproducing in this connection one of Buber's own
verses:

[33] *Werke*, iii. 38; *Hasidism and Modern Man*, 107.
[34] *Werke*, iii. 38; *Hasidism and Modern Man*, 108.

We are sounds spoken by the Primordial Mouth.
Yet we are words only, not sayings.
When shall we become sayings that fall
Into one sentence with which the Primordial Mouth will be satisfied?[35]

According to Buber's picture of it, holy intention in Hasidism has two faces and one role. As a '*kavvanah* of receiving', it cooperates in the redemption of the world in so far as it is directed towards using, handling, and consuming things in holiness, towards realizing, that is to say, the inner value and dignity of what is external. As a '*kavvanah* of giving', it co-operates in the redemption of the world in so far as it is directed towards making and creating in holiness, towards giving, that is to say, external expression to what is internal. For in the final resort, as Buber writes, it is 'through holy making and holy use that the redemption of the world is effected'.[36]

4. *Worship* 'What is the worship of the heart?' the ancient commentator asks, apropos of the text 'And worship him with all your heart' (Deut. 11: 13). His answer: 'This is prayer.'[37]

When the rabbis identified worship in this way, their chief purpose was to urge, now that the Temple was destroyed, that the worship formerly offered there should be replaced by worship 'of the heart', the 'heart' being the one remaining site worthy for the worship of God. It was even suggested that Israel's later situation in this regard was an improvement on the older one, and that prayer is dearer to God than good works and sacrifice.

For many ages, worship had nevertheless been associated with the institutional and communal worship of the Sanctuary, and its link with these is indelibly stamped on the Jewish religious memory. But so, too, is the worship of the beginnings of time, before temples and their rites were ever thought of, when God called and man replied, and when man cried out and God 'was there with' him; when it was enough for Adam to hear the 'sound' of God walking about in the Garden to recognize his Presence there, and when Moses had only to hear his Voice to inaugurate with God what was to be the dialogue of dialogues. Each of these stages in the development of the relation between man and God, from the forefathers' spontaneous and intimate conversation

---

[35] Hans Kohn, *Martin Buber: sein Werk und seine Zeit*, 3rd edn. (Melzer Verlag, 1961), 240.

[36] *Werke*, iii. 38; *Hasidism and Modern Man*, 108.   [37] *Taan.* 2a.

with him to the solemn observances governed by laws and ordinances when Israel communed with heaven as a nation, left its mark on Jewish teaching concerning the proper worship of God.

Hasidism honoured them all. By the time it appeared on the scene of history, religious thought had admittedly moved on still further to include the doctrine of the indwelling Presence, but the movement's attitude towards worship never loses sight of the past. On the contrary, it reverts to it constantly, not only reproducing the biblical record, but infusing it with its own characteristics of religious existentialism and extra inwardness, drawing from it new lessons. As an example, Rabbi Uri of Strelisk comments on the text 'And Abel brought he too . . .' (Gen. 4: 4): 'He brought his own "he," his own self. It is only when a person brings himself too that his offering is valid.'[38]

Rabbi Mosheh of Kobryn (d. 1858) voiced the same argument. He was once reciting on a Sabbath the Additional Prayer that replaces the sacrificial offering of Sabbaths and Feast Days, and when he reached the words 'Lead us into our land, there we will bring to You the offerings of our obligations,' he fell unconscious to the ground. Later in the day, at the evening meal, he came again to the prayer 'There, we will bring to You the special offering of this Sabbath, here we have no Sanctuary and no sacrifice.' At this point, his love for God blazed into words and he cried: 'Lord of the world, we, we, we ourselves! We desire to bring ourselves to You in place of the offering! Then they all understood why he had fallen down in the House of Prayer as though deprived of life.'[39]

The recollection that worship was formerly offered to God on an altar is used by another Hasidic teacher to press home his message that it is best to offer oneself to God in spontaneous silent communion with him rather than in the polished phrases of formal prayer. Citing the text 'Make for me an altar of earth . . . But if you make for me an altar of stones, do not build them up squared, for if you have swung over it your iron tool, you have profaned it' (Exod. 20: 24–5), Rabbi Israel of Rizhyn (d. 1850) said: 'The altar of earth is the altar of silence, the altar most pleasing to God. But if you make an altar of words, let them not be hewn and chiselled, for with proud arts you profane it.'[40]

Sincerity and simplicity in the sphere of personal relation with God are constantly emphasized in Hasidism, but there was no neglect on

---

[38] *Werke*, iii. 533; *Tales of the Hasidim: Later Masters*, 145.
[39] *Werke*, iii. 558; *Tales of the Hasidim: Later Masters*, 169.
[40] *Werke*, iii. 452; *Tales of the Hasidim: Later Masters*, 59.

the part of its teachers to preach the necessity of worship by the people as a corporate body, to offer the prayer of 'all Israel'. Their attitude towards this other aspect of worship is typified by an interpretation advanced by the *zaddik* Menahem Mendel of Kotzk (d. 1859). Asked why, in the passage 'Worship YHWH your God and He will bless thy bread' (Exod. 23:25), the writer first uses the pronoun 'your', and follows it with 'thy', the rabbi explained: 'To worship means to pray. When a man prays, even if he is alone in his room, he should first bind himself to all Israel. So in every true prayer, it is the community that prays. But when a man eats, even with many others at table, each does the eating for himself.'[41]

Both these teachings attempt to re-formulate the words of the Bible so that they acquire new meaning and reality, but the favourite topics of kabbalah are treated similarly. The supreme subject of thought being unity, it is extended into the concept of worship: the kabbalists' view of true prayer is that which asks for the restoration of the unity of the One God. God's Being has fallen into duality, into one part removed from his creatures and one part dwelling in creation. It is in man's power, by means of his worship, to return the indwelling Presence to its Source. The Hasidic masters inherited this belief and accepted it as their own, adding to it the admonition that a Hasid should regard his troubles and sorrows as springing from the distress of the exiled divine Presence. If he would remember to live as someone who desires to satisfy the needs of the Shekhinah, his own would also be stilled.

This, quotes Buber, is the meaning of worship to the Hasid. 'Through his own need and deficiency, he learns the deficiency of the *Shekhinah*, to pray that the deficiencies of the *Shekhinah* may be made good, and that through him, the praying man, the union may occur of God and his *Shekhinah* . . . For everything, Above and Below, is *one* unity.'[42] Another *zaddik* said: 'Men think they pray before God, but this is not so, for prayer itself is Godhead.'[43]

5. *Ardour*   It has not been easy to unravel Buber's understanding of this counsel of perfection, the trouble being that he—and many of the Hasidic texts to which he appeals—seems to deal with two very different conditions as though they were identical. By *hitlahavut*, a

---

41   *Werke*, iii. 670–1; *Tales of the Hasidim: Later Masters*, 282.
42   No source given; *Werke*, iii. 28–9; *Hasidism and Modern Man*, 88–9.
43   *Werke*, iii. 29; *Hasidism and Modern Man*, 89.

term derived from the Hebrew root *lahav*, to burn, and said by Scholem to be one of the comparatively few religious expressions originating in Hasidism itself,[44] he understands a condition best rendered in English by 'ardour'. But he clearly includes in the same category the religious phenomenon we recognize as ecstasy, which has a Hebrew name of its own, *hitpa'alut*,[45] and is not mentioned by him at all.

As is well known, after certain experiences of his youth, Buber came to disapprove of mystical extremes such as trances, ecstasies, and the like, but there is no denying that Hasidism, following a tradition going back without a break to the beginnings of Jewish mysticism, viewed them as peak experiences towards which the holy should learn to rise rung by rung. Influenced by the kabbalistic notion of God as the supreme Nothing which preceded the existence of Something, Hasidic mystics do not in the main bring back from their transports accounts of any *unio mystica*, but tend to express the limit towards which they have been brought as one of Nothingness. Theirs is the altar of silence, the 'altar of earth'. But because of their ability to empty themselves of all except cleaving and holy intention, theirs is the power to perform a miracle greater even than that of transforming Nothing into Something: they transform Something into Nothing.

The creation of heaven and earth is the development of Something out of Nothing, the descent of what is Above into what is Below. But the holy, who set themselves apart from existence and cleave always to God, see and comprehend him in truth as though he were Nothing as before the creation. They change Something back into Nothing. And this it is that is the more marvellous: to raise up what is Below. As it is written in the Gemara: 'The last miracle is greater than the first.'[46]

Every Hasid was exhorted to discover the way to worship and serve God best suited to himself, but once arrived at the rung of Nothingness, every way was open to him. As one *zaddik* expressed it, he needed only to stand ready, like a messenger boy, for whatever God asked him to do.

The Baal Shem himself was noted for his moments of ecstasy. He once broke into a fit of violent trembling while he was praying, and when two of his congregation went to assist him, they noticed that his face 'shone like a torch, and the eyes were wide open, and staring like

---

[44] See Scholem, *Major Trends in Jewish Mysticism*, 342.
[45] See Jacobs, *Hasidic Prayer*, 23.
[46] *Werke*, iii. 25; *Hasidism and Modern Man*, 82.

those of a dying man'.[47] Rabbi Shmelke of Nikolsburg, who died
twenty years after Israel Baal Shem, was also carried away during his
devotions, but in his case ecstasy caused him to depart from the
customary liturgical chants, and to sing 'new melodies, miracle of
miracles, which he had never heard before, nor had any other human
ear. And he had no idea of what he was singing, or how, since he was
bound to the world above.'[48] Without doubt, all these stories relate to
the religious trance proper. It is also quite plain that it was a state
which Hasidism deliberately cultivated through dancing and chanting
during the services, and through the *kavvanah* or intention directed at
deep contemplation of words and letters, of which it is explicitly said
that it induced 'the great ecstasy'.[49] One source is quoted as remarking
of the ecstatic that he 'makes his body into a throne of life, and life into
a throne of the mind, and mind into a throne of the soul, and the soul
into a throne of the Light of God's Glory. And the Light streams
round about him, and he sits in the midst of the Light and trembles
and rejoices.'[50]

All this belongs to the category of *hitpa'alut* or ecstasy. *Hitlahavut*,
defined as 'a burning enthusiasm in which the soul is aflame with
ardour for God whose presence is everywhere',[51] is both less and more
than ecstasy, depending on one's understanding of these matters. It
would seem on the face of it less remarkable to 'burn' for God than to
drop senseless at the mere thought of him. Yet without a preliminary
burning, would there be any fall into unconsciousness? Moreover, it
can be argued that whereas ecstasy belongs to the other side of the
divide between this world and another, and as far as one may judge
from its effects, to death rather than to life, to an admitted Nothing
rather than to Something, ardour belongs to present existence, and its
force and warmth are active here. For whatever ecstasy may be, ardour
is essentially love. Its burning, *pace* the mild and respectable 'enthusiasm' of the *Encyclopaedia Judaica*, is the passion of the Song of Songs.
Who better than Jeremiah has succeeded more movingly in putting
into words what is meant by this all-consuming and irrepressible
adoration of God?

> If I say I will not mention him,
> or speak any more in his Name,

[47] *Werke*, iii. 165; *Tales of the Hasidim: Early Masters*, 49.
[48] *Werke*, iii. 301; *Tales of the Hasidim: Later Masters*, 182.
[49] See above, p. 169.   [50] *Werke*, iii. 32; *Hasidism and Modern Man*, 95.
[51] *Encyclopaedia Judaica*, 'Hasidism', vol. vii, col. 1405.

> there is in my heart as it were a burning fire
> shut up in my bones,
> and I am weary with holding it in,
> and I cannot. (Jer. 20: 9)

It is a love whose 'burning fire' purifies and re-creates, as the great Rabbi Nahman of Bratslav taught. In the one great flame of ardour, he says, the loves and passions that are part of the 'evil inclination' are melted down and re-directed towards God.

'Create in me a new heart O God' (Ps. 51: 12) . . . Purity of heart is attained through having the heart on fire for God, blessed be he. Through this is the heart purified. For if a man is to counteract his burning and glowing in sin or evil lusts, God forbid, through which his heart becomes unclean, he must set his heart on fire to burn for God, blessed be he. As it is written, 'All that has been through fire you shall pass through fire' (Num. 31: 23).[52]

Ardour as Hasidism understood it is a love the radiance and force of which win immediate forgiveness from God. Rabbi Shalom Shakhna of Probitsch (d. 1803) said: 'It is written, "A psalm of David", and afterwards, "as he had gone in to Bathsheba" (Ps. 51: 1). Rabbi Shalom explained the verse thus. With the same sincerity and ardour with which he had gone in to Bathsheba, so did David make his *teshuvah* to God and recited his psalm to him. For this reason he was forgiven instantly.'[53] Finally, this ardour is a love which, because God is conceived as The Place of the world, seeks and embraces him in the world. There are two kinds of love, a *zaddik* said.

There is the love of a man for his wife, which it is seemly to conduct in secret and not in a place where there are onlookers, since this love can only be consummated in a place apart from others. And there is the love for relations and children, which requires no concealment. Similarly, there are two kinds of love for God. There is love through Torah, prayer, and the fulfilment of the commandments, which it is seemly to conduct in quietness and not publicly, so that it does not lead to a love of glory and to pride. And there is love in time, when a person mingles with other living creatures, speaks and listens, gives and takes, and in secret cleaves to God and does not cease to think of him. And the latter is a higher stage than the former. And it is said of it, 'Who gives you to me as a brother that sucked at my mother's breasts. If I were to find you in the streets, I would kiss you, and they would not be able to mock me.'[54]

---

[52] Quoted in Jacobs, *Hasidic Prayer*, 123.

[53] *Werke*, iii. 443; *Tales of the Hasidim: Later Masters*, 51.

[54] *Werke*, iii. 27; *Hasidism and Modern Man*, 86–7.

6. *Joy* Hans Kohn, in his description of Hasidism as a 'mystical religiousness, a joyful world-orientated mysticism', emphasizes that it was not a new religion, nor even a reform of Judaism. Situated firmly within the traditional religious framework, it accepted without question its teachings, and sought only to inject into the beliefs it had inherited a 'new immediacy, a heartfelt sincerity'.[55]

Kohn's remarks apply just as well to the Hasidic doctrine of joy as to the rest of its outlook. The stress on joy was not a new import into religious thinking, but age-old, with roots as deeply embedded in the Bible, where God himself is projected as a God of joy rejoicing in his works, as in every other element of the Jewish faith. Music, song, dancing, rejoicing, joyful shouts, joyful noises, jubilation, exultation— one forgets until one actually looks for it how constantly joy, and even ecstatic joy, recurs in page after page of biblical literature. The psalmist urges, 'Make a joyful noise to YHWH all the earth! Break forth into joyous song and sing praises!' (Ps. 98: 4). Deutero-Isaiah's rapture is still more electric:

> Sing, O heavens, for YHWH has done it!
> Shout, O deep places of the earth!
> Break forth into singing, O mountains,
> O forest, and every tree in it!

Another psalm strikes a quieter, more personal note:

> I will sing to YHWH as long as I live,
> I will sing praise to my God whilst I have being.
> May my meditation be pleasing to him,
> for I rejoice in YHWH. (Ps. 104: 22–4)

Ecclesiastes offers advice of an earthier kind—which was nevertheless appealed to later by the rabbis in support of their promotion of joy as the only fitting condition of the human soul for the indwelling there of the Presence.[56] 'And I commend enjoyment, for man has no good thing under the sun but to eat and drink and be merry; for this will go with him in his toil through the days of life which God gives him under the sun' (Eccles. 8: 15).

More weighty than all these recommendations is the actual commandment to rejoice given in Deuteronomy, where joy is presented not so much as a counsel as an obligation. 'You shall eat before YHWH

---

[55] Kohn, *Martin Buber*, 75.   [56] *Shab.*, 30b.

your God,' the biblical writer orders, 'and you shall rejoice, you and your households, in all that you undertake' (Deut. 12: 7, 18).

In subsequent centuries, the same intoxication with God and his creation is so conspicuous in the Jewish liturgy and prayers, and especially in the Sabbath liturgy, that joy is sometimes represented as the key to the whole Hebrew cult. Most of the sages expressed their delight in life, and not only advocated that the joys of the senses, of nature, of achievement, should be found delectable, but that it was positively wrong not to appreciate them. Rav, the Babylonian master who flourished in the first half of the third century AD, is recorded as having said: 'Man shall be called to account for whatever his eyes have beheld *and of which he did not partake.*'[57] God has made these things for man's enjoyment, and to fail to take pleasure in them is to fail in gratitude to him. 'Blessed is he', wrote the talmudist, 'who has not left his world deficient in anything, and has created in it goodly creatures and goodly trees for the enjoyment of mankind'.[58]

Joy is considered so essential to the right worship of God that there has been through the ages a perceptible bias against asceticism, even in its moderate forms. In the opinion of Rabbi Akiva, the renowned second-century teacher and martyr (sawn in two by the Romans while reciting the prayer 'Hear, O Israel'), it is not permissible to inflict harm of any kind on oneself.

Hasidism, for all the added richness of texture brought to it by kabbalah, reverted in the matter of joy once again to the purity of its biblical meaning. The Hasid rejoiced in all that he undertook, as prescribed by Deuteronomy. He ate with joy, prayed, worked, and made love with joy. He worshipped with joy and with dancing and singing. He died with joy. Menahem Mendel, the Rabbi of Rymanov, fulfilled this ideal. When he lost his daughter very shortly after suffering the death of his wife, Menahem Mendel's followers hoped that news of the second disaster could be kept from him for a little while. But he saw his son-in-law enter the House of Prayer in tears, and guessed what had happened. Whereupon he turned to God and prayed: '"Lord of the world, You have taken my wife from me. Yet I could still have rejoiced in my daughter. Now You have taken her too and I can rejoice in You alone. Therefore, I will rejoice in You." And he recited the main prayer of the Sabbath in a transport of joy.'[59]

It was explained that there are two sorts of joy and two sorts of

---

[57] *PT Kid.*, 4: 12, 66d.   [58] *PT Ber.*, 43b.
[59] *Werke*, iii. 528; *Tales of the Hasidim: Later Masters*, 137.

sorrow. There is the true grief of the broken heart as opposed to
moroseness; and there is true joy as opposed to the empty frivolity of
the pleasure-seeker. The Rabbi of Berdichev's answer to the question
concerning the correct way to worship God, with sorrow or joy, was:

There are two kinds of sorrow and two kinds of joy. When a man broods over a
misfortune which has befallen him, and crouches in his corner despairing of
help, this is the unseemly moping of which it is said, 'The *Shekhinah* dwells not
in the place of melancholy.' The other kind is the honest grief of one who
knows what he lacks. The same is true of joy. One who is deficient in inner
substance, and in his empty pleasures does not perceive it, or attend to making
good his deficiency, is a fool. The truly joyful man, however, is as one whose
house has burned down, and who has suffered anguish in his soul, but who
then begins to build a new house, and whose heart rejoices over every stone
that is laid.[60]

Dejection was anathema to Hasidism, the Baal Shem describing it in
his *Testament* as 'a great hindrance to the worship of God'.[61] He
believed that physical pleasure can lead to spiritual pleasure, and
taught that every physical act is a religious act when it is performed in a
spirit of cleaving. Joy in God and in all God's deeds arouses God's own
joy; and when God rejoices, his pleasure flows back into the created
world in the form of blessings. There is even an instance recorded by
Buber of joy being revered for itself, apart from either God or religion.
The Hasidim of Lublin once taxed their Rabbi, Jacob Isaac, for
consorting with a man they knew to be a wrong-doer, and for spending
long hours talking to him. How could he behave in such a way? Jacob
Isaac said:

I know what he is as well as you. But you also know my love of joy and my
hatred of melancholy. And this man is so great a sinner. Others regret it the
moment they have sinned, grieve for a moment, and return to their folly. But
he knows no grief and no melancholy reflections, but dwells in his joy as in a
tower. And the radiance of his joy overwhelms my heart.[62]

This sort of joyful response to no matter what cause sprang from an
overall joy in life and in the world, 'in every hour of life in the world as
that hour is'.[63] But it would be a great mistake to conclude that Hasidic

[60] *Werke*, iii. 351; *Tales of the Hasidim: Early Masters*, 231.
[61] *Zevaath Ribesh* (1963), 9.
[62] *Werke*, iii. 436–7; *Tales of the Hasidim: Early Masters*, 315–16.
[63] *Werke*, iii. 80; *Tales of the Hasidim: Early Masters*, 3.

joy was in any way *for the sake* of the world as it is. It was for the sake of God. As Buber paraphrases the Hasidic attitude:

The world in which you live, as it is, and nothing else, ensures your relation with God . . . And your nature, the person you are, is your particular way of access to God, your particular ability to arrive at it. Do not allow your pleasure in beings and things to discourage you; but do not allow it to become encapsulated in beings and things, but press forward, through them, towards God. Do not be angry with your desires, but grasp hold of them and bind them to God. You are not to kill your passions; you are to make them work in holiness, and rest in holiness, in God. Every non-sense that offends you in the world begs for its sense to be discovered by you. And every contradiction that distresses you in yourself waits for your word to expel it. Every primordial sorrow desires to be admitted into your enraptured joy. But it is not for your joy that you strive. It will be granted you if you strive 'to give joy to God'. Your joy arises when you desire nothing other than God's joy, nothing other than joy itself.[64]

The Hasidim rejoiced. They played their fiddles and danced; they drank their wine and smoked their pipes. But their rejoicing was a delight in the present—because of the Presence believed to be dwelling in it. Their aim was not to 'be happy', but, as Rabbi Elimelekh phrased it, to make God himself 'sing'. 'It is written in the psalm, "For it is good to sing to our God" (Ps. 147: 1).[65] Rabbi Elimelekh interpreted this: "It is good when man manages to make God sing within him." '[66]

––––––

Besides the six major counsels of perfection, which all have to do with man in his relation with God, Buber selects six secondary Hasidic recommendations mainly concerned with man in relation to himself.

1. *Reflect on yourself* The first exhortation asks that a person should thoroughly examine his life to ascertain what he has done with it and where he now stands. Hasidic lessons on this topic mostly use the story of Adam and Eve. Having disobeyed the divine commandment, the first parents later

heard the sound of YHWH God walking in the garden in the cool of the day, and the man and his wife hid themselves from the Presence of YHWH God among

---

[64] *Werke*, iii. 81; *Tales of the Hasidim: Early Masters*, 4.
[65] *Ki tov zammerah elohenu.*
[66] *Werke*, iii. 375; *Tales of the Hasidim: Early Masters*, 254.

the trees of the garden. But YHWH God called to the man and said to him, 'Where are you?' And he said, 'I heard the sound of You in the garden and I was afraid because I was naked, and I hid myself.' (Gen. 3: 8–10)

The moral drawn from the story is that Adam hid from YHWH God because awareness of the divine Presence made him fear that he would be called on to answer for his disobedience. He knew God was present because he had heard his 'sound', but he did not emerge from his hiding-place until YHWH God 'called' him. He then confessed his fear.

Adam's descendants also hide from God's 'sound'. Their lives become a cleverly engineered place of concealment inside which they can ignore it. When they refuse to look for the purpose of their existence, or into the record of their gains and failures to establish where they have done right or wrong, they are hiding themselves.

According to this myth, it is into such conditions of induced obscurity that YHWH God calls, and to respond to his sound is to overcome the fear of accepting responsibility for one's deeds. It is to acknowledge the authority of a tribunal outside the self. To answer the question, 'Where are you?' is also to take the first step towards entering into living communion with God.

Rabbi Isaac Meir (d. 1866) taught, quoting from the *Sayings of the Fathers*, that the Hasidim must consider three things. He told them: 'Know from whence you come, where you go, and before whom you are to answer.'[67] He held that it is of the greatest importance to confront and settle these problems for oneself, otherwise there is a danger that they may have to be faced suddenly and unexpectedly, perhaps in circumstances of anguish or stress; and with no answer ready, there may seem to be no way out from the dilemma in which one finds oneself. A person may be asked (as Jacob warned his servant that Esau might ask him), 'Whose are you? Where are you going? And whose are these before you?' (Gen. 32: 18). If he does not by then know whose he is, and in which direction he goes, and what he has so far done with his life, he may experience such despair that he will no longer hear even the sound of YHWH God, let alone his Voice. Moreover, once awareness of God's sound is lost, no movement towards *teshuvah* is possible.

The recommendation to think about oneself is, needless to say, also closely associated with the doctrine of the presence. Meditating on the words of the psalm, 'I will not give sleep to my eyes nor slumber to my

[67] *Pirke Abot*, 3: 1.

eyelids until I find a place for YHWH (Ps. 132: 4), Rabbi Barukh ben Jehiel of Mezbizh (d. 1811), a grandson of the Baal Shem, breaks off to comment: 'until I find myself and establish myself as a place prepared for the descent of the *Shekhinah*'.[68] Whereas Adam had hidden himself, Rabbi Barukh understood that he had to find himself. He had to find himself in order to establish himself. In contrast to Adam, who was unready for God and on hearing his sound took refuge among the trees, he must establish himself as a place ready for the indwelling Presence. For God to be The Place of the world, man must first become a place of God.

2. *The particular way* The second precept teaches that there is no general way to serve God; each individual has to find and cultivate his own unique vocation. Every human activity, whether buying and selling, writing books, driving lorries, building houses, washing clothes, if it is done in a spirit of cleaving, can lead to God. The saintly Rabbi Meshullam Zusya of Hanipol (d. 1800) once explained that eating can be a way to worship God. Asked why it is that Abraham is said in the Bible to have 'stood over' the visiting three angels while they ate the food he had prepared for them, his reply was: 'Whoever eats in (a spirit of) consecration, redeems the holy sparks exiled in the food. But the angels know nothing of this worship unless man teaches them. This is why it is said of Abraham that he "stood over them" (Gen. 18: 8). He caused the consecration of the meal to come down on them.'[69]

The Hasidic recipe for serving God is simple and pleasant: each person has to discover what he most likes doing, and then do whatever it may be as well as he can, and with holy intention for the redemption of the world. Each must therefore observe and know himself. To discover his own special talent, he must think of what gives him most pleasure and stimulates him most strongly. '"There is in everyone something precious that is in no one else." But a man can only discover what is "precious" in himself if he truly comprehends his strongest feelings, his central desire, that within himself which stirs his inmost being.'[70] Such feelings and desires are frequently to be found in the darkest depths of the psyche, and it is one of the wisest of all the teachings of Judaism that the huge energies of the libido must be included as valuable and important ingredients in the worship of God.

[68] *Werke*, iii. 204; *Tales of the Hasidim: Early Masters*, 88.
[69] *Werke*, iii. 358; *Tales of the Hasidim: Early Masters*, 248.
[70] *Werke*, iii. 721; *Hasidism and Modern Man*, 142.

To learn what stirs the inmost self and what constitutes its central desire, the passions must also be consulted, with their sexuality, greed, ambition, possessiveness, love, hate, envy, power, and the rest.

Man, of course, often only knows his strongest feelings in the form of the particular passion, in the form of the 'evil inclination' which would lead him astray. In the nature of things, a man's greatest longing will fall on those things he encounters which promise to satisfy the longing. What he has to do, therefore, is direct the very energy of that feeling, that very impulse itself, away from the fortuitous to the necessary, away from the relative to the absolute. It is thus that he finds his way.[71]

The argument is typically Hasidic. By serving God in his own particular way, man helps to perfect his own self. He chooses to offer to God what he does best, and thereby fulfils the duty of every Jew to develop himself as best he can. A *zaddik* said:

It is the duty of every man in Israel to know and consider that in his nature he is unique in the world, and that there has never been another like him. For had there been another like him, he would not need to be in the world. Each individual is a new thing in the world, and must perfect his own nature in this world. For truly, it is because this does not happen that the coming of the Messiah is delayed.[72]

In accordance with his intrinsic uniqueness, each man's particular way will also be unique and new. The pupils of one of the earlier *zaddikim*, Yehiel Mikhael of Zloczov, were once puzzled by a text in the Book of Elijah which exhorts the Jew to struggle ceaselessly so that his works may measure up to those of the forefathers, Abraham, Isaac, and Jacob. To the young men, the admonition seemed absurd and impertinent. Rabbi Jehiel calmed them. Each of the patriarchs, he explained, had served God in a new way, special to himself and in harmony with his own personality, the one offering a worship of love, another of strict justice, another of beauty. The meaning of the text is that every Jew should try to do as they did, and renew the light of the Torah and the worship of God, not by repeating what had already been done, but by doing what remains to be accomplished.[73]

Every man, being a 'new thing in the world', must 'Sing to YHWH a new song' (Ps. 96: 1).

---

[71] *Werke*, iii. 721; *Hasidism and Modern Man*, 142.
[72] No source given; *Werke*, iii. 719–20; *Hasidism and Modern Man*, 139–40.
[73] *Werke*, iii. 265–6; *Tales of the Hasidim: Early Masters*, 147.

3. *Determination* A Hasid once decided to fast for a week, from Sabbath to Sabbath. By Friday, he was so thirsty he thought he would die, and seeing water nearby, ran up to drink. However, as he hurried along, it struck him that since he had only a few more hours of fasting to endure, it would be a pity to falter for want of a little more courage. Rather pleased with himself for showing such self-control, he therefore held back. Immediately, new qualms assailed him: would it not be better to break his fast than to commit the sin of pride? Sooner than allow this to happen, he consequently returned to the water for a drink—only to find that his thirst had left him. Later, he called at the house of his *zaddik*, presumably expecting to be commended for his perseverance. But when the Seer of Lublin noticed him standing at his door, he had only one word to say to him: 'Patchwork!'[74]

Buber uses this anecdote to exemplify the virtue of resolution. Rabbi Jacob Isaac, far from being impressed by his pupil's persistence, had found it deficient. Instead of making a firm decision before embarking on his ascetic exercise, the young man had zig-zagged between one uncertainty and the next. If before starting he had unified himself and his effort, the result would not have been patchwork, but all of one piece, like himself.

One of the six sons of an eccentric rabbi named Israel of Rizhyn (d. 1850) once came on some young man playing draughts. When he asked if they knew the rules, they were too embarrassed to answer at once, so he himself supplied a list of three. The first, he told them, 'is that two moves must not be made simultaneously. The second is that you can only move forwards and not backwards. And the third is that when you are on top, you can go wherever you like.'[75] Each of these rules was broken by the vacillating student of the Seer of Lublin. He should have decided on the one move of maintaining his fast, but had tried to combine it with a second move of containing his pride. He should have moved forwards resolutely, but had moved backwards irresolutely. Yet none of this would have diminished his endeavour if only he had been 'on top' of himself. If he had been unified within himself, his departures from the rules would themselves have formed part of a unified exercise.

4. *Begin with yourself* Whereas the advice to reflect on oneself is designed to conduce to self-knowledge, encouragement to begin with

[74] *Werke*, iii. 437; *Tales of the Hasidim: Early Masters*, 316.
[75] *Werke*, iii. 725; *Tales of the Hasidim: Early Masters*, 150–1.

oneself means that a person should put his own house in order before attempting to set the world to rights. The peace and harmony of society at large depend on the peace and harmony of the individual heart.

Such was the teaching of Rabbi Isaac of Vorki (d. 1848), whom Buber portrays as a noble figure memorable for his enlightened wisdom.[76] Engaged one day in a discussion, the rabbi contradicted a remark to the effect that the well-being of a household turns on the servant, and that if he is efficient and honest, all prospers as it did in the hands of Joseph. Once, said the rabbi, he had thought the same, but his teacher had insisted that everything depends on the master of the house. Rabbi Isaac explained how he had come to change his mind.

In my youth, you see, I had great trouble with my wife, and although I was able to put up with her myself, I was sorry for the servants. So I went to my teacher, Rabbi David of Lelov, and asked him whether I should confront my wife. He replied, 'Why do you speak to me? Speak to yourself.' I had to think over what he had said for quite a time before I understood. But then I did understand when I remembered a saying of the holy Baalshem Tov: 'There are thought, word and deed. Thought corresponds to one's wife, word to one's children, deed to one's servants. He who arranges these three aright within himself, for him everything turns to good.'[77]

The lesson learnt by Isaac of Vorki is that, contrary to the customary belief, conflict does not spring from motives of which the opposing parties are conscious, and which derive basically from the situations and events in which they are involved. But neither is the other explanation wholly satisfactory, that the source of conflict is to be found in certain unconscious complexes, and that its motives are merely symptoms of a sickness. Hasidism accepts that external discord points undeniably to inner turmoil, but instead of tracing it to isolated complexes of one kind or another, it involves the whole man. The Hasidic masters maintained that to distinguish this element from that in the human psyche, and to separate one process from another, is an impediment to understanding man as a whole, an understanding which alone can lead to real change and healing, first of the individual, and subsequently of relation between the individual and others.

Another difference between the Hasidic and the secular approach to the problem of conflict is that in Hasidism man is not viewed as an

---

[76] *Werke*, iii. 148: *Tales of the Hasidim: Later Masters*, 46.
[77] *Werke*, iii. 680; *Tales of the Hasidim: Later Masters*, 290.

object of study and research, but as a subject in control of his own condition and destiny. As Rabbi Bunam said, alluding to the words of the sages, 'Seek peace in your own place': 'You can seek peace nowhere except in yourself, until you find it there. We read in the psalm, "There is no peace in my bones because of my sin" (Ps. 38: 4). Not until a man has found peace in himself, can he go on to seek it in the world.'[78]

Having recognized that the situations of external conflict in which he is implicated are externalizations of a conflict within himself, he must first solve his own personal problem. As a changed individual, at peace with himself, he will then be able to live at peace with his fellows. But where should he look for the source of inner discord? According to Buber's re-wording of the doctrine of the Baalshem, the roots of all disharmony in the self lie in a failure to ensure a right order of precedence in respect of the three fundamental elements of personal existence. Inner conflict, he writes, 'is conflict between three principles in the nature and life of man: the principle of thought, the principle of word and the principle of deed. The origin of all conflict between me and my fellow-men is that I do not say what I think, and I do not do what I say.'[79]

Thought is the marriage-partner of the master of the household. Word is the offspring of them both and should be subject to them both. And deed is the servant of all three. Such is the order which the individual has to establish and maintain in himself if order and peace are to exist in the society of which he is part.

5. *Do not be preoccupied with yourself* It would seem contradictory to ask people with one breath to reflect on themselves, and with the next not to be preoccupied with themselves. Yet the intention is clear. Hasidism demands self-knowledge and self-integration, but it warns against the temptations of self-absorption. Rabbi Haim of Zans (d. 1876) was not one of the greatest of the *zaddikim* and was indeed once rebuked for his egocentricity. The day following the marriage of his daughter to the son of Eliezer of Dzikov, a fellow *rebbe*, Haim hurried along to his new relative hoping that now that they were part of the same family group, he could indulge with him in a pleasant orgy of introspection and self-castigation. 'O relative,' he started, ' "now that you are close to me, I can tell you what troubles my heart. See, my hair

---

[78] *Werke*, iii. 729; *Hasidism and Modern Man*, 157–8. [79] Ibid.

and beard are already white, and I have still not done penance!" "O relative," was Rabbi Eliezer's answer, "you think only of yourself. Forget yourself and think of the world." [80] In addition to the familiar Hasidic twist which Eliezer injects into his advice ('Forget yourself and think of the *world*', where one expects to read 'Forget yourself and think of *God*'), it is clear from his response that he not only felt that Haim was exaggerating his faults and underestimating the penance he had assuredly already done; he was also conveying to his lugubrious relation that he should not plague himself with memories of wrongs committed, but should direct the energy spent on self-reproach towards doing what he had been born to do in the world.

Another cause of the disapproval of undue preoccupation with past misdeeds expressed by Hasidic teachers is the sensible one that it leads to a condition of spiritual ill-health. With too much meditation on sin, the masters argued, one becomes bogged down in sin. The Rabbi of Ger (d. 1866), himself a humble and self-critical man, warned his congregation on the Day of Atonement:

He who constantly discusses and considers a wrong that he has committed, does not cease to think of the base thing he has done, and whatever one thinks, therein one is; one's soul is well and truly there in whatever one thinks. He therefore is present in his baseness. He will certainly not be able to make his *teshuvah*, for his spirit will coarsen and his heart grow fusty, and he may in addition be overcome by melancholy. What would you? Stir the mud here, stir the mud there, it remains mud. Sinned, or not sinned, what does heaven get out of it? During the time that I ruminate over it, I can string pearls for heaven's joy. Therefore we read, 'Turn from evil and do what is good' (Ps. 34: 15). Turn from evil completely, do not brood on it, but do what is good. You have done wrong? Counteract it by doing what is right. [81]

Believing every human soul to be whole in itself, and part of a whole, and looking forward to the perfection of the whole through the perfection of the constituent parts, Hasidism discouraged exaggerated introspection because it wished to ensure that the greater cause should not be overlooked on account of absorption in the smaller. Rabbi Menahem Mendel of Kotzk once observed that he required only three things from his people: 'Not to peep outside yourselves. Not to peep into others. And not to have yourselves in mind.' [82] As interpreted by

---

[80] *Werke*, iii. 599–600; *Tales of the Hasidim: Later Masters*, 214.

[81] *Werke*, iii. 699; *Tales of the Hasidim: Later Masters*, 306–7.

[82] *Werke*, iii. 671; *Tales of the Hasidim: Later Masters*, 282.

Buber, Menahem Mendel's admonition not to 'peep outside yourselves' is intended to caution people to preserve and sanctify their souls in their own way and in their own place, and not to envy alien ways or places. That they are not to 'peep into others' means that they are to respect the mystery of their fellow-beings and not attempt to penetrate or exploit it. And that they are not to have themselves in mind means that they are not to place themselves, either in private or in public life, at the centre of their own attention.

6. *Here where one is* A person should sanctify his soul *in his own place*. The world, so the teaching goes, is made holy by the presence in it of the Shekhinah. Therefore, existence on earth is not, as some religions maintain, a dream in which people have to grope their way. Nor is it the unreal antechamber to a real life in another world. Present life is no less true and no less important than life in the world to come. More than this, life in the minuscule space allotted to each one is of no less value than life in the world as a whole.

According to Rabbi Simha Bunam (d. 1827), Rabbi Eisik, son of Rabbi Yekel of Cracow, dreamt three times that he would find riches in a particular situation not far from the royal castle in Prague. He went there to search for the treasure, but dared not start digging because sentries were posted nearby. After a short time, a captain of the guard noticed him waiting around and asked him what he was looking for. Rabbi Eisik recounted the story of his dream. His companion laughed heartily when he heard it and told him that precisely the same experience had occurred to him. He had dreamt that he travelled to Cracow to the house of a man called Eisik son of Yekel, and found treasure under his stove. But of course, he had not been so silly as actually to go there to see if the dream were true. Think how stupid he would have looked, searching about in a place where every other man is called Eisik son of Yekel! Rabbi Eisik, when he heard this, said nothing, but went straight home and dug the treasure from under his stove. And with it he built a synagogue which he called 'the *shool* of Reb Eisik son of Reb Yekel'. ' "Pay heed to this story," Rabbi Bunam used to add, and listen to what it tells you: that there is something which you cannot find anywhere in the world, not even in the house of the *zaddik*, and yet a place exists where you can find it.'[83] The treasure we look for, Buber suggests, is fulfilment of our life on

---

[83] *Werke*, iii. 629–30; *Tales of the Hasidim: Later Masters*, 245–6.

earth. We become restless. We imagine that if we go somewhere else, or do something else, we will discover it. But all the time it is lying under our feet. Our treasure is to be found here where we are.

It is said of one holy man that the streets of heaven were as bright to him as those of his own home town. Characteristically, Hasidism reverses the analogy and teaches that it is far better to find the streets of one's own town as bright as those of heaven, for it is where we live that we have to release the hidden light of God's indwelling Presence and allow it to shine.

Nothing leads to greater fulfilment than to live in real and true relation with the people, creatures, and things of one's own immediate environment. And nothing more reliably ensures participation in true existence than to perform one's daily tasks with holy intention. For the fundamental meaning of life on earth is that God's Kingdom should be brought into being through the realization and actualization of his indwelling Presence. When Rabbi Menahem Mendel of Kotzk asked some learned men where God dwells, they laughed and quoted the well-known text to the effect that the whole world is full of his Glory. Menahem Mendel would not accept this slick answer. According to him, God takes up his abode wherever he is admitted. And the only dwelling-place which every individual is qualified to prepare for God, and into which he can admit him, is the place, the situation, in which he himself stands.

———

One last aspect of Hasidism needs to be mentioned, one that permeates Judaism through and through: the idea of unity. From God's own unity, to the unity of those who imitate him, to the longed-for unity of all things in God, the notion of the One has engaged the minds of Jewish thinkers from the beginning until now.

For Hasidism, which drew not only on biblical teaching, but on the centuries of religious thought produced by the study of the Bible, the concept of unity comprised the very warp and woof of existence. It reached into every corner of life, so that holy and profane, beginning and end, this world and the world to come, were viewed as simultaneously one, and requiring to be made one (like God and his indwelling Presence).

The Hasid, as we have seen more than once, was concerned for God's destiny in the world rather than for the world itself or for man himself. He accepted the doctrine of God's unity and uniqueness, and therefore, in the spirit of authentic religiousness taught by the Baal Shem Tov, set out to realize it in life—by realizing his own unity and uniqueness as the person he was. He acknowledged the doctrine of God's perfect wholeness, and therefore applied himself to realizing wholeness in life—by realizing perfectly his own humanity. He did not set for himself a goal of super-human holiness, but aimed to become 'humanly holy' to God.[84]

Cleave to God, worship God, in humility, joy, with holy intention and love. Know yourself, begin with yourself, avoid concentrating on yourself, be resolute, find your particular vocation, make your own place holy by admitting God into it so that he may be present with you there. This, in briefest summary, is the Hasidic recipe for the sanctification of present existence. Its language may be a far cry from Buber's, but it must nevertheless be listened to and heard if Buber's own message is to be understood. The perfect man in Hasidism is one who, through imitating God in his attributes of unity and helpful love, *becomes* perfectly man.

Hasidism says the worlds can fulfil their destiny to become one in so far as the life of man becomes one. How is this to be understood? Is a perfect unity of living existence conceivable except in God himself? Israel's confession of faith in the unity of God does not merely state that there is no God beside him, but also that he alone is unity. Here, the interpreter must insert a word. If man can become 'humanly holy', i.e. as man, to the extent and in the manner of man, and indeed, as it is written, 'to me', i.e. before the Face of God, then he, the individual man, can, in accordance with the measure of his personal potential, and in the manner of his personal ability, become one before the Face of God. Man cannot approach the divine by reaching beyond the human. He can approach it by becoming the person he, this individual, was created to become. This seems to me to be the everlasting kernel of Hasidic life and Hasidic teaching.[85]

[84] *Werke*, iii. 940; *Hasidism and Modern Man*, 31.
[85] *Werke*, iii. 947; *Hasidism and Modern Man*, 43.

15

Presence as Religiousness

BUBER'S perfect man is also one who becomes perfectly whole, perfectly what a human being should be, by living in relation with what is Above and what is Below, but the road he walks is not that of Hasidism. Buber's prescription is not for a religion centred on the Presence of God, but for religiousness in the form of man's presence with present existence. On the other hand, his understanding of this religiousness cannot be grasped apart from the religion of Hasidism. To ignore or overlook the association of the everlasting *You* with the Jewish and Hasidic concept of the Deity is to place the supreme *Vis-à-Vis* at the mercy of every sort of intellectual and theological distortion. Likewise, to be unaware that the radical and all-pervasive Jewish consciousness of the unity of God underlies Buber's preoccupation with unification in its various aspects, is to allow its psychological and philosophical implications to be mishandled so that they may dominate and even obliterate the religious connotations integral to the idea of unity.

It is interesting that none of Hasidism's counsels and values are lost sight of entirely when collated with Buber's.[1] Some become less obvious because Buber lays his emphasis elsewhere. Some gain in significance and topicality. Even the Hasidic virtue of ardour, although formally stripped of the element of ecstasy, continues to emit its glowing warmth in the love of God and his creation written into every page on the life of dialogue.

It might seem that because of Buber's habit of reasoning from earth upward, from man to God, his path must be in direct conflict with that of Hasidism, which leads from heaven downward, but when the two are studied side by side, it becomes clear how much the reverse is true. The point of departure may differ, but the journey covers the same ground.

The Hasidic life is accepted from God, is ruled by God, and is

[1] The only possible exception is joy (*simhah*), of which there is little sign in Buber's writings.

directed towards God. God is its beginning and its end. Assuming without question that the foremost duty of the Jew is to love and imitate YHWH, it teaches that this love and imitation demand, and inculcate, a corresponding care and love of YHWH's creation, and that the effect of such behaviour may be seen in a growth of resemblance to YHWH in his followers and worshippers. Therefore if, for the sake of clarity, we were to divide the Hasidic way into stages, the first would be God. The second would be the worship of God through a life of service and love in the world. The third would be, in consequence of the service and love, a reflection of the attributes of God in his faithful servant.

Buber's way is on the face of it quite different. His traveller does not ostensibly take off from a belief in God. His starting-point down the road of life is marked by uncertainty, and in place of the relation implicit in an untroubled faith in an omnipresent and all-powerful Supreme Being, his first stage is relation with the things, events, and persons of everyday existence. The second stage is that, his *I* having learned how to 'say you', i.e. how to enter into and maintain what Buber calls '*you*-relation', he develops a measure of personal integrity and maturity. The third stage is that, having become a whole and integrated *I*, he can, if he so desires, move on to relation with the everlasting *You*.

The two sequences are easier to follow when seen together side by side.

The Hasidic way

1. Relation with God.
2. A life of care and service in the world for God's sake.
3. The realization in man made perfect of God's own attributes.

Buber's way

1. *I–you* relation.
2. The realization and unification of the *I*.
3. *I–You* relation.

The dissimilarities are striking. One way begins with God–man relation, the other ends with it: or so it would seem, until one realizes that it is an unspoken assumption in Buber's scheme that from the start some sort of sense must exist, however flickering, of the presence of *You*. Otherwise, how would a person catch, as Buber asserts, glimpses of the supreme *Vis-à-Vis* in the finite *you* addressed and encountered? Again, the progress from Hasidic stage 1 to stage 2 is identical with Buber's progress from stage 3 back to stage 1. For of course there is no ultimate *I–You* relation any more than there is an ultimate attainment of holiness in Hasidism. Both ways are without end. Hasidism is intended to lead to an ever-increasing likeness to God the Helper—and hence to an even greater capacity for service and love in the world and an ever stronger faith in God. Buber's life of dialogue is intended to be perfected in *You*-relation—and hence move on to ever more intimate and responsible *I–you* relation, and to an ever more marked and substantial growth of personal integrity and unity. Finally, the Hasidic stage 3 is the effect of stage 2, just as Buber's stage 2 is the outcome of stage 1, the realization of God's attributes being, in effect, the realization and unification of the self.

Buber's substitution of *you*-relation for plain relation with God as the beginning of his way has nevertheless three far-reaching logical consequences which distinguish it sharply from Hasidism's religion of Presence.

The first is that whereas one who starts out from a belief in God has him for helpful Companion, Counsellor, and Guide into the second stage of the way, and on into the third, Buber's man has no sure and steadfast conviction of this kind to support him for a good part of his journey. He is granted only 'intimations' of an everlasting *You*; he can hear no more than his 'breathing' in the *vis-à-vis* of the world. He has to look about in his environment of time and circumstance for what signals there may be of eternity. And even when he reaches true and perfect relation, he still 'knows' nothing.

The second consequence is that the religious agnosticism implied in Buber's approach precludes any conventional *imitatio dei*. We cannot imitate what we do not know. Where contact with God is made at the end of the journey and not at the beginning, understanding of his nature will come from material gathered along the way, which will also probably include traditional teachings. It is not possible in any case to imagine supreme Presence except out of the experience and practice of presence. We cannot envisage an ultimate Wholeness and Unity except out of the experience and practice of wholeness and unity. We come to our *You* not empty-handed, as psychological and spiritual paupers. We are what we behold, and we behold what we are, as Ruysbroek writes.

The third and even more surprising consequence of Buber's teaching is that where relation with *You* is postulated as the effect of relation with *you*, and not its cause, *I–You* relation itself has no independence. The three spheres of relation as set out in *I and You* are (1) that of man and the natural world; (2) that of man and man; (3) that of man and the things of the mind or spirit, the *geistige Wesenheiten* of art, knowledge, and example (of which more later). These three are precisely what they are explained to be. No fourth sphere is allocated to 'God'. The everlasting *You* in this schema is as it were the supreme Knot beyond and transcending every relational bond, towards which they all lead and into which they are tied.[2]

What happens to the crucial Hasidic doctrine of the sparks in Buber's formulation of the life of dialogue, to the myth that nothing exists, material or immaterial, which is not a 'shell' containing a fragment of God's indwelling Presence dispersed at the time of the creation of the world? How much remains of the conviction that 'mending' is man's primary task, repairing God's broken unity?

In Buber's thought the allegory of the sparks is not abandoned but re-composed. Where kabbalism speaks of the transcendent God and the indwelling Presence, Buber treats of the indwelling presence of *you* and the everlasting *You*. Where in Lurianic kabbalah the Presence is a fragment of the dispersed light of 'Without End' (*Ein-Sof*), in Buber's thought the many presences of *you* are to be joined in the Presence of *You*. Where the sparks have their substance from God, the *you* of finite relation gives of its substance to the everlasting *You*.

It is again a matter of where one begins. In both myths, whatever comes down returns upward, and whatever goes up, comes down.

Also of great significance is Buber's application to the life of dialogue of the stimulating hypothesis that creation, revelation, and redemption are dynamic, that they are continuous processes demanding man's collaboration. Each is represented as inseparable from *you*-relation.

To consider creation first. Entry into immediate relation is creative, causing *you* to 'be there' where formerly no *you* existed and with it the *I* of *I–you* relation (which is quite different from the *I* of *I–it*). Creativity extends, furthermore, to time. No present time exists except while I say *you*. People and things regarded objectively from the stand of *I–it*

---

[2] Martin Buber, *Werke*, 3 vols. (Kösel–Lambert Schneider, 1962–4), i. 81; *I and Thou*, trans. R. Gregor Smith, 2nd edn. (Scribner–T. & T. Clark, 1958), 6. Elsewhere, Buber drafts this arrangement slightly differently as a life-relationship to the world and to things; a life-relationship to men, individuals as well as to the many; and a life-relationship to 'that which shines through all this and at the same time radically transcends it, the Mystery of Being which the philosopher calls the Absolute and the religious God, but which even for him who rejects both connotations cannot factually be eliminated from his situation'. See *Werke*, i. 375; 'What is Man?', *Between Man and Man*, trans. R. Gregor Smith (Fontana, 1961), 215.

consist of qualities and quantities belonging to the past, of characteristics already acquired. A tree is judged valuable if it *has grown* straight
and tall. A person is found useful because he *has won* influence in
appropriate places. A cat is acceptable because it *has proved* itself a
good mouser. Present time comes into being only in the direct presence of *I* with *you*.[3] When he enters the world of relation, a person has
a Now which was not formerly there: indeed, he possesses a present
only in so far as he possesses a *you*-world.

Revelation is also an essential ingredient of *I–you* relation. In
whichever sphere it is established, lines of communication open along
which the spirit travels to and fro. Nothing can refuse to become *you*,
and similarly nothing can refuse to serve as a channel of revelation. In
the life of dialogue as Buber expounds it, the only limits to revelation
are human insensitivity and lack of awareness.[4]

Redemption is equally part of *I–you* relation. Not only does it
continually redeem the *vis-à-vis* from the exile of its own dispersion,
but it reunites it with the *I* to which it belongs. Conversely, the saying
of *you*, which requires the whole presence of the *I*, redeems the *I* from
its own dividedness and disunity.

These observations concerning creation, revelation, and redemption
in Buber's scheme take into account only *I–you* relation on the three
levels of man and nature, man and man, and man and ideals or ideas,
but they all apply equally to perfect relation. To say *You* is creative,
causing the supreme *Vis-à-Vis* to 'be there', as well as the *I* of the basic
word *I–You*. It is revelatory. It is redemptive, redeeming the everlasting *You* from its own disunity, but also from its separation from the
indwelling *you* of the world.

When Hasidism and Buber's life of dialogue are collated, one
shared word stands out: presence. Or more precisely, presence and
Presence as manifestations of human and divine love. The Hasid was
persuaded by his sense of the Presence of God to be present with the
world. Buber hoped to pass on the lesson that to be present with the
world leads to consciousness of Presence.

---

[3] *Werke*, i. 100; *I and Thou*, 33.
[4] *Werke*, i. 183; 'Dialogue', *Between Man and Man*, 27.

16

I *and* you

BEFORE coming properly to grips with the first stage of Buber's way, a word has to be said apropos of his rather lax use of the two terms 'encounter' (*Begegnung*) and 'relation' (*Beziehung*). One would assume, given the carefulness with which he uses language, that these two lynch-pins of his vocabulary cannot be synonyms. Yet a search through the literature devoted to Buber's work will give the impression that 'relation' and 'encounter' are bandied about almost indiscriminately, and that for the most part they either have the same significance, or are so nearly identical as makes no difference.

Sometimes, it is true, the distinction between them has been recognized, but in the two instances which come immediately to mind, it has been done in a way that generates more confusion than it clears up. Malcolm Diamond, in his explanation of Buber's contention that the *I–it* attitude is insufficient for human existence, adds: 'Beings elicit a deeper response from man, the I–Thou relation which is grounded in encounter and engagement.'[1] This would seem to imply that 'encounter' and 'engagement' are not the fruits of relation, but the ground out of which it grows. You have your 'encounter' or 'engagement', and after that your 'I–Thou relation'.

Another writer, Emmanuel Levinas, offers a similar interpretation. In his opinion, 'I–Thou relation is nothing but a realization of the meeting.'[2] So here again, relation is represented as a secondary development. And even 'the meeting' is defined rather curiously by this author as a 'momentary present which cannot be connected to other temporal instants in order to form a history or biography'. As for relation, it is a 'fulguration of moments without continuity, not a coherent connection of parts nor a final possession'.[3]

In all fairness, it should be repeated that whatever uncertainty exists in this area of Buber's thought is largely his own fault. He does, in fact,

[1] M. Diamond, 'Dialogue and Theology', in P. A. Schilpp and M. Friedman, eds., *The Philosophy of Martin Buber* (Open Court, 1967), 236.

[2] Emanuel Levinas, 'Martin Buber and the Theory of Knowledge', in Schilpp and Friedman, *The Philosophy of Martin Buber*, 144.   [3] Ibid.

explicitly discriminate between relation and encounter, as we shall see, but not emphatically enough, and certainly not consistently enough. It may be that, as in his treatment of the divine Name, he was carried away by the larger perspectives of his insight, and forgot that most of us would need to be guided step by step to where he had arrived in one stride. If, in any case, an explication is required beyond what appears in *I and You*, it can be found in the answer he gives to an enquiry put to him by the French existentialist philosopher, Gabriel Marcel. Marcel is worried about the aptness of the word *Beziehung*, relation, for the sense Buber intends, yet has to confess that he can think of no alternative. Nevertheless, if relation is to be understood as a 'connection between two terms' or between 'data capable of being treated as terms', how, he asks Buber, can *I* and *Thou* be thought of in this way? Surely, *Begegnung*, encounter, is a better choice?[4]

Buber replies:

The question is asked whether the German term 'Beziehung' (rendered more or less accurately by 'relationship' in English), and in particular the French word 'relation', correspond to what I mean, where discontinuity is an essential element. The question is a valid one, and it is quite understandable that the term 'Begegnung' (encounter) should be thought more suitable. But 'Begegnung' signifies only something actual. A person who remains with someone he has encountered, encountered him in effect earlier. But the event is over; he no longer encounters him. The concept of 'Beziehung', by contrast, opens up the possibility—only a possibility but a possibility nonetheless—of latency. Two friends, two lovers, must repeatedly experience how *I–you* is succeeded by *I–him* or *I–her*; but does it not often seem in those moments as though a bird with a broken wing is trying secretly to fly? And does not an incomprehensible and, as it were, vibrating continuity manifest itself at times between *you*-moments? In the relationship of the true believer to God, the latent *You* is unmistakable; even when he is unable to turn to him with a wholly collected soul, the Presence of God is primordially real to him.[5] One can only try to

[4] Gabriel Marcel, 'I and Thou', in Schilpp and Friedman, *The Philosophy of Martin Buber*, 44.

[5] In Hasidism, relation with God was understood to swing from a state of *katnut*, meaning 'smallness', to *gadlut*, 'greatness'. 'From R. Israel Baal Shem onwards, *devekuth* was understood in empiric, psychological terms as occurring in alternations of exaltation and lowness, high and low tide, climax and anti-climax of the spiritual life. The low tide was usually termed *katnuth* and the high tide *gadluth* . . . Dissipation of the spirit and lack of spiritual concentration are the marks of the former, even as intensive concentration of the soul upon God is the mark of the latter, which is considered throughout Hasidic literature as the ideal state. Various theories developed in Hasidism concerning the role of this lowness of spirit in which *devekuth* diminishes or ceases

overcome the lack of an adequate designation by combining the skeleton-word 'Beziehung' with other more concrete and restricted terms, such as 'Begegnung', contact, communication, depending on the context. It can be replaced by none of them.[6]

Is this not quite straightforward? Without formally defining either notion, Buber intimates that relation is a state of being connected with another, of being aware of another, in such a way that withdrawals into the distance of *it*-ness retain a possibility of future closeness. Encounter, on the other hand, is not a psychological state, or an attitude of mind, or a personal condition, but an *event*.

And is it not also plain from Buber's answer to Marcel that, contrary to the statements of Diamond and Levinas, *I–you* relation is neither a realization of encounter, nor grounded in encounter, the corollary being that encounter comes first and relation second? The very reverse: relation comes first. Considering that encounter between *I* and *you* undoubtedly constitutes the high peak of relational life, this may seem strange, but on reflection, the conclusion is logical. Encounter signifies 'only something actual'. It cannot last. Relation endures, or can do so; the moving away of the *I* into the position *I–it* may be the prelude to a new *I–you*.

In sum, relation can exist without encounter. But encounter cannot occur except from a state of relation.

And what is encounter? It is what happens when two *I*s move towards each other as *you*. It is the coming together of two *I*s with two *you*s. It is the entry of two *I*s into existential communion with one another.

Encounter is a privilege bestowed on me. I myself, of my own volition, enter into the position of relation and thereby fulfil the 'act of my being, my being's act'.[7] Encounter, however, is not done by me, but granted to me. '*You* encounters me by grace: it is not found by seeking ... *You* encounters me. But I enter into immediate relation with it.'[8] It may

---

altogether as a consequence of the great spiritual effort preceding it': J. G. Weiss, 'R. Abraham Kalisker's Concept of Communion with God and Man', *Journal of Jewish Studies*, 6/2 (1955), 91.

[6] M. Buber, 'Antwort', in P. A. Schilpp and M. Friedman, eds., *Martin Buber* (Kohlhammer, 1963), 603–4; 'Replies to my Critics', in Schilpp and Friedman, eds., *The Philosophy of Martin Buber*, 705.

[7] Martin Buber, *Werke*, 3 vols. (Kösel–Lambert Schneider, 1962–4), i. 85; *I and Thou*, trans. R. Gregor Smith, 2nd edn. (Scribner–T. & T. Clark, 1958), 11.

[8] Ibid.

be recalled that in *I and You* Buber observes of *you*-relation that it does more, and is capable of more, than *it* knows, that it is the very 'cradle of real life'.[9] And if we ask what 'real life' is, what do we hear? That 'all real life is encounter'.[10]

This would seem on the face of it to be the perfect summary of Buber's teaching on relation and encounter, but further thought rouses doubts and we find ourselves faced with yet another problem. Are we to deduce that where there is no encounter, life is 'unreal', that life's 'reality' is linked to the momentary blessedness and privilege of encounter between *I* and *you* (and *You*)? This is hardly in line with other pronouncements by Buber on the subject of reality.

On the other hand, it appears to be in encounter rather than in relation pure and simple that the creative, redemptive, and revelatory processes take place which Buber associates with the dialogical life. It is from the great and little encounters between *I* and *you* and *I* and *You* that new creation, new redemption, new revelation derive.

The basic premiss of Buber's exposition of the life of dialogue is that throughout our existence we alternately move towards, and away from, the people, things, and events which make up our life. We either approach close, and from that stand lose sight of qualities, quantities, faults, virtues, values, and dimensions. Or we retire to where we can focus on whatever is before us, and from that distance carry out the indispensable functions of learning, watching, experiencing, evaluating, etc. Moreover, passing from relation to irrelation and back again, two quite different *I*s come into play, the *I* of *I–you* and the *I* of *I–it*.

It is a mistake to suppose that anything pejorative is attached by Buber to irrelation. Nothing is wrong with the objectivity of *I–it* . . . as long as it is able to change to *I–you*, and does not become so habitual that entry into relation is impeded. On the contrary, irrelation is inevitable and good, if only for the reason that *I* cannot be present with *you* except by leaving the world of *it*.[11] 'That the first (*I–it*) is the

---

[9] *Werke*, i. 83; *I and Thou*, 9.
[10] *Werke*, i. 85; *I and Thou*, 11.
[11] R. E. Wood, in *Martin Buber's Ontology* (North Western University Press, 1969), describes the two basic movements of *I–you* and *I–it* as '*Rückbiegung*, or bending back to oneself, and *Hinwendung*, or turning towards the Other' (p. 37). This is quite incorrect. The passage on which he bases his interpretation has nothing to do with the swing between objectivity and presence, but is a discussion on what constitutes genuine

prerequisite of the second (*I–you*), arises from the fact that it is possible
to enter into relation only with a being that is at a distance from us: or
more exactly, with one that has become an independent *vis-à-vis*.'[12]

In Buber's view, the relational impulse is innate. Before birth, the
baby is attached to its physical mother, but also to the great Mother,
the 'undivided pre-form primordial world',[13] and its first instinct on
coming into the world is to replace this inborn *you*. It feels, tastes,
watches, and 'speaks' to the things of its new environment, not as
objects, but as co-existing beings. True relation is impossible at this
stage because the baby is unaware of being separate from what sur-
rounds him. But once he becomes conscious of himself as an *I* distinct
from the rest, and therewith acquires an *it*-world out of which he can
step into relation, his life-long swing between *I–you* and *I–it* has
started on its course.

A few further preliminary remarks are called for.

I–you is exclusive. I can address only one *you* at a time: though the
occasional rare spirit has been able to include all in his *I–you*, to
love all men. (But this anticipates perfect relation, which must await
discussion until later.)

Next, *I–you* relation is direct. Preconceptions, needs, judgements,
desires, phantasies, come between *I* and *you*. To say *you* to a *vis-à-vis*, I
must be present with the whole of myself, accepting whatsoever or
whomsoever is there, as it is there, in the manner that it is there, at that
actual moment of time.

Further, *I–you* relation, although it is not 'only something actual'
like encounter, is transient in the sense that it is never permanent. Its
duration can be quite brief, and it can even die; but when it endures, it
alternates by necessity between actuality and latency. Nothing exists
that cannot become my *you*; but likewise, every *you* (apart from the

dialogue. Cf. 'Dialogue', in *Between Man and Man*, trans. R. Gregor Smith (Fontana,
1961); *Werke*, i. 195–7. Sometimes, Buber writes here, what seems to be dialogue is
really a monologue, a bending back to the self, instead of a turning towards the partner in
conversation. The same word, *Rückbiegung*, appears towards the end of *I and You* in the
context of bending back towards the Revealer instead of heeding his revelation, Buber's
intention here being to stress the temptation to be concerned with God rather than with
the world. See *Werke*, i. 157; *I and Thou*, 115.

[12] *Werke*, i. 412; 'Distance and Relation', in *The Knowledge of Man*, ed. M. Friedman
(Allen & Unwin, 1965), 60.   [13] *Werke*, i. 95; *I and Thou*, 25.

everlasting *You*) must repeatedly retire into the distance of irrelation and become an *it*.

Lastly, *I–you* relation entails reciprocity. I affect my *you* and my *you* affects me, even when the effect is imperceptible to either or both.

MAN AND NATURE

One of the specialities of the life of dialogue—an enormous advance, some may agree, on the usual preachments of religion—is that it presupposes a living relationship of love embracing not merely one's fellow-men, but things of the spirit and the mind, and also animate and inanimate nature, the beasts, plants, and elements of the material universe. This latter relation, as Buber expounds it, takes place below the level of speech; this saying of *you* is wordless. And certainly the things and creatures of nature have not themselves the ability to 'speak' as we understand speech. But relation here is as direct, exclusive, and reciprocal as *I–you* relation elsewhere. I address myself to my *vis-à-vis*, whether vegetable, animal, or mineral, as 'one being alone, and each one only as being'.[14] There is no imputation whatever of any mystical rapport with 'nature' as a whole. Relation with a *vis-à-vis* is immediate. To adopt the illustration in *I and You*, I cannot say *you* to a tree, and at the same time consider it in terms of profit as timber, or of adornment as an addition to my garden, or of study as an object of botanical research. When I say *you* to a tree, I am simply present with it; its whole unique self is present with me and to me.

---

[14] *Werke*, i. 100; *I and Thou*, 32. R. E. Wood, mentioned above as being under the impression that the *I–it* attitude is a bending back towards the self, makes another mistake in describing the sphere of relation with nature as 'the region of the subhuman'. 'Sub-liminal' is the term Buber employs, referring not to the natural world itself, but to communication with it. The *limen*, as has been explained, is that of speech. See Wood, *Martin Buber's Ontology*, 42. The same book also provides the reader with a totally misleading chart in which we see man, above him God, below him nature, and in the middle, a little square for the Between and for the 'forms' of 'acting', 'thinking', and 'doing'. Such an arrangement is definitely not Buber's. In his synthesis, nature, man, and spirit are three gates forming one great portico to relation with the everlasting *You*. If a sketch were to be drawn at all, it would show a man, and beyond him gates bearing the legends 'natural world', 'human world', and 'world of the spirit'. And from the man's mouth, three *you*s would issue, each passing through its own gate and meeting in the supreme and all-embracing *You*. As for the 'Between', figuratively speaking this can best be described as the dash in *I–you*, the space between *I* and *you* where whatever happens, happens. The Between is the loving road of the spirit, over which its journeys to and fro between *I* and *you*.

Reciprocity in this area is less easy to grasp. There can be little doubt that animals, for instance, can on their own humble level affect and be affected by *I–you* relation. They can even achieve fleeting *I–you* encounter. But not everyone will accept that the same is feasible in the vegetable world. Yet evidence has been produced suggesting that plants are more sensitive than we imagine. The effect of *you*-relation, according to this, is to be seen in their health and growth,[15] which is presumably what Buber means when he contends that reciprocity is manifested here as one 'of being itself, one that is solely being'.[16] In regard to the inorganic, it is even harder to know what to conclude. Buber laments at one point that so much can never break through the 'crust of thing-ness', seeming thereby to imply that the inanimate is incapable of reciprocity. Nevertheless he makes this remark while regretting that one of his most important insights—that the *I* is not 'inside' the self but indivisible from *I–you* and *I–it*—did not occur between himself and the piece of quartz he was at that time holding in his hand, but in himself alone. Are we to understand that he felt this to have been his fault, and that the event could have been one of reciprocal relation if he had managed it differently?

Of the creative, revelatory, and redemptive forces at work in *I–you* encounter with nature, little needs to be added to what has already been said. Here, too, all is a potential channel of revelation, and here too, redemption is from multiplicity into unity. Here, too, creation is the causing of the *vis-à-vis* to 'be there' by being there with it. 'The living wholeness and unity of the tree, denied to the sharpest gaze of the investigator and disclosed to one who says *you*, is there precisely when *he* is there; he permits the tree to manifest it, and the existent tree does so.'[17]

Buber appends an observation to the second edition of *I and You* which, although he makes it apropos of relation with animals, is perhaps applicable to *you*-relation in every area of the natural world. Some people, he notes, have the ability to evoke a specially strong reaction in living creatures, and the more genuine their saying of *you*, the stronger it is. Such persons are 'on the whole not "animal", but spiritual by nature.'[18]

[15] See Peter Tompkins and Christopher Bird, *The Secret Life of Plants* (Allen Lane, 1974).
[16] *Werke*, i. 163; *I and Thou*, 126.   [17] Ibid.
[18] *Werke*, i. 152; *I and Thou*, 123.

MAN AND MAN

This is the one relational sphere in which *you* is said and heard in the form of speech. As it is the theatre in which we are most at home, it is also much easier to recognize here all that Buber writes about *I–you* relation and encounter and their effects. When I confront a human *vis-à-vis* as my *you*, we read,

and say to him the basic word *I–you*, he is neither a thing among things nor composed of things. He is not a *he* or a *she* among neighbouring *he*'s and *she*'s, a point inscribed in a world-grid of space and time. He is not a character to be described and experienced, a loose bundle of named idiosyncrasies. Distinct and all of a piece, he is *you* and he fills the heavens. Not as though nothing exists apart from him, but all else lives in *his* light.[19]

In this setting, we can see more realistically than in the sphere of nature or the immaterial that the presence of *I* with *you* is essentially a display of love, and we understand better Buber's meaning when he distinguishes love from feelings of love. Love is a stand which I occupy, feelings are what I 'have'. Love is between *I* and *you*, not an emotion directed by an *I*-subject towards a *you*-object.

Similarly, it is more convincing to argue in terms of human love, including sexual love, against the tendency to wrap encounter in mystic veils as a union or identification of *I* with *you*. What seems a coalescence of *I* and *you* in sexual encounter is never in reality a cancellation of duality, but, as Buber writes, merely the 'bewitching dynamic of relation' which leads lovers mistakenly to imagine themselves one.[20]

Probably, Buber's most important dictum on the subject of love is that it is 'the responsibility of an *I* for a *you*' (see p. 240 below). This is another of his puns, but one which can for once happily be translated into English: *Antwort/Verantwortung* = response/responsibility. In the life of dialogue, address is at the same time response, and response is assumption of responsibility. More simply: to respond to a *vis-à-vis* as *you* is to make oneself responsible for that *vis-à-vis*. To be present with *you* is to offer help, a comfort, and support to *you*.

Later, Buber realized that some human relationships cannot accommodate the reciprocity which he had thought integral to true relation between persons. Specifically, the teacher, the psychotherapist, the minister of religion, needs to confront his pupil, patient, or client as *you* if his services are to be effective. Whoever goes for instruction, or

---

[19] *Werke*, i. 83; *I and Thou*, 8.   [20] *Werke*, i. 136; *I and Thou*, 87.

for mental or spiritual help or advice, must be accepted as he is in a spirit of directness and open-mindedness. But if someone in such a role becomes the *you* of those who come to him for help, and especially if *I–you* encounter happens between them, his effective offices become impossible. No teacher or healer of any kind can admit a pupil or patient into the closeness of encounter and continue to act as a healer or teacher. These are functions which 'can only be performed by one who lives *vis-à-vis* and yet apart'.[21] Reciprocity infringes especially the 'sacral authenticity' of the task of the priest or minister; but in general, all *you*-saying in relationships where the specific aim is for one party to exercise an effect on the other 'exists by virtue of a mutuality which is obliged never to become total'.[22] Thus not only is encounter excluded from these cases; *I–you* relation itself has to suffer modification.

Buber believed that although we live in an age and a society in which the odds are in any case weighted against easy and spontaneous interpersonal relation, the psychologists have contributed to its deterioration. In a debate on the factors militating against it, he refers to the tendency to analyse personality, to subject it to processes of reduction and deduction, on the assumption that since mind and body have been put together they can also be taken apart. Not only is the so-called unconscious, which is amenable to objectivization, treated in this way, but so is the 'psychic flow', which can 'never in fact be considered as objectively existent'.[23] The reductionist trend characteristic of the modern view reduces the rich variety and multiplicity of the human person to structures everywhere recurrent and surveyable, and the deductive method deduces human development, and indeed what a man is actually becoming, from genetic formulae. The quality of 'person', that 'unremittingly close *mysterium*',[24] has been levelled, and it no longer comes easily to us to accept another human being in all his wholeness and uniqueness, as he is.

Buber's own principles are directly contrary to these. They take into account, as we have seen, that with one swing of the pendulum the *I* analyses, deduces, and reduces, but view this as only one part of the dual movement *I–you/I–it*. From the beginning, the *I–you* instinct takes precedence over its yoke-fellow. We have in us not an inborn *it* but an inborn *you*. And as we say *you*, we do the very reverse of unravelling our *vis-à-vis*. We corroborate and call into presence his whole 'presence and thusness'.

[21] *Werke*, i. 168; *I and Thou*, 133.   [22] *Werke*, i. 168; *I and Thou*, 134.
[23] *Werke*, i. 279; *The Knowledge of Man*, 80–1.   [24] Ibid.

MAN AND THE IMMATERIAL

Of the three spheres of relation, the region of the *geistige Wesenheiten* is probably the least well known, no doubt partly owing to the variety of ways in which this term has been done into English. Sometimes it is rendered 'intelligible forms', sometimes 'spiritual beings' (R. Gregor Smith in the first and second editions of *I and Thou* respectively). Sometimes it appears as 'forms of the spirit' or simply 'forms' (R. E. Wood). Sometimes we find it as 'intelligible essences' (Maurice Friedman). One or two of these are more acceptable than the others, but none is exactly right. Yet it is hard to think of an improvement. The allusion is to the immaterial entities or immaterial beings of art, knowledge, and example, those which have already entered the world as the works of artist and scholar or as a living exemplary person, and those which still inhabit the realm of 'the genesis of word and form' and may loosely be called 'ideas', though Buber rejects this interpretation as too passive.

In this sphere of the immaterial, relation is supra-liminal: it occurs above the level of speech. Our *vis-à-vis* is 'wrapped in cloud yet self-revealing'. We 'feel' ourselves called and, unable to utter *you* with our lips, we respond—to art by way of making, to knowledge by way of thinking and to example by way of doing.

———

For art, Buber finds a formula which must have pleased him, since he repeats it at least twice. Art, according to this, is 'work and witness to relation between *substantia humana* and *substantia rerum*'.[25] Art is 'the Between given, and made into, form'. The poem, the painting, the musical composition, do not spring from the artist's own self. The source of his work is not his own independent imagination. Artistic creation arises from encounter with an immaterial entity not yet in the world but 'wandering about among us' and waiting to be given substance.[26] The painter, poet, or musician can say *you* to his *vis-à-vis* and then withdraw without doing anything further. Or, committing himself fully and exclusively, he can struggle with total dedication to give to his *you* the presence which it asks of him.

Encounter in this field illustrates with particular clarity the need for

[25] *Werke*, i. 81; *I and Thou*, 6.
[26] *Werke*, 441, quoting *Werke*, i. 418; 'Man and his Image-Work', in *The Knowledge of Man*, 165, quoting 'Distance and Relation', in *The Knowledge of Man*, 66.

immediacy and exclusiveness in relation between *I* and *you*. All else but *you* must be eliminated. All lines, colours, and words must go, all shapes and sounds which are not the *you* encountered. The idea cannot be described, but only substantiated, yet it is seen, not as an 'inner' thing among other 'inner' things, but as that which is there. Tested objectively, it is of course not there at all. But for the artist, nothing could be more present. And his relation with it is real, entailing real reciprocity. His *you* affects his *I*, and his *I* affects his *you*. Once endowed with actuality, the *vis-à-vis* is brought from the immaterial into the material world, and the artist's *you* becomes an *it*. But the *you* remains alive in the 'shell' in which it is confined. It needs only new encounters with other *I*s to be released from its *it*-ness and to be *you* once again.

Response to knowledge, the second immaterial entity, is made by way of thought. The thinker encounters an idea not yet in the world, and gives himself over (or not, as his choice may be) to realizing it. He will do so not in the same way as the artist, but in words or numbers. Otherwise, the story is the same. Banished into the objectivity of the mathematical formula or the written work, his *you* must subsequently bide the time when it will be redeemed through a new encounter.

With the third immaterial entity, qualified by Buber in non-religious language as 'pure action, action without arbitrariness',[27] we pass to another level entirely, one requiring more careful reflection, particularly since its significance seems to have been overlooked even more thoroughly than the others. Once more, any uncertainty must regrettably be ascribed to Buber himself, who in spite of laying much emphasis on it and insisting that here we have something incomparably superior to the immaterial entities of art and knowledge, has failed to enlarge on it sufficiently.

The argument, as far as we can understand it, is that in the same way that the spirit of art and knowledge, within and without the world, await relation and encounter, so does the spirit of human example. Within and without the world—the example within represented by a living exemplary man, and the example without, by a departed exemplary man known only through the teachings attributed to him—the spirit of 'pure action' wanders among us hoping for a response.

Kees Waaijman, a Dutch Carmelite whose exhaustive, intelligent, and highly penetrating study of *I and You* is without doubt second to

---

[27] *Werke*, i. 105; *I and Thou*, 42.

none,[28] concludes from the relevant passages that Buber presupposes, as a first stage, a response on the part of the exemplary one himself to his everlasting *You* made through the medium of his life. As a second stage, I encounter as my *you* that life-lesson, outside the world as an idea, or inside it embodied as a living person, and in turn express a response through the medium of my own existence.

This is a faithful reproduction of Buber's own explanation, but is harder to grasp than his presentation of encounter with the other immaterial entities because of the additional complication of an encounter, prior to the one between *I* and *you*, between my *you* and his everlasting *You*. That response to the everlasting *You* precedes my own *you*-response to that person.

Thus, where a past life is concerned, I enter into relation, by means of the teachings accredited to it, with a life lived 'without arbitrariness'. I say *you* to an ideal, not of what is or of what should be, but of 'how to live in the spirit, in the face of *You*'.[29] I can subsequently allow my *you* to recede to the status of an *it*, in which case I will take note of the teaching, make sure that its words are on my bookshelves, and be interested to establish the teacher's place in history. I may even go so far as to venerate or worship him. Alternatively, I will commit myself to encounter with that life and to fulfilling its demands of me. I will respond with my own life. I will bring my *you* back from its absence from the world into a new presence in the world by means of my own 'pure action'. I will become the place of its exile, from which it will be redeemed afresh, as an immaterial entity already in the world, by other *I*s.

And as I give presence to my *you* through my own presence, I make a reality of the Presence in which it was itself lived and from which it is forever inseparable.

The most remarkable feature of this whole pattern of authentic religiousness as Buber sees it is its scope. To become a real and unified person, and to be able, as such, to establish and maintain real relation with the everlasting *You*, I am expected to have learnt how to live in relation with present existence. The wholeness of the perfect man

[28] Kees Waaijman, *De Mystiek van ik en jij: een nieuwe vertaling van 'Ich und Du' van Martin Buber met inleiding en uitleg en een doordenking van het systeem dat fraan ten grondslag ligt* (Bijleveld, 1976).

[29] *Werke*, i. 105; *I and Thou*, 42.

requires a loving response to, and acceptance of responsibility for, life in its entirety—in its several parts, and in each component of its parts. Relation in the sphere of nature is not to be a general appreciation of the natural world, but an acknowledgement of the quiddity of whatever natural *vis-à-vis* confronts me, and a presence with it. Relation with my fellow-beings is not to be an undefined solicitude for the human race— though it must be this too—but a developing habit of presence with individual persons in the spirit of love. Relation with the immaterial world of the mind and spirit is not to be a detached interest in cultural, intellectual, and 'spiritual' matters, but a presence, if not with know- ledge still unformulated, then with knowledge already extant; if not with art as yet unrealized, then with art already given form and shape; if not with the exemplary awaiting embodiment, then with the exem- plary living among us.

Nothing mystical is involved. On this point Buber insists. Whoever possesses a candid heart and the courage to proffer it will recognize that *I–you* relation and encounter are part of life as we know it. It may sometimes be necessary to abandon earlier modes of reasoning in order to understand it, but not the 'primal norms that determine human thought and reality'.[30]

[30] *Werke*, i. 166; *I and Thou*, 130–1.

17

The Real and Unified I

THE second stage of Buber's way is that, from having cultivated the habit of relation, the *I* becomes more real and more unified. These conditions are inseparable from one another, since a real *I* must be unified, and a unified *I* must be real, but they are not identical.

THE REAL *I*

It is probably true to say that no words appear more persistently in Buber's exposition of the dialogical life than reality (*Wirklichkeit*) and presence—meaning also that which is present, and present time (*Gegenwart*). Response and responsibility are crucial too, but these others occur again and again throughout his work, attended by a battery of ancillary verbs, adjectives, and nouns, many of them puns impossible to reproduce in English. Presence is probably the richer of the two in this respect, but reality also has its quota.[1] From beginning to end, Buber's teaching on reality, his *Wirklichkeitslehre* as Hans Kohn calls it, is forced on our notice. Everywhere there are references to 'lived reality', to the 'real and effective', to the 'central reality of the every day hour on earth'. In *Daniel*, the warning is given that whoever 'fails to realize, remains himself unreal', and that 'there is no reality other than that realized by one who realizes himself and the whole of existence'.[2] In *Paths of Utopia*, Gustav Landauer is said to have believed that religion will become real as a result, and not as a cause, of a changed society. Society will not be transformed because religion has become a reality. The transformed society will cause its religion to be real. (This matches Buber's own hypothesis that true relation with the everlasting *You* does not precede, but follows from, true relation with *you*.) In *Eclipse of God*, it is contended that present-day religion is

---

[1] e.g. *Verwirklichung*, realization; *verwirklichen*, to realize; *entwirklichen*, to empty of reality; *wirken*, to work, act upon, effect; *Wirkung*, operation, effect; *wirksam*, effective; etc.

[2] Martin Buber, *Werke*, 3 vols. (Kösel–Lambert Schneider, 1962–4), i. 43.

notable for its unreality; it is thought and not done. We read also in this book that the unreal *I* of irrelation which predominates in our times, the *I* that makes all, takes all, succeeds in all, and arrogates all to itself, separated from any bond of *you*-relation, has come between man and the light of heaven. The first essential, therefore, if we are to lift the veil behind which God's Face is hidden, is to return to reality from unreality.

Reality is, as he himself admits, central to Buber's thought. He insists that he has no teaching (so much for the *Wirklichkeitslehre!*), but claims: 'I point to something. I point to reality.'[3]

When we search for what he means by this, we discover at once that for Buber the real is what is done. Nothing can possess the quality of being real, of having actual existence, unless it is made real by me. Nothing can be real for me unless I myself realize it. No tree is real until I endow it with reality as *you*, no fellow human being, no work of art, no knowledge, no ethical ideal. Realization is an act performed by me, a deed done, within the context of *I–you* relation.

But if *I–you* relation evokes the reality of *you*, it does no less in regard to the reality of the *I*. If my real presence with a *vis-à-vis* calls out its own real presence, the latter in its turn gives reality and presence to my *I*. The *I* becomes real 'through its participation in reality. The more complete the participation, the more real it becomes'.[4] 'I become through *you*.'[5] This is the first step. Not 'I become real', and not 'the *I* becomes', but simply, 'I become'. My infant personality, resting in the lap of a world consisting solely of *you*, an existence still quite empty of *it*, moves gradually towards awareness of itself as an *I* separate from its environment; until the moment comes when, having briefly confronted myself as *you*, I launch myself at last into a life-long alternation of *I–it* and *I–you*.

'Becoming *I*, I say *you*.'[6]

For various reasons, I may not become *I* through *you*. I may be unable to develop a real *I* through genuine *I–you* relation. My condition may then be diagnosed as genuine mental illness. But there is

[3] *Martin Buber*, ed. P. A. Schilpp and M. Friedman (Kohlhammer, 1963), 593; P. A. Schilpp and M. Friedman, eds., *The Philosophy of Martin Buber* (Open Court, 1967), 693. See also Buber, *For the Sake of Heaven*, trans. L. Lewisohn (Meridian/Jewish Publication Society, 1958), xiii.

[4] *Werke*, i. 121; *I and Thou*, trans. R. Gregor Smith, 2nd edn. (Scribner–T. & T. Clark, 1958), 63.

[5] See below, p. 239.   [6] Ibid.

another, less grave, state of ill-health which Buber calls the sickness of the unreal *I*.

The unreal *I* is an *I* that has become so settled in the separateness required for the exploitation and manipulation of people and things that it now functions much more readily out of relation than in it. An individual to whom this has happened has become in his own eyes a particular being distinct from other particular beings. The swing between relation and irrelation has in his case developed an irregularity of balance which tips him too constantly in the direction of irrelation. He does not feel part of the world. He says 'my' much more often that he says 'our'. He says 'my' work, 'my' genius, 'my' way.

The real *I* is the opposite of all this. It is the *I* of a person who turns with far greater promptness to relation than to irrelation. He feels that he exists to the extent that he coexists. Without surrendering anything of the sense of his own uniqueness, he regards himself as one among others, as a member of the body of the created world.

Nobody is purely an unreal *I*, and nobody purely a real *I*, but in all of us, one tendency dominates over the other.

Buber illustrates these two types of *I*—or, as he calls them, these two poles of humanity—by three historical personalities, each a genius in one or other of the three spheres of relation.

The poet Goethe was able to enter into 'pure communion' with nature. He could 'speak' to it and hear its unceasing speech to him. He could place himself side by side with the things of the world of nature and be present with them in the 'one reality'. Consequently, his *I* retained its own reality even when relation and encounter with his *you* had ended.

Socrates was another such person. Famous above all for his ability to communicate with his fellow-men, even in front of the judges and during the last hours of his life, this great philosopher believed in their reality. A human partner in dialogue was for him a real *you*. Therefore, like Goethe, his *I* was never wholly deprived of reality.

The third example is Jesus. For Buber, the *I* of Jesus as it appears in the sayings attributed to him by tradition is real in the sense that where Goethe and Socrates could align themselves habitually and with perfect ease with the *you* of nature and of their fellow-men, Jesus could do the same with the *You* of his Father in heaven. Jesus' *I* belongs by right to the realm of perfect relation, where every finite *you* is gathered in and embraced in a *You* which is at once indwelling and transcendent. When the Jesus of the Gospels says *You*, there can be no doubt that his

I is the *I* of *I–You* relation. He may have been stirred at times by his unreal *I*, but the characteristics proper to the real *I* always take precedence. Always, he addresses himself to the world from the position, not only of relation, but perfect relation.

All can do as Jesus did, is Buber's comment. All can say *you* and become a real *I*. All can also say *You*. All can say Father and become thereby the Father's child.

THE UNIFIED *I*

It will be seen that once the essentials are grasped, Buber's notion of what constitutes a real *I* is not very complex. The same is true of the unified *I*. C. G. Jung, in a letter written to Buber in 1960, complains in connection with differences they have had on the subject of God that Buber has no concrete experience of depth psychology, and that when he accuses Jung of gnosticism, he is confusing it with psychiatric observation, 'of which he obviously knows nothing'.[7] Whether Jung was right in rejecting the charge against himself is neither here nor there, but he was correct in asserting that his correspondent had no practical knowledge of psychiatry. Buber never pretended to enter into the human condition further than a certain depth; his approach to it is always upward and outward rather than inward and downward. Nevertheless, although the unification of the *I* as he explains it demands no plunges into the unconscious, collective or otherwise, no exhaustive and exhausting searches for roots and causes, no very thorough analyses of the forces making for personal disintegration, it would be an error to confound simple with simplistic. Buber may not have been a professional in this field, but his knowledge was not negligible. He was in constant touch with psychologists and psychiatrists, and kept abreast of contemporary expert opinion. But as has been said, and independently of how much or how little he knew of treating the sick human psyche, he was against the analytical approach to the personality as a matter of principle.

In *I and You*, Buber disposes of the self-unification sought by oriental mystical religions such as Buddhism through immersion in a self believed to be the seat of All-Being. Not only is there no such unity of being. This spiritual way is a negation of *you*-saying because the *I* cannot say *you* to itself, and it has no bearing on real life because it

[7] C. G. Jung, *Letters: 1951–61*, ii (Routledge & Kegan Paul), 570–3.

regards as an illusion what we know as reality. It certainly leads to a 'unification of the soul', but to one that induces not greater and closer contact with *you* and *You* but less relation altogether.

The problem is to know what Buber means by the 'unification of the soul'. Is the 'soul' the '*I*', and is the unifying of the one identical with the becoming one of the other? Sometimes, it would certainly seem so, for instance in this passage from *I and You*: 'The unified *I*: for as I have said earlier, there is in lived reality a unification of the soul . . .'[8] On the other hand, the unification of the soul is portrayed as a happening, a kind of blitz-union, a sudden inrush and concentration of power and energy, accompanied by renewed vision and intensified resolution. It is depicted as a person's great opportunity, the decisive moment which qualifies him for the 'work of the spirit'.

Assembled into unity, he can at last go out towards successful encounter with mystery and salvation. But he can also savour the bliss of unity to the full, and without applying himself to the supreme task, fall back into fragmentation. Everything on our way is decision—intended, intuitive, mysterious—but this one made in the inmost heart is the primordially mysterious decision, with the most powerful impact on destiny.[9]

What causes such an enormous effect? Not God, we are told. Or rather, it is not an event that takes place between man and God, but in man alone.

The 'unified *I*', by contrast, is a personal condition reached by positive endeavour. It is in every sense 'all there'. It is all there in itself, inasmuch as it does not attempt to erase the 'dross' of human nature and to preserve only what is 'pure'; and it is all there with present existence, inasmuch as it does not turn away from a presumed external illusion for the sake of a presumed higher internal reality. It is an *I* that enters as a whole into whole *I–you* relation: which in turn confirms its wholeness and adds to it.

The presence of existence before which I am placed changes its shape, its appearance, its revelation; it is other than myself, often frighteningly so, and other than I expected it to be, often frighteningly so. If I confront them, enter into them, really encounter them, with the truth that is to say of my whole being, then, and only then, am I 'properly' there. I am there if I am *there*; and the whereabouts of 'there' is at each moment determined less by me than by the changing shape and appearance of the presence of existence. If I am not

---

[8] *Werke*, i. 138; *I and Thou*, 89.
[9] *Werke*, i. 136; *I and Thou*, 86.

really there, I am guilty. If to the call of present existence, 'Where are you?', I answer, 'Here I am!', but am not really there—that is to say, not there with the truth of my whole being—then I am guilty.[10]

This homily based on the story of YHWH God calling to Adam in the Garden uses without ambivalence the language of religion, and specifically of biblical religion. With the emphasis laid on being 'properly' there, on 'I am there', on 'I am not really there', the presence of *I* with *you* is deliberately associated with the divine Name YHWH = HE IS THERE, and the unified *I* is thus made part of the Jewish *imitatio dei* in general, and of that of Hasidism in particular.

Immediately, part of the enigma seems solved. The unified soul and the unified *I* are not different, but refer to the same condition. It is simply that the one term is couched in the language of Hasidism, and the other in Buber's own dialogical jargon. Yet the unease persists, fuelled chiefly by the contention that the soul's unification takes place in independence. The 'becoming one' is positively asserted to be an occurrence that takes place within the self, a flashing thunderclap, overwhelming but transient. The soul is as it were shocked into wholeness and unity, and from that point on, is fit to proceed, if it so desires and determines, towards full encounter with 'mystery and salvation'.

We are thus forced to conclude, first, that our later assumption is incorrect, and that the two unifications refer to two distinct states. Secondly, and somewhat more daringly, we are led to associate the unified *I* with relation, and the unification of the soul with encounter. Any other interpretation entails a contradiction of Buber's own principles. The notion of a self-unification of any kind happening in isolation leaves no space for the work of the spirit whose operations he places in the Between, i.e. between *I* and *you*. It would therefore play no part in this highly important moment. But more fundamentally, such a theory runs directly counter to Buber's basic law of the life of dialogue, according to which there is no *I* in itself; in all we do, and in all that happens to us, we occupy the position either of *I–it* or of *I–you*. Now it stands to reason that an event as galvanic as Buber presents it can never be the outcome of the objectivity inherent to *I–it*. This blitz-unification of the soul must be a response to *you*, and indeed to an encounter with *you*. But if the everlasting *You* is ruled out, what other

[10] *Werke*, i. 363; 'What is Man?', in *Between Man and Man*, trans. R. Gregor Smith (Fontana, 1961), 203.

vis-à-vis can have such an effect? Allusions to 'decision' and 'work of the spirit', and indications that such unity is a necessary preliminary to perfect relation, do not appear to point to a *you* from the natural or human spheres of relation: though, on second thoughts, why not? It would seem, however, that the instant unification of which Buber writes must come from encounter with one or other of the immaterial entities of art, knowledge, and example, and that in the circumstances, the most plausible of the three is the last.

This is our own attempt to fill in the gaps of Buber's rather sketchy outline. Self-unification as an event happens in the event of encounter, and may lead to the event of supreme encounter. The unified *I* as a condition derives from, and leads to, *you*-relation, and possibly also to perfect *You*-relation.

———

On the age-old problem of good and evil and their place in human life, Buber has a great deal to say that is characteristic of his treatment of the human personality.[11] He does not explore their roots or manifestations in any detail or analyse the issue. He views it *en large*, within the setting of existence in general rather than in the narrower confines of the inner individual self.

In the religious tradition which he inherited, man becomes one and whole by uniting his two 'inclinations' or 'urges', the evil inclination which impels him towards sensuality, possessions, success, and power, and the inclination which draws him towards the good, towards God. The right worship of God requires the service of both. If you are to love YHWH your God with 'your whole heart' (Deut. 6: 5), you must love him 'with your two united inclinations. The evil inclination must be included in man's love of God. So, and only so, will it become perfect. So, and only so, will it become again as it was created, "very good".'[12] In his time, the Baal Shem Tov taught his followers that the greater the man, the greater his 'urge', and that if they were to become pure and holy, they must 'learn pride and not be proud, know anger

---

[11] Though not so much, some may think, as to justify the prominence given to it by Maurice Friedman in *Martin Buber: The Life of Dialogue*, 3rd rev. edn. (Chicago University Press, 1976). In line with biblical rabbinic and Hasidic tradition, Buber undoubtedly accords it prime importance, but it is hardly the overriding preoccupation that Friedman suggests.

[12] *Werke*, i. 625; *Images of Good and Evil*, trans. M. Bullock (Routledge & Kegan Paul, 1952), 41.

and not be angry'. They would then become whole in all their 'qualities' and make of their 'urge' a 'chariot for God'.[13]

Rabbi Yehiel Mikhael of Zloczov (d. 1786) imparted a similar
teaching. Interpreting the verse from Genesis, 'Let us move away and
go, that I may go before you' (33: 12), he told his listeners:

So speaks the evil inclination secretly to man. For it ought, and desires to,
become good by stimulating him to overcome it and make it good. And its
secret request to one whom it labours to seduce is this: 'Let us move away from
all this shamefulness and enter into the service of the Creator, so that I too may
go and ascend with you stage by stage, even though I may seem to stand before
you and disturb you and hinder you.'[14]

The same understanding is evident in the comment of Rabbi Shalom
Shakhna of Probitch (d. 1803) to the effect that God forgave King
David instantly because he made his *teshuvah* with the same passion as
when he made love to Bathsheba.

At the root of this accumulated wisdom is the conviction that the so-
called evil urge is not evil in itself, but is made evil by being separated
from its fellow. The two inclinations belong together. They are seen as
a pair of oxen yoked in the service of God. The power of the one must
combine with the force of the other. Other traditional representations
of evil see it as the lowest degree of the good, and as the throne on
which goodness rests, but always as being first and foremost a failure to
be turned towards God.

In Buber's version, these concepts are rendered faithfully into the
language of *I–it* and *I–you*. *I–it* is not evil in itself, but can become evil
if it is divided from its life-companion, *I–you*. The destiny of *I–it* is to
cooperate with *I–you*, not to function independently. Also, failure to be
directed towards God becomes in the idiom of the life of dialogue
simply a failure to be directed towards present relation.

Evil as a reality is evil done. It is whatever is carried out in a spirit of
irrelation, in obedience to the arbitrary whims and desires of the evil
urge. In Buber's own words, it is a lack of 'direction, and whatever is
done in and out of it by way of grasping, clutching, swallowing up,
forcing, seducing, exploiting, humiliating, tormenting, and destroying
whatever presents itself'.[15] Evil, which Judaism interprets as an

[13] *Werke*, iii. 16; *The Tales of Rabbi Nachman* (Souvenir, 1956), 13.
[14] *Werke*, iii. 263; *Tales of the Hasidim: Early Masters*, trans. Olga Marx (Schocken,
1947), 145.
[15] *Werke*, i. 643; *Images of Good and Evil*, 71.

absence of God, takes the shape in Buber's thought of an absence of *you*.

Good, by contrast, is what is performed in a spirit of relation, directed towards the needs of 'present existence'. It represents a choice on my part between what I want, and what I believe is required of me. But the good inclination does not function independently. According to the wise teaching of the ancients, it makes use of the powerful energies of the 'evil urge', 'so that all the strength and passion with which evil can be done is included in that deed'.[16]

This is a notion which Buber develops at some length in connection with the unified *I*. I am not to destroy parts of myself. I am not to attempt to obliterate even those features which I consider objectionable in myself. I must redirect their enormous vitality and energy away from the desire to have, use, and exploit, and channel it instead into the deed which I choose to do, as opposed to the deed I merely find myself doing because I want to do it. If I gather my whole self into unity in this way, whatever I resolve to do will be a deed which, in the Baal Shem's words, is not patchwork but 'of one piece'.[17]

The unification experienced in encounter is momentary. It is a prelude, at best, to a unity fought for and more lasting. But although reality and unity come more easily and naturally to some than to others, the realization and unification of the *I* is never final. The most we can hope for is that they will grow and deepen.

In the same way that the soul unified from birth will nevertheless be assailed from time to time by inner difficulties, so one who has striven very hard for unity can never attain to it completely. But everything I do with a unified soul affects my soul in return, works in the direction of a new and higher unification; each such achievement leads me, although by all manner of detours, to a unity more *constant* than that which preceded it. Thus in the end, one reaches the point where one can rely on one's soul because its dimension of unity is so great that it overcomes contradiction as though it were child's play. Even then one must remain watchful, but it is a relaxed watchfulness.[18]

These words do not in fact refer specifically to the life of dialogue. They are intended to interpret the Baal Shem's teaching that the unification of the soul must extend to man *in toto*, body and spirit. The soul cannot be truly one, the founder of Hasidism maintained, unless

---

[16] *Werke*, i. 643; *Images of Good and Evil*, 71.

[17] *Werke*, iii. 724; *Hasidism and Modern Man*, trans. M. Friedman (Horizon, 1958), 148.

[18] *Werke*, iii. 725; *Hasidism and Modern Man*, 150.

all the physical powers are likewise unified. Nothing of the self must be omitted. Whatever we do must be done with all our 'members'.

Whatever we do. For that is what ultimately matters. Wholeness of mind and body, and the binding together of *I–you* with *I–it*, are not psychological or spiritual conditions to be pursued for their own sake, but because they are the prerequisites of the whole and unified human deed.

18

I *and* You

'NOT before one can say *I* in reality—finding oneself, that is—can one in perfect reality—to God, that is—say *You*.'[1] Buber could not be more explicit. Furthermore, the corollary is that until one can say *I* in reality, until one is oneself real, one risks saying *You* to what is unreal and not God. This aspect of man–God relation deserves more attention than has been accorded to it hitherto.

Conventional thinking is given a second jog by Buber's contention that perfect relation is the fruit and not the source of every other relation. The proposition that love of God is the fount of all other love is replaced by another claiming that love of the world is a precondition of the love of God.

Buber denies that perfect relation is the prerogative of a spiritual elite. In no sense is it the privilege of a few specially gifted spiritual men and women. He abhors in any case the opposition of 'spiritual' to 'material'. To live in relation with *You*, he says, is basically a robust 'doing', an active, effective participation in the work of revelation, creation, and redemption, and is within the reach of all.

ENCOUNTER WITH *YOU*

Encounter with *You* is again distinguished from relation with *You*, but as before, not over-clearly. The coming together of *I* and *You* as an event, and the condition of living 'before the Face', flow in and out of each other in Buber's writings and are not easy to disentangle. It may therefore be best if we first determine what encounter with *You* is *not*, and what it does *not* entail by way of preparation.

Against the teachings of the mystics, occidental and oriental, supreme encounter does not require in Buber's view a preliminary retreat from the world. It does not call for an insulation of the self against the

[1] Martin Buber, *Werke*, 3 vols. (Kösel–Lambert Schneider, 1962–4), i. 220; 'The Question to the Single One', in *Between Man and Man*, trans. R. Gregor Smith (Fontana, 1961), 63.

experiences of real life so that the excitements of a more elevated spiritual order may be more keenly enjoyed. An experience, however lofty, is always an experience, and belongs as such to the world of *it*, while *You*—the infinite *You* and the finite *you*—can never be experienced. Besides, to abandon human society and the business of everyday existence for refuge in a realm of ideas and values is to take flight into the void. Ideas relate always to the substance of life. When the reverse is attempted and life's substance is made to relate to ideas, they can never become present to the *I*.

Supreme encounter demands in addition no prior turning away from the self. The *I* does not have to reject itself in order to encounter *You* but the very opposite: it has to have become healthily real and whole.

Not needed, in short, are any of the lessons taught across the centuries, in the east and the west, on how to make ready for encounter with the Supreme Being by submerging into the self, and by disciplining, mortifying, purifying, abasing, and depriving the self. None of these recipes leads one step out of the *it*-world into the world of *you* and *You*.

Equally bold is Buber's rejection of commonly held notions on the nature of *I–You* encounter as an event. In no way is it a mystical union: *I* cannot become one with *You* any more than *I* can be unified with *you*. In no way, either, is it a unilateral *coup de foudre*, as is obvious from the word 'encounter'. In no way is it a possessing of *You* on the part of *I*: the everlastingly present God does not allow himself to be possessed.

What are we left with?

As far as the preliminaries are concerned, the path to Presence, as Buber traces it, passes by way of presence. Less cryptically, he substitutes for spiritual exercises, meditation, contemplation, and other techniques of mysticism a single condition: a total acceptance of presence, by which he means a total acceptance of the presence of what confronts us, at the present time, within a parallel acceptance of the One Presence.

Of *I–You* encounter itself all he says is that 'something happens'. Whether as a puff of wind, or as a wrestling bout, it 'happens'. Travelling down the road of presence, I encounter the everlastingly Present One as he journeys towards me. Thus although I go forward of my own free will, my encounter with him is a grace. Buber illustrates this combination of will and grace in encounter with the story of the meeting on Mount Horeb. When he sees the burning bush, Moses is curious and decides to investigate. Consequently, he is able to answer, Here I am! when God calls Moses! Moses! But he might just as easily have wondered about the strange phenomenon and moved on with his sheep, without stopping.

The effects of what Buber terms this 'act of pure relation',[2] this 'religious act', are described with a corresponding delicacy and diffidence. A person does not emerge from a moment of supreme encounter the same as he entered it. He has in him, from then on, something new, something added, something that was not previously there, something related to consciousness of God's Presence, which gives him strength. Love has been offered and received, but offered to what or to whom, and received from what or from whom, he cannot say. But existence henceforth can never again be without meaning: a meaning, furthermore, which pertains to the present time, and not to whatever may lie on the other side of death.

On the functioning of creation, redemption, and revelation in *I–You* encounter, Buber is more discursive. To begin with the first of these great works, the effect of *I* on *You* is as creative as that of *You* on *I*. The real and unified *I* calls into being the supreme *Vis-à-Vis*—which makes God's Presence dependent on man's presence with him. Remarkable though this speculation may seem, it is by no means singular in Jewish (or Christian) tradition. One ancient source comes to mind even more outspoken than Buber. Interpreting Psalm 123 with the help of Isaiah 43: 12, 'You are my witnesses says YHWH and I am God', the midrashist comments: 'That is, when you are my witnesses, I am God. And when you are not my witnesses, I am as it were not God.'[3]

Buber's proposition is no more startling than this. Certainly, man needs God. But equally, I AM THERE needs man in order to be there; his need constitutes the very meaning of human life. However impertinent it may appear to talk about a developing or emerging God, so Buber writes in *I and You*, 'that there is a coming into existence of the existent God, this we know quite surely in our hearts'.[4]

As for the more familiar creative action in encounter on the part of *You*, Hillel, one of Israel's saints and scholars from the early first century AD, has the *mot juste*. God says, according to him: 'If I am

---

[2] *Werke*, i. 152; *I and Thou*, trans. R. Gregor Smith, 2nd edn. (Scribner–T. & T. Clark, 1958), 109.

[3] *Midrash on Ps.*, 93:1.

[4] *Werke*, i. 133; *I and Thou*, 82.

there, all are there. And if I am not there, who is there?'[5] One source, that is to say, represents God as confessing that the Presence of his divinity depends on his people's presence with him; the second reverses the situation and gives God to indicate that unless his Presence is with them, his people have no presence.

Redemption as an element of encounter with *You* is, as before, difficult to distinguish from the creative and revelatory activities, but Buber probably succeeds best in clarifying this point in a short work published in 1930. Reintroducing his idea of redemption as a deliverance into unity from the exile of plurality, fragmentation, he links it to the concept of redeeming what he calls the 'moment-gods' recognized here and there in various circumstances and on various occasions, and of reuniting them into the unity of the One God. In encounter with *You*, the many accumulated insights into the nature of our supreme *Vis-à-Vis* come together and merge. Out of the darkness of unknowledge where we bear witness to the everlasting *You*, takes shape a single divine Identity. Out of 'the givers of signs, out of the speakers of sayings in lived life, out of the moment-gods, comes into existence for us as an identity the Lord of the Voice, the One'.[6] With the Lord of the Voice comes into existence also his word, for it goes without saying that where encounter between *I* and *you*, in every sphere of relation, is seen as a source of revelation, that between *I* and *You* must be the fount of revelation *par excellence*.

———

A short digression will not be out of place at this point.

Gershom Scholem, described many times in these pages as the foremost expert in the field of Jewish mysticism, will not accept Buber's denial that his concept of revelation in the 'here and now', and his association of revelation with encounter, are esoteric in any way. Insisting that revelation thus formulated is 'purely mystical', Scholem pronounces it as 'one of Buber's most astounding illusions' that he had 'quit the realm of mysticism and even overcome it'. On the contrary, he asserts, everything Buber writes falls conclusively and entirely within the kabbalist concept of revelation, with one exception: for the mystics, historical revelation implies mystical revelations, in that the one is unfolded in the others. There is nothing of this in Buber's outlook.

[5] *Suk.* 53*a*, quoted in C. G. Montefiore and H. Loewe, eds., *A Rabbinic Anthology* (Meridian, 1963), 13.

[6] *Werke*, i. 188; 'Dialogue', in *Between Man and Man*, 33.

'He recognizes one revelation alone, mystical revelation, though he declines to give it that title.'[7]

In Scholem's view, Buber does not consider mystical revelation as developing from historical (biblical) revelation, but as happening independently in, as it were, its own right. To press this opinion home, Buber's crucial statement on revelation is quoted from *I and You*. We reproduce it from the German as it appears in Scholem's essay.

This is the everlasting revelation in the here and now. I know of none whose primordial phenomenon is not the same. I believe in none. I believe in no self-naming of God, in no self-defining of God before men . . . That which is, is there. Nothing more. The everlasting source of strength flows on. The everlasting touch lingers. The everlasting voice sounds. Nothing more.[8]

Reading these lines, how can we do other than agree with Scholem's conclusion? Certainly, there is nothing noticeably biblical or historical here. Faced with such evidence, he cannot but be justified when he asserts that Buber broke away 'above all from the Sinaitic revelation'.[9]

But stay. What has been omitted?

Nothing less than the revelation on Sinai itself: *ehyeh asher ehyeh*! The sentences dropped by Scholem are: 'The word of revelation is: I AM THERE SUCH AS I AM THERE. That which reveals is that which reveals.'[10] In no way is Buber divorcing revelation in the here and now from historical revelation. In no way is he defining it as some vague and novel 'that which is' being there. Basing himself directly on the Bible, he is asserting that the everlasting word of revelation is 'I am there such as I am there', God's words to Moses from the burning bush. In other words, there seems to be not even this difference between Buber's concept of revelation and that of the kabbalists!

This particular misrepresentation is undoubtedly curious, but if we study Scholem's own qualifications of mysticism, it is hard to understand why he associates Buber with it at all. To select a few statements taken at random, we read that mysticism 'postulates self-knowledge, to use a Platonic term, as the surest way to God who reveals himself in

---

[7] G. Scholem, 'Martin Bubers Auffassung des Judentums', in *Judaica*, 2 (Suhrkamp, 1970), 173; 'Martin Buber's Conception of Judaism', in *On Jews and Judaism in Crisis* (Schocken, 1976), 157.

[8] Ibid. See also 'Reflections on Jewish Theology', in *On Jews and Judaism in Crisis*, 273.

[9] Scholem, 'Martin Buber's Auffassung des Judentums', 174; 'Martin Buber's Conception of Judaism', 157.

[10] *Werke*, i. 153; *I and Thou*, 112.

the depths of the self'.[11] The same page includes a statement to the effect that mysticism, while it starts with the religion of the individual, 'proceeds to merge the self into a higher union'.[12] Earlier in the same work, Scholem informs us that mysticism 'strives to piece together the fragments broken by the religious cataclysm, to bring back the old unity which religion has destroyed, but on a new plane, where the world of mythology and that of revelation meet in the soul of man. Thus the soul becomes its scene and the soul's path . . . its main preoccupation.'[13]

If this is mysticism, in what sense can Buber be said to be in sympathy with it, on the subject of revelation or of anything else? He writes about self-knowledge, but not about knowledge of the self as the surest way to God; according to him, the way to God is through knowledge of what is not the self, won through love. He does not accept that the self can be merged into a higher union; he rejects it as a possibility altogether. He is not preoccupied with the 'soul's path'; his emphasis is on its deed. His mature belief was that all contemplation of the secrets of heaven, all search for enlightenment, all cultivation of closeness to God, is wholly without value unless and until whatever understanding is obtained through them is translated into the reality of 'lived life'. Encounter between *I* and *You*, with its revelation of Presence, is not intended, so Buber thought, to act as a spiritual magnet drawing the *I* and holding it ineluctably fixated on God. Encounter is certainly an exclusive affair between a person and his *Vis-à-Vis*, but the inclusiveness proper to perfect relation forbids it from remaining so. The word uttered in encounter with the everlasting *You*, as Buber understands it, is a summons; but it is also a sending back again into the world to make a reality there of what has been heard. Yet again and again, the attraction to remain concerned with God prevails over the duty to be concerned with God's creation. When this happens, the *I* no longer confronts its everlasting *You*, the supreme Knot into which every other *you* is tied, but what Buber calls an ' "*it*-God" set in a context of thingness'.[14]

Scholem quarrels with Buber on another point. The prophets, the former maintains, have transmitted revelation as they received it. Or rather, what they have passed on is what was given to them.[15] Buber

[11] G. Scholem, *Major Trends in Jewish Mysticism* (Thames & Hudson, 1955), 18.
[12] Ibid.   [13] See ibid. 7–8.   [14] See *Werke*, i. 157; *I and Thou*, 115.
[15] See Scholem's gloss introduced into a citation of Buber's text: *Judaica* 2, 175; *On Jews and Judaism in Crisis*, 159.

contradicts this theory. To the scandal of the fundamentalists, he opposes the idea that a person can serve as a speaking-tube for the Almighty. However true and faithful the *I* may be to its encounter and relation with the supreme *You*, the message it subsequently proclaims cannot be identical with what entered its own inner ear. In Buber's view, every listener modifies all that he hears when he comes to repeat it for the benefit of others. He adds to it something of himself. This is true of the mighty and convulsive revelations marking the turning-points of history, but also of the little revelations of everyday life. The great and the humble friends of God—Moses being the first and foremost friend of them all[16]—mediate and participate in the act of revelation. Hence the phenomenon that as human nature changes, so does the form of the One God to whom the one everlasting revelation alludes.

LIVING BEFORE THE FACE

All encounter—with *you* and with *You*—is ephemeral. It comes. And it goes.

All relation is also impermanent. But where in the case of *I* and *you* it alternates between actuality and a latency in which *you* becomes (temporarily perhaps) an *it*, in the latency of perfect relation, my own presence may waver, but never the Presence of *You*. The supreme *You* can never move to the distance of an *it*. It is by nature everlastingly *You*.

The other great difference between *you*-relation and relation with *You* is that where the first is exclusive, so that I can only say *you* to a single *vis-à-vis* at a time, it is of the essence of perfect relation that it is simultaneously all-exclusive and all-inclusive. My *You* is unique. But in saying *You*, I utter every other *you* of my life.

To live in perfect relation is in Buber's eyes to live religiously: which is not necessarily the same as what Jews understand by 'being religious'.

On reflection, it is remarkable how largely unnoticed Buber's distinction has been between religion and religiousness. It is almost as though, compared with his contributions to modern thought on the life of dialogue in all its philosophical, educational, social, and political ramifications, the fact that he looked for the assimilation of religion into religiousness was of no very great moment. He never, needless to

---

[16] Exod. 33: 11.

say, implies that the man of religion is *de facto* excluded from the authentically religious life. On the contrary, he goes out of his way to salute those who are able to accept inherited beliefs and still remain in direct contact with God. It is against religion itself that he takes up his cudgels.

Buber's antipathy to religion has admittedly not gone wholly unnoted. In 1974 Donald M. Moore published a book entirely devoted to it.[17] More influentially, the great Paul Tillich himself alluded to Buber's 'freedom from ritualism', and went so far as to approve of his 'openness to the secular' in the name of the 'Protestant Principle'. Buber, he maintained, anticipated an emphasis which has appeared in the latest phase of Protestant theology: freedom from religion, including the institutions of religion, for the sake of 'that which religion points to'.[18]

Others, too, have noticed Buber's position *vis-à-vis* religion, but for the most part only as it were in passing. Or else they have chosen to jib at his distaste for theology and metaphysics, which is not the same. As an example, the Jesuit Pedro Sevilla bridles at Buber's 'unduly rigorous judgment regarding any metaphysics that is applied to God'. It is 'a rash and harsh charge', he complains, 'to say that metaphysical concepts applied to God have nothing to do with what the Bible gives us regarding God'. Yet the strictures against religion itself expressed by our nevertheless 'ever faithful follower of the God of the Hebrew Bible' seem to upset Fr. Sevilla hardly at all.[19]

Whether or not, in any case, the truth has filtered through that Buber preached the abandonment of institutional religion, its present downward slide really cannot to any measurable extent be imputed to him or to his interpreters. It can hardly be argued that the minicrusade for the dialogical life fought on our bookshelves over the last forty years or so has included an equally fervent holy war against the formal and organized worship of the Deity.

Yet Buber made no secret of his mistrust of religion. In a BBC interview on 14 December 1961, he described himself as very glad that the word 'religion' occurs nowhere in the Bible. And whilst not

---

[17] Donald M. Moore, *Martin Buber, Prophet of Secularism: The Criticism of Institutional Religion in the Writings of Martin Buber* (Jewish Publication Society of America, 1974).

[18] Paul Tillich, 'Martin Buber', in J. Owen and J. Richmond, eds., *A Reader in Contemporary Theology* (SCM Press, 1967), 57.

[19] Fr. Pedro Sevilla, *God as Person in the Writings of Martin Buber*, Logos 4 (Ateneo University Publications, 1970), 157.

actually proclaiming 'nulla salus *nisi* extra ecclesiam',[20] he let it be known in the writings of his youth, maturity, and old age, that he considered the life of the spirit to be threatened rather than promoted by adherence to a particular religious cult of whatever persuasion.

His primary objection was to religion's own nature. That it should set itself apart from the secular as a sacred speciality, with a code and regimen centred on the divine in much the same way that those of a businessman are centred on trade—this was intolerable to him. Separate like this, it cannot help but see itself as the preserve of a God equally separate, a Being to be placated and entreated by *its* worship, obeyed by means of *its* laws, known best, defined best, and expounded best by *its* theologians. The real concern of religion is not with God, but with man's intercourse with God. And since the latter not only takes place in the world, but is about the world, the aim of organized religion should be to sanctify this dialogue, not in buildings set aside for the purpose, and not in the language of established liturgical formulas, but by way of what is *done* in house, office, factory, and field. In what purports to be a reformulation of Spinoza's view but on this point is in fact also his own, Buber uses twice in the same paragraph the phrase 'prime peril'. It is a 'prime peril', he writes, 'indeed the utmost of man's perils and temptations, that something of the human side of the intercourse becomes separate and independent, rounds itself off, becomes seemingly complete and reciprocal, and sets itself up in place of true intercourse. Man's prime peril is "religion".'[21]

The sequence is always the same. The laws, precepts, beliefs, and rites of religion serve at the beginning of their history genuinely to sanctify human life and further true converse with God. Little by little, however, they move off into an independence and introversion and self-acclamation which not only cease to confirm the meaning of earthly existence as before, but actually divorce men from it. From then on, life and the public worship of God run along side by side but separate: except that by then, 'God' has become little more than a 'plastic semblance'. The real Partner in the discourse between earth

---

[20] At times he nevertheless comes very close to doing so. See e.g. below, p. 266, his advice in *I and You* to one who finds that prayer in religion has degenerated to such an extent that he can no longer 'with his whole undivided being' enter into immediate communion with God.

[21] *Werke*, iii. 744; 'Spinoza, Sabbatai Zevi and the Baalshem', in *Hasidism*, trans. Greta Hort (Philosophical Library, 1948), 99.

and heaven is no longer there. 'The gestures of communion beat in the empty air.'[22]

Individual prayer follows the same pattern. Where originally it is directed to a Being addressed as *You* in the human half of a living dialogue, it tends eventually to decline into spiritual exercises and experiences which, instead of flowing back into existence and enriching it, run along a channel leading exclusively to 'God'—as though God would wish the love that prompts them to be offered only to him. When the world disappears, Buber insists, so does God. 'Only the soul is there. What it calls God is only an image inside it. The dialogue it conducts is a monologue in two parts.' And again he reiterates: 'The real Partner of the intercourse is no longer there.'[23]

In effect, unreality is the principal characteristic of contemporary religion, according to Buber. He totally rejected the *'spiritual'* (his italics) theory that it is the one force able to mend the broken links between spirit and world. Itself unreal, an affair of the divided spirit, religion can do no such thing. As he describes it, it is now no more than 'a favoured compartment of life's superstructure, a chamber among the upper rooms especially full of atmosphere. A whole embracing man's life it is not; nor in its present state can it become so. It cannot lead men to unity because it has itself fallen into duality. It has itself become adapted to this duality of existence. It would have itself to return to reality before being able to affect contemporary man.'[24] Because religion as a reality is not about God but about God-and-man, and because the human situation as a reality is located in the created world, religion can only be really effective when the divine object of its faith is a reality with whom people, in their places in the world, live in true relation. Once they put their faith in religion itself, a religion centred on a divinity as it supposes him to have been in the past, then the relation thought to exist between God and his worshippers takes place only in the believer's mind, 'a mind containing, in effect, images that have become independent: independent "ideas".'[25]

The second major charge laid by Buber at religion's door is that it interferes with the necessary immediacy of relation between man and God. On this topic he expresses himself with, if possible, even greater

[22] *Werke*, iii. 745; 'Spinoza, Sabbatai Zevi and the Baalshem', 99.
[23] *Werke*, iii. 745; 'Spinoza, Sabbatai Zevi and the Baalshem', 99–100.
[24] *Werke*, ii. 850; 'The Man of Today and the Jewish Bible', in *The Writings of Martin Buber*, ed. Will Herberg (Meridian, 1965), 240.
[25] *Werke*, i. 511; *Eclipse of God*, trans. Norbert Guterman (Gollancz, 1953), 21.

passion and indignation. The function of the religions, he claims, is to act as a barrier to revelation. The lesson they teach is that God's word has been uttered and recorded for all time in their sacred writings. It has moreover also been, and continues to be, authoritatively interpreted by them. The man of religion has only to listen and read, and he will be told exactly what God said, and when, and what God's words signify.

But this is to deprive present existence of its power to speak. By pinning revelation to past sacrosanct occasions, religion robs God of his 'mouth' in the present time. By interposing itself between man and God, it ensures that the only Face man sees is that of its own tradition, and the only Voice he hears, its own. If nothing, Buber fulminates, can conceal our fellow-beings from us more effectively than ethics, nothing can hide God from us more successfully than religion.

Principle here, dogma there. I am able to appreciate dogma's objective compactness, but behind them both lurks a war, profane or holy, against the situation's dialogic power, the once-and-for-ever opposing the unpredictable moment. Even when its claim of origin is uncontested, religion has become the most elevated form of invulnerability to revelation.[26]

This whole process of the degeneration of religion into a system sure of itself, and believing in itself, is nevertheless part and parcel of God's passage through history as an *it*, a 'thing'. The forms we lend him come and go through the ages, each following the same career.

A new and powerful revelation, an encounter between a particular *I* and his everlasting *You*, stimulates the people to whom it is communicated to make a profound *teshuvah*, to turn back from irrelation to relation—with the world in all its three relational spheres, and with the divine form newly come into existence. People settle down to living in 'perfect relation'. God's form becomes for them a reality, with deeds and ways which they can imitate. It becomes a medium through which they can genuinely commune with their everlasting *You*. The laws and worship they devise in his honour and service are part of a whole life lived with and before him, sanctifying relation *with* him by sanctifying relation with existence *in* him.

As a second stage, religion then develops a momentum of its own and begins to turn on its own axis, whereat the form of God at its heart falls progressively more silent and inert. And because it is no longer heard to be saying anything or seen to be doing anything, religion

[26] *Werke*, i. 191; 'Dialogue', in *Between Man and Man*, 36.

having restricted its activity to a past deed re-done and a past word
constantly re-stated, it finally dies. While religion concentrates on
securing its own health and growth, the divine form it is intended to
serve and proclaim loses its vitality, and in the end its life. The
revelation associated with it does not disappear because religion preserves it. But once the form held up for veneration is dead, the
revelation grows unreal and ineffectual. And so ends the second stage
of God's journey through time as a 'thing'.

The third part of the way sees a return to the beginning: an eruption
out of human consciousness of a new divine form, a new revelation,
and a new and overwhelming *teshuvah*. Such is Buber's picture of the
course of God's forms through history.

But why, we ask, does the reality of the earliest phase give way to the
later unreality of religion? How does the nebulous, tenuous, but vital
sense of Presence become transmogrified into a corpus of 'knowledge'
which religion formulates and lays down and a code of conduct prescribed in terms of laws?

The cause, we hear, is the human dread of uncertainty and insecurity. People need to know that they can count on being safe, on being
never alone, on being sure that 'someone' is keeping a constant eye on
their well-being. In perfect relation, there is none of this knowledge.
Far from being able to depend on a continuing well-being and serenity,
one who lives in the Presence is only too aware of its power to visit with
wrath and rebuke as well as love. And owing to the limitations of
human nature, even that Presence itself cannot be relied on. I will
sometimes not perceive that my *You* is with me. I will feel exposed to
hazard and isolation. It is a Presence of which my own absence is
necessarily a part.

At the beginning, before religion takes over, existence on these
terms is accepted happily. But inevitably, the periodic losses of comfort
and the solitariness of the religious situation becomes intolerable. A
protection has to be invented against the recurring remoteness of *You*,
against the defencelessness, and against disaster and death. People
therefore persuade themselves into believing in an unvarying, unceasing 'God-having' in time (and beyond it). They convince themselves
that they 'have' God always and that they are unassailably safe because
they have faith that this is so. And as a shield against the absolute
solitude of *I* before *You*, which likewise eventually becomes unbearable
to many, they provide for themselves a continuous 'God-having' in
space in the form of the religious community. They become members

of a company of the faithful, all obedient to the same teachings, performing the same rites, and fulfilling the same legal duties.

The effect is the one hoped for. The sharp edge of fear and the threat of the unexpected and the unknown are blunted. With the knowledge of faith as a supporting staff, a body of laws as guide, and the solidarity of fellow-travellers, life's road takes on the appearance of a well-trodden and well-signposted way leading from a known starting-point to a foreseen destination.

But danger! danger! danger! was Buber's cry as long ago as 1913. 'Let your motto be God and danger!'[27] Dread and trepidation are never to be escaped if religion is to be real. All religious reality begins with

life between birth and death becoming incomprehensible and awesome, with the shattering of all security by Mystery: not relative mystery, inaccessible only to the structure of human knowledge and therefore primarily discoverable, the as yet unknown, but essential Mystery, to the essence of which inscrutability belongs: the Unknowable. Through this dark door (which is indeed a door and not a dwelling-place as some theologians opine) the believer enters into an everyday, sanctified from then on, as into the room where he is to live with the Mystery, directed and guided towards the concrete situation of his life. That from this point on he accepts the situation as given to him by the Giver: this is what biblical religion calls 'the fear of God'.[28]

The knowledge enjoyed in perfect relation is not the knowledge of religion—i.e. a knowledge of God's existence, laws, nature, purposes, and desires—but the knowledge of love, of which the New Testament writer says, 'Beloved let us love one another, for love is of God, and he who loves is born of God and knows God.'[29] It is the 'true knowledge' of Rabbi Nahman of Bratslav, who saw no separation between the so-called sacred and the so-called profane, or even between living and dying. But in the end it is knowledge of unknowledge, as the Baal Shem taught.[30]

What is this unknowledge more precisely?

It is the voluntary surrender of whatever may obstruct immediate presence of *I* with *You*, between whom must intervene nothing thought, nothing hoped for, nothing imagined, nothing desired, nothing anticipated, and nothing known. In the case of a *vis-à-vis* from the world of *you*, knowledge returns when a *you* returns to the status

---

[27] *Werke*, i. 45.   [28] *Werke*, i. 529–30; *Eclipse of God*, 50–1.
[29] 1 John 4: 7.   [30] See above, pp. 135–6.

of *it*. But in perfect relation, where the everlasting *You* can never be an object of thought, the unknowledge needed for *I–You* encounter persists into the major part of life which is lived without that encounter.

There may be no lasting 'God-having' in the religious life as Buber depicts it, but this is not to say that it has no continuity at all. Living before the Face, we create a special continuity of time, for as we utter the *You* which embraces every other *you*, including the *you* of our life as it passes from present moment to present moment, we bind time together into a flowing whole. 'Time in human life thus shapes itself into a fullness of reality, and although it neither can nor should overcome the *it*-connection, it becomes so permeated by relation that it acquires in man a radiant and irradiating constancy.'[31]

Also, although there may be no community of 'God-having' in perfect relation, this does not mean that no enduring community exists in it at all. On the contrary, it possesses the one true guarantee of spatial continuity, which is that 'people's relation to their true *You*, the spokes leading from every *I* to the Centre, form a circle. It is not the periphery, the community, that comes first, but the spokes, the common relation with the Centre. This alone ensures the genuine continuance of community.'[32] It is not the sharing of certain beliefs about God that creates the community and holds it together, but common communion with the everlasting *You*.

The one authentic temporal continuity is where the separate moments of time are joined to form a lifetime of relation. And the one genuine spatial continuity is where space is assembled into a community united at its Centre. Only while these two exist and endure, 'only then does a human Cosmos conceived in the spirit out of the age's world-substance exist and endure about the invisible altar.'[33] For, as we have said earlier, in the life of dialogue which goes to create the perfect man, and is lived by the perfect man, none of the virtues promulgated by the Baal Shem (except possibly joy) is entirely lost sight of. Cleaving appears as a cleaving to *You* in a spirit of love and responsibility for the world, as a 'profound involvement with the world before the Face of God'.[34] The burning ardour of encounter is there, and so are the holy intention of taking, in the form of accepting what is

[31] *Werke*, i. 156; *I and Thou*, 114–15.
[32] *Werke*, i. 156; *I and Thou*, 115.
[33] *Werke*, i. 156–7; *I and Thou*, 115.
[34] *Werke*, i. 152; *I and Thou*, 108–9.

given as coming from the hands of the Giver, and the holy intention of giving, in the form of encounter with the immaterial entities, the sources of human creativity. Humility is there as awareness of being a part and not the whole, as existing because coexisting. And worship is also there with prayer, sacrament, sacrifice, and altar.

Prayer in life lived before the Face is a communion between *I* and *You* in which reciprocal help and presence are asked for and offered.

Sacrament is 'the austere sacrament of dialogue, in which God can be tasted even though a person rejects with all his might that "God" is there'.[35] Sacrifice is the surrender of the 'little will' to possess, use, and exploit, for the sake of the 'greater will' to do what is hoped, but not known, to be right, in a spirit of trust and love. And the invisible altar on and before which these offerings are presented is the hearth of the created world made into a true home.

To live in perfect relation is to watch for what may be seen, and to listen for what may be heard, in order to do whatever may be asked.

How are we to understand the Hasidic teaching that the worlds can fulfil their destiny to become one in so far as the life of man becomes one? Buber's answer is:

If man can become 'humanly holy', i.e. as man, to the extent and in the way of man, and indeed as it is written, 'to me', i.e. before the Face of God, then he, the individual man, can to the extent of his personal capacity, and in the manner of his personal potentiality, become one before the Face of God. Man cannot approach the divine by reaching beyond the human. He can approach him by becoming the man that he, that individual, was created to be.[36]

Nor is this all. For he was not created to perfect himself alone, or even to perfect God alone, but to perfect the world. In his imitation of the supreme Helper he must himself become a helper—a helper in the spirit, as Buber describes it, a teacher of life's meaning, a liberator of the goodness concealed in the world. This is the person, so Buber thought, for whom the world cries out. 'It is he, the perfect man, the true helper, who matters to the world. It is for him that the world waits, for him that it waits ever anew.'[37]

---

[35] *Werke*, i. 191; 'Dialogue', in *Between Man and Man*, 36.
[36] *Werke*, iii. 947; *Hasidism and Modern Man*, trans. M. Friedman (Horizon, 1958), 42–3.
[37] *Werke*, i. 973; *Hasidism and Modern Man*, 69.

And what part is institutional religion to play in this, the stifler of
revelation, the divider of the indivisible, the barrier to true dialogue
with the everlasting *You*?

The reply is given without ambivalence (and this may account for
the muted attention paid to Buber's solution by so many of the men
of religion who in other respects pay him such reverent homage).
Religion should renounce itself.

Religion that is real, we read in *Eclipse of God*, or religion wishing to
become real, will work for its own obliteration. From specializing in
God, it will wish to be transmuted into life. It will hope for redemption
from the specifically 'spiritual' and desire God so to enter the whole of
man's business on earth that all shall become sacrament, all temple, all
priesthood. Confessing itself to be an exile, it will look and work for his
Kingdom, not beyond the grave, but in this world, in human life 'lived
without arbitrariness before the Face of God'.[38]

[38] *Werke*, i. 527–8; *Eclipse of God*, 48.

Postscript

Turn to me and I will turn to you.

ZECH. I: 3

Turn us to You, O Lord, and we shall turn.

LAM. 5: 21

THIS enquiry began with the allegory of the legendary Breton book, *Ar Vif, The Living One*, that huge volume, big as a man, its red pages covered with black script which stays invisible until *Ar Vif* has been fought and conquered. We would wrestle with the red pages of Buber's writings, we said. We would grapple with the black letters to discover their meaning.

What have we found? How have we deciphered them? What is the real concern of these literary and teaching endeavours of a lifetime? To promote a new divine form in place of the God gone into eclipse? To offer a new ideal of personal and social existence? To stir the human religious instinct into new life?

In every case, no. They are, of course, also intended, but viewed from near to, and not from afar, the black characters of Buber's written work spell primarily the one word *teshuvah*; *teshuvah* which throughout this book I have stubbornly given in its Hebrew form rather than translate it into the loaded 'conversion' or the alien 'turning'; *teshuvah* which calls for a whole book of its own and is here to be compressed into paragraphs.

What is *teshuvah*?

Teshuvah is when a person, in anguish and despair, prostrates himself beside the ruins of all that he thought he possessed, and from his loss, fear, isolation, alienation, and dereliction, cries out to his *You* to be there with him.

'Turn!' has been the cry of all the prophets. It is the word with which the Baptist's preaching began, and that of Jesus and his apostles. They have all called for *teshuvah*, the word falsely rendered as *metanoia*, with its implications of a spiritual process, a change of mind. *Teshuvah* is a turning to God of the whole man.

Teshuvah is not a return to a sin-free condition. It is a turn-about to face in an opposite direction. It is the beginning of a different journey, not along a way ordered by God, but along a path taken by God's own indwelling Presence. One who makes his *teshuvah* follows in the footsteps of God.

Teshuvah in Buber's terms is all of this and something more. It calls for a turning to perfect relation by means of other relation. It demands that the *you*-world should take precedence over the *it*-world, but also that the *you*-world and the *it*-world should both be sanctified by relation with the everlasting *You*.

Buber's *teshuvah* envisages the Kingdom of God as one in which human beings show loving response and responsibility towards nature, singly and as a whole, with its soil, rocks, seas, rivers, plants, and animals; towards fellow-beings, singly, nationally, globally; and towards the things of the mind and spirit—art, knowledge, and holiness. If man can learn to live like this, as a helper working hand in hand with the divine Helper, he will not feel a stranger here as now, not alone, not at the mercy of unseen powers. The son will have returned to his Father's house.

————

Sleeping on the hearth of the living world
yawning at home before the fire of life
feeling the presence of the living God
like a great reassurance
a deep calm in the heart
a presence
as of the master sitting at the board
in his own greater being
in the house of life.[1]

[1] *Complete Poems of D. H. Lawrence* (Heinemann, 1964).

APPENDIX

I *and* You

THE first of the three parts into which this book is divided deals with the whole field of relation and irrelation—*I–you*, *I–it*, and *I–You*—with special emphasis on the relation termed *I–you*.[1]

Quotations throughout are translated directly from the original. References are accordingly to *Werke*, i (1962), the initial volume of Buber's collected works in German, and afterwards to the corresponding passage in the English translation by R. Gregor Smith, *I and Thou* (Scribner–T. & T. Clark, 2nd edn. 1958). For the sake of brevity, these are given simply as G (German) and E (English), followed by the page number. No additional reference is given to the more recent rendering of the work by Walter Kaufmann, *I and Thou* (Scribner–T. & T. Clark, 1970, 1971).

PART ONE

Ours is a dual world inasmuch as our attitude towards it is a dual one. We adopt a stand of closeness to it, and as it were say *you* to it, or we move back from it and see it as an object separate and apart from us, an *it*. Whichever we do, the *I* that says *you* is different from the *I* that views the world as an *it*. Accordingly, we have a dual *I* as well as a dual world. There is no *I* in itself. When we say, *I*, we are either an

---

[1] Readers may be interested in the criticism of one of Buber's contemporaries, Florens Christian Rang. A letter from him to Buber reads: 'Your language . . . inclines far too much towards the scholarly. Because of this, and contrary to what it wishes to say, which is ultra-concrete, it becomes abstract; and with the language, so also the train of thought. A word such as "relation"—one of your basic words—is no praying word . . . But . . . how do you arrive at such a pale word as "relation"? Answer: Because you proceed from the assumption that *I–you* (and *I–it*) exist on the human plane even without God—expressible on the level of common speech . . . This is my most important quarrel with your method of presentation . . . The truth is that there is no *I–you* but only *You* (spoken to God), out of which the *I* is no more than an echo.' *Briefwechsel* ed. Grete Schaeder, 3 vols. (Lambert Schneider, 1972–5), ii, no. 106.

I-saying-*you*, an *I*-with-*you*, or we are an *I*-objectively-viewing-*it*, an *I*-apart-from-*it*.

———

When I say *you*, it is not to 'something' or 'someone'. Where one 'something' is, there is another 'something'. To say *you* is to enter into exclusive relation with a unique *vis-à-vis*.

We necessarily experience the world. But experience by itself cannot bring the world to us. To experience is to experience 'something'. Besides, an experience is only *in* us. It is never *between* us and what is experienced. Experience belongs to the *it*-world.

———

These are the realms of possible *you*-relation: nature, humanity, and the spiritual (*geistige Wesenheiten*). In the first, our *you*-saying takes place below the level of speech; in the second, by way of language; in the third, we hear nothing yet feel called, and we respond by way of creating, thinking, and doing. Our *you*-saying here is above the level of speech. But 'in every sphere, through everything that becomes present to us, we look towards the hem of the everlasting *You*. We hear its breathing in each. With every *you*, we address the everlasting *You*, in every sphere in accordance with its own way' (G p. 81; E p. 6).

———

In relation with the world of nature, I can see a tree as a picture, or feel it as a movement of veins and roots, or classify it as a species, or define it in terms of scientific laws. I can even reduce it to mathematical proportions. While I do any of this, the tree remains for me an *it*. But I can also say *you* to the tree; that is, I can be present with it so that it is wholly present to me—in its colour, form, movement, species, law, number, and all.

The same happens with human relation. I can stand apart from someone to estimate and appreciate his qualities and peculiarities and to place him in a context of time and space. He is then an *it* for me. But I can also confront him as my *you*, in which case, whole and unique, 'he fills the heavens. Not as though nothing exists but him, but all else lives in *his* light' (G p. 83; E p. 8).

I do not experience him because experience needs the distance of irrelation. I am simply there with him.

Similarly in relation with the immaterial essence, art. An artist's composition does not originate in his own soul but from encounter between himself and form. Form takes shape before him and demands that he should realize it. His response, if he gives it, will be made with the single-minded dedication of himself to the task facing him. 'To make is to draw out, to invent is to find. To shape is to uncover. By translating into reality I expose. I lead form into the world of *it*. My work is a thing among things, to be experienced and described as a sum of qualities. But from time to time, it can confront personally one who views it receptively' (G p. 84; E p. 10).

———

It is a grace that I encounter *you*. I do not find *you* by seeking. But I say *you* as an act of my own volition, as an act of my being.

I can only say *you* with the whole of myself. But I cannot become whole by my own efforts alone. Neither can I do so without them. 'I become through *you*. Becoming *I*, I say *you*. All real living is encounter' (G p. 85; E p. 11).

———

I–*you* relation is a presence of *I* with *you* in which nothing is allowed to intervene—no ideas, no preconceptions, no fantasies, no purposes, no desires, no aims, no anticipations. It cannot occur until all these have fallen away.

———

Present time exists only where presence, relation, and encounter exist. Objects, with their qualities, dimensions and values, etc., belong to the past. They have become what they are. But the *vis-à-vis* to whom I say *you* is never present to me as other than he, she, or it *is* at the actual moment.

———

Relation is reciprocity. My *vis-à-vis* affects me and I affect my *vis-à-vis*.

In the case of the artist this is easy to understand. His *you* induces him to create and he in turn affects his *you* by giving it reality. He brings it into the *it*-world, where it will become a thing among other things, but also a potential *you* to countless others, to whom it will impart happiness and inspiration.

Among human beings, reciprocity of relation is not too simple to define, mainly because we tend to confuse *you*-saying with feelings. Feelings accompany the metaphysical and metapsychical fact of love but do not constitute it. In addition, the feelings that accompany love can be very diverse. Jesus' feelings for the beloved disciple were not those he felt for the man possessed of the devil; yet the love was the same. I 'have' feelings; love happens. Feelings reside in me; I reside in my love.

To one who takes his stand in love, people become loosed from their involvement in the hustle and bustle of life. Good and bad, clever and silly, beautiful and ugly, one after another they become real to him, and *you* . . . Love is the responsibility of an *I* for a *you*. Herein lies the similarity, not to be found in any feeling, between all who love, from the humblest to the greatest, from the blessedly protected whose life is completed in that of a single beloved person, to him who, nailed life-long to the cross of the world, dares that monstrous thing—to love all men. (G pp. 87–8; E p. 15)

Reciprocity of relation in the natural world must remain a mystery. But if we believe in the simple magic of life, we shall get to understand the meaning of that watchfulness, that 'craning of the neck', which we find among living creatures. 'Every word is bound to mislead. But look. Beings live all around you, and whichever one of them you approach, you come always upon being' (G p. 88; E p. 15).

———

Why so much talk about love? Isn't hatred relation?

No. *You*-relation requires the whole acceptance of a *vis-à-vis*. Hatred is blind. Only part of a person can be hated. 'Nevertheless, one whose hatred is direct is closer to relation than one who neither hates nor loves' (G p. 89; E p. 16).

———

Every *you* must inevitably return to the *it*-category. Nothing and no one can remain indefinitely present to me in *I–you* relation. Even in love, the presence of *I* with *you* is alternately actual and latent. This is the melancholy of our lot.

———

In the beginning is relation.

The life of the so-called primitive is rich in presence. It is apparent even in his language. 'There where someone cries, O mother, I am

lost,' is the Zulu version of our word 'far'. And compare our own
greeting formulas with the Kaffir's 'I see you', or its American variant,
the ridiculous and sublime 'Smell me!'

The elementary excitements of natural man derive from relational
events and relational situations. The moon does not disturb him until
contact with it is followed by evil or good fortune. Once he has been
touched by it in this way, he retains from the experience, not a visual
concept of the moon as it is, but, to begin with, only an image of the
excitement caused by its effect on his body, an image from which
another concept, one of the moon as a person, a *he* or a *she* separate
from him, emerges little by little.

With the passing of time, such encounters accumulate in the memory and arrange themselves there in a certain order. As they do so, the
ingredient most important to self-preservation and knowledge—that
which produces an effect—acquires dominance and independence.
The less important—the unshared and changing *vis-à-vis* itself—
retreats, becomes isolated, is gradually viewed from a point of irrelation, and is then fitted into groups and classes.

The unchanging partner, the *I*, is the last to make an appearance. It
comes into being after the verb in 'I-affecting-you' and in 'you-
affecting-me' has changed into a noun and become personalized.

So although relation can be resolved into *I* and *you*, it does not
derive from their juxtaposition; it is pre-*I*. Irrelation, by contrast,
ensues from juxtaposing *I* and *it*; it is post-*I*. 'Once the sentence, "I see
the tree"[2] is uttered in such a way that it no longer records a relation
between man-*I* and tree-*it*, but perception of a tree-object by human
consciousness, the barrier between subject and object has been
erected. The basic word *I–it*, the word of separation, has been spoken'
(G p. 93; E p. 23).

———

The development of *I–you* relation and *I–it* irrelation may be observed
more clearly in the human child.

Before birth, the infant rests in the womb, not only of its mother of
flesh and blood, but also of the great Mother, the undivided primordial
world. It is enfolded in natural relation. At birth, these bonds are

2 Franz Rosenzweig to Buber: 'If only you had not prattled on with the devilish *I*-It of
the philosophers, but had used the blessed *He*–It of children, and Goethe and the
Creator. For never as long as the world has existed has anyone said, "I see the tree."
Only philosophers say that.' *Briefwechsel*, ii, no. 108.

broken, in the first instance suddenly and catastrophically, in the second, little by little. The baby is given time to find its way towards a new relation by encountering through its senses the bright strange world into which it has been born.

It is not true that a child is first aware of something as separate from it, and subsequently establishes relation with it. 'The struggle for relation, the cupped hand into which the *vis-à-vis* nestles, comes first. Relation to it, a wordless pre-form saying of *you*, comes second' (G p. 96; E p. 27).

In the beginning is relation. But the *a priori* of relation is the inborn you. 'Relation is the realization of the inborn *you* in what is encountered. That it is conceived as a *vis-à-vis*, accepted exclusively, and finally addressed as *you*, is based on the *a priori* of relation' (G p. 96; E p. 27).

The longing for a *vis-à-vis*, with all the fulfilments and disappointments associated with it, is indissolubly linked to a child's development. But it will never be understood correctly unless its cosmic and metacosmic origins are remembered. For it reaches back into the primordial world from which, even though born into this world, it has still to emerge by entering into relation. 'Man becomes *I* through *you*' (G p. 97; E p. 28).

Vis-à-vis come and go, relational situations materialize and disperse, and increasingly the child becomes aware of its *I*. At first, it is merely something that reaches out for *you*, but eventually the tie snaps and the detached *I*, having briefly confronted itself as a *vis-à-vis*, takes possession of itself and enters into relation in full self-awareness.

It cannot adopt the stand *I–it* until this stage has been attained. Relationships may have repeatedly faded, but the *vis-à-vis* did not for that reason become an object of experience. It became an object *per se*. But once the *I* has changed into an experiencing and using subject, it can move in on all those objects *per se* and settle down with them in a condition of irrelation.

An *I* of the conjunction *I–it* places itself in front of people, things, creatures, and events instead of face to face with them in reciprocal effectiveness. It isolates them without any of the exclusiveness belonging to *I–you* relation, and it masses them together without any sense of universality. In the *it*-world, all is experienced as a sum of qualities, all is given a place in a context of space, time and causality, all is accorded measurability and conditionality. My *you* appears in space also, but in one that is the background to its exclusive self and not its measure and bound. It appears in time also, but in a span determinable only in terms of itself. It appears also as acting and acted upon, but not as linked to a sequence of cause and effect.

It is part of the fundamental truth of this world that only *it* can be coordinated. *You* recognizes no system of co-ordination. The other part of the truth, without which the first is useless, is that

an ordered world is not world order. There are moments of silent depth when world order is seen as presence. Then, the melody is heard in flight whose indecipherable score is the ordered world. These moments are immortal and most transient. Nothing of them can be preserved yet their power enters creation and the knowledge of man. The rays of their power penetrate the ordered world and dissolve it again and again. As in the history of the individual, so in that of the race. (G p. 99; E p. 31)

We see existence as consisting of things. We see beings as things. We see what happens as events. We see things as possessing qualities and events as possessing moments, all of them measurable by, and comparable with, other things and events. This is an ordered world and in some degree dependable. It has density and duration. Nevertheless, whilst it allows us to accept it as 'truth', it does not give itself to us. No encounter takes place there. And although life would be impossible without it, if we should die in it, we should be buried in nothingness.

The alternative is that a person confronts what is and what happens as a *vis-à-vis*. 'Never more than one reality, that is, and each as reality alone. What is, reveals itself to him in what happens; and what happens, happens to him as what is' (G p. 100; E p. 32). This world is not dependable. It is tenuous and transient. It is not outside but deep inside—though if I try to move it into my 'soul', I lose it. It is my present. Without it, I have no present. It teaches me to encounter and how to be constant in encounter. And it leads me, 'through the grace of its coming and the sorrow of its going, to the *You* in whom the extended lines of relation meet' (G p. 100; E p. 33). It does not help to sustain life. It helps only to offer me an intimation of eternity.

The *it*-world possesses coherence in space and time. The *you*-world possesses no coherence at all in space and time. 'The individual *you*, after relation has run its course, *must* become an *it*. The individual *it*, by entering into relation, *can* become a *you*' (G p. 101; E p. 33).

We cannot live purely in the present, in a state of presence. We can however live purely in the past. Indeed, it is only in the past, in the *it*-world, that we are able to organize a life for ourselves. Yet—in all earnestness—whoever lives with *it* alone, is not man.

PART TWO

The second section of *I and You* deals mainly with the withdrawal into distance which Buber calls *I–it*, and with the damage which follows when it is allowed to prevail over the instinct to enter into the closeness of *I–you* relation.[3]

The world of irrelation is continually growing, for mankind as a whole as well as for the individual. Each civilization adds to it out of its own experience and out of the *it*-world of other civilizations, as Greece took over that of Egypt and western Christianity that of Greece. Our basic commerce with *it* is experience (which increases its substance) and use (which applies it to its various ends, i.e. the preservation and relief and provision of the necessities of human existence). Immediate experience is decreasing, it is true. Instead, we acquire information *about* things and people. And utilization is taking the place of use. Nevertheless, the ability to experience and use is improving all the time. Meanwhile, our capacity for relation, by virtue of which alone we are able to live in the spirit, is diminishing.

———

'Spirit in its human manifestation is man's response to his *you*' (G p. 103; E p. 39). The response can be made in the forms of speech, art, and deed. But spirit is one. Spirit is word. Just as language is not in man but man in language, and speaks from out of it, so spirit is not in the *I* but between *I* and *you*. A man lives in the spirit if he can respond to a *vis-à-vis* by saying *you* to it with his whole being. As it happens, the more powerfully he responds, the more forcefully his *you* is changed into an *it*. But this is a source of human greatness for it is the means by which 'knowledge, art, image and example come into being in the midst of the living' (G p. 104; E p. 40).

[3] Another comment by Rosenzweig to Buber: 'I'll take the bull by the horns straight away. With I–It you present I–you with a cripple as an opponent. That this cripple rules the modern world makes no difference to the fact that it is a cripple. You have eliminated *this* It quite easily, of course. But it is the false It, the product of the great illusion not

Every *you* that has turned into an *it*—as a scientific theory, a musical composition, or an ethical code, for example—is destined to regain its original *you*-ness through fresh encounters. But this destiny is thwarted by those who perceive it only as *it*. An idea which comes to a thinker in a flash of understanding is, in that moment, his *vis-à-vis*, his *you*. But as he analyses, compares, and describes what he has come to know, the *you* becomes an *it*. As such, it can be re-encountered by someone else as *you*, or it can remain as it is, its destiny unfulfilled. In the same way, an artist's *you* will not be released from the painting or musical piece into which it has been banished except by someone who detects in it more than a matter of technique, style, or financial value.

Response in the third category of image and example is made in the language of deed. It is to perceive as *you* the example of men and women who themselves responded to their *You* through the medium of their very life. Whether that life kept the law or broke it—both are necessary if spirit is not to die on earth—it is there to teach those who come after 'not what is, nor what should be, but how to live in the spirit, before the Face of *You*' (G p. 105; E p. 42). It is always ready to become their *you*. But where living relation is rejected, so is the lesson of the teacher who teaches it. He is accorded a place in history. His words are relegated to the library. He is admired and even adored. But O lonely face! O living fingers on the unheeding brow! O dying footsteps!

———

Improvement in our ability to experience and use mostly involves a lessening of our capacity to enter into relation.

One for whom spirit has become a source of personal advantage takes his stand in irrelation and divides his life into the neatly separate preserves of institutions and feelings. He works, negotiates, transacts

three hundred years old in Europe. Only with *this* It is an I not said but *thought*. No I is said with the *spoken* It. No human I, in any case. What I as a man say, if I say It correctly, is HE [HE written like this means God, as in the Rosenzweig–Buber Bible translation]. The basic word *I–it* can obviously not be said with the whole being [*Wesen*]. It isn't a basic word. It's at most a basic thought: no, a top thought, a thought top, a philosophical point. So if It is *nevertheless* quite real, it must be in a basic word that is equally spoken with the whole being [*Wesen*] by *him* who speaks it. From his viewpoint, this basic word is *I*–It [as an opposition of Creator God and created world]. From ours, HE–It. Say once, "Who slays and brings back to life," and you have said this basic word and said it *wesentlich.*' *Briefwechsel*, ii, no. 103.

business and the like in the institutions, in the company of other human heads and limbs, and he recovers from the institutions in feelings. Feelings are where he 'indulges his affection, hatred, pleasure, and, as long as it is not too sharp, his pain' (G p. 106; E p. 43). However, neither the separate *it* of institutions nor the separate *I* of feelings knows anything of the presence of people. Neither of them is concerned with present time. Institutions, even the most modern, only know the past, what is over and done with. Feelings, even the most lasting, only know the scurrying moment, the not-yet. Neither of them has any access to real life.

Those who regret that institutions conduce to no public life suggest that all they need is an injection of feelings. The state should be replaced by the community of love, where people live together because they choose to. But true community does not exist because people have feelings for one another. True community originates

first, from their all being in living reciprocal relation with a living Centre, and secondly, from their being in living reciprocal relation with each other. The second derives from the first but is not given with the first alone. Living reciprocal relation includes feelings but does not spring from them. Community is built from living reciprocal relation; but the builder is the living operative Centre. (G p. 108; E p. 45)

The same is true of institutions of the so-called private life. They cannot be renewed from feelings, though not without them either. The sole source from which marriage can be renewed is the source from which it flows: that 'two people reveal *you* to one another . . . This is the metaphysical and metapsychical *factum* of love, that is simply accompanied by feelings of love' (G p. 108; E p. 46).

True public life and true personal life are two sorts of attachment. For them to come into being and endure, feelings and institutions are necessary. But even in combination, they do not make for human life. 'It is the third element that does this, the central presence of *You*. Or more exactly, the central *You* perceived in the present' (G p. 108; E p. 46).

———

But isn't modern life bound to be plunged in irrelation? Aren't the economy and the state inconceivable except as based on a renunciation of 'immediacy' between human beings? Aren't the achievements of the

economist and the politician due precisely to the fact that they regard
people, not as *vis-à-vis*, but as potential sources of work, money, and
aspiration? Wouldn't a reversal of these tactics mean exchanging the
expertise, which alone makes life possible for a vastly increased
humanity, for cloudy fanaticism?

Human public life can as little dispense with the distance of irrelation as can the individual himself—whilst the presence of *you* hovers
over it like the spirit over the waters. There is nothing unnatural or
wrong in the desire for profit and power as long as it is linked to, and
supported by, a desire for relation. But once state and economy deny
spirit, they deny life. An injection of some kind of 'immediacy' will not
help. No tinkering with the peripheries can take the place of a living
relation to the Centre. 'The structures of human public life derive
their vitality from the richness of relational energy penetrating their
members, and their embodied form from the binding of this energy in
the spirit' (G p. 110; E p. 49). The statesman or businessman obedient
to the spirit is no fanatic. He knows it is beyond his ability to treat
everyone with whom he has to deal with as *you*. But he does so as far as
he is able.

So, too, work and property cannot be redeemed of themselves. Only
spirit can do it, by transforming them into *vis-à-vis*. When spirit is
present, work is infused with meaning and joy, and property arouses
respect and the capacity to offer sacrifice.

It is important that state institutions become freer, and those of the
economy more just, but not for the problem of real life with which we
are at present concerned. But whether 'spirit, the *you*-saying and *you*-
responding spirit, remains in life and reality; whether that of it which is
still to be found in human public life becomes further subject to the
state and the economy or independently effective; whether that of it
which still lingers in human personal life becomes part of public life:
this is decisive' (G p. 111; E p. 50).

It will not come about by dividing existence into distinct compart-
ments, one of them labelled 'the spiritual life'. This would deprive
spirit of all reality. For spirit does not affect itself but the world.
Spirit's task is to redeem the world, and itself in the world. And this,
'the dissipated, feeble, degenerate spirituality which passes for spirit
today can only do by attaining once more to the essence of spirit: the
ability to say *you*' (G p. 112; E p. 51).

———

In the *it*-world, causality is limitless. All appears to be caused or causative. Yet causality, which is of fundamental importance to science, need not oppress one who is able to leave the *it*-world for the world of *you*. There, where the reciprocal effect of *I* and *you* is unaffected by causality, and where a man decides on his own right action, he knows he is free. 'Only one who is acquainted with relation and knows the presence of *you* is qualified to decide. And whoever decides is free because he has stepped before the Face' (G p. 112; E p. 51). Confronted with a variety of alluring possibilities, a man chooses what he believes he is meant to do. Moreover, in order that the rejected tempting alternative will not generate trouble in himself, he harnesses the force of its 'undiminished passion' to the performance of the deed chosen. The energies of the so-called 'evil inclination' are directed into the service of the good.

Assured of his freedom, one who makes decisions cannot be disturbed by causality. He knows that life is by nature a swing from the presence of relation to the remoteness of irrelation and back again.

He is content to be able to set foot again and again on the threshold of the sanctuary wherein he may not stay: indeed, it is for him an intimate part of the meaning and destiny of this life that he has constantly to leave it. There, on the threshold, response kindles in him ever anew—the spirit. Here, in the unholy and needy land, the spark has to prove true. What is known here as necessity cannot frighten him since there he has known the true necessity, destiny. (G p. 113; E pp. 52–3)

Destiny goes hand in hand with freedom. To one who sets aside 'goods and garments' and 'stands naked before the Face', destiny appears as the counterpart to freedom.

No indeed, to one who returns to the *it*-world bearing the spark of relation, causality is no worry. In times of health, men of the spirit infect their fellow-beings with confidence so that all of them, even the dullest, can become aware of the presence of *you*. But in times of sickness, the *it*-world is cut off from the warmth of *you*-relation, and human life consists of objects not present but remote from man. He then loses his freedom, and the previously familiar and unfrightening causality takes on the appearance of a crushing and inescapable fate.

Every great civilization rests on an original relational event, a response to *you*, an essential act of the spirit. But the creativity and freedom stimulated and inspired by it lasts only as long as that *I–you* relation continues to be repeated in the life of the individual. Once a civilization is no longer centred on that endlessly renewed act of relation, it rigidifies into a world no longer present but caught in the grip of fate.

The sickness of our own time is unlike that of any other and yet part of them all. History is not a record of succeeding civilizations measuring the same circuit of death. A nameless path runs through their rising and falling. It is not one of progress or development. It is a descent—which can also be described as an ascent—into the spiritual underworld to the point where there is no longer any backwards or forwards, but only the breakthrough: *teshuvah*.

Nowadays, belief in fate is more obstinate than ever. We have a law of survival which lays down that all must participate in a universal struggle or perish; a psychological law which postulates the formation of the human personality from inborn habitual instincts; a law of civilization which ordains the unalterably uniform genesis and decline of historical structures. We seem in short to be yoked to a course of events impossible to escape, to be carried along on the conveyor belt of a progressive continuum. In this scheme of things there is no room for freedom, and none for *teshuvah*, the most real of all the revelations of freedom, with its power to change the face of the earth. No allowance is made here for overcoming the universal struggle, for mastering the instincts, for lifting the class taboos, for rejuvenating and changing the historical structures through *teshuvah*.

Yet nothing can become fate except belief in fate—because it suppresses the movement of *teshuvah*. The *you*-world is not closed, whoever turns in its direction as a whole and unified person becomes aware of freedom. 'And to become free from belief in the absence of freedom is to become free' (G p. 117; E p. 58).

As power over an incubus is obtained by giving it its real name, so the *it*-world must surrender to whoever knows its essential nature. But how can someone whose *I* has become empty of reality summon the strength to address the incubus by its name? How is his ability to enter into relation to be resurrected when this spectral *I* tramples the grave under which it lies? How can he gather himself into one whilst he suffers from the sickness of the divided *I*? If he lives in arbitrariness, how can he become conscious of freedom?

As freedom and destiny go hand in hand, so do arbitrariness and fate. The free man is one who wills without arbitrariness. 'He believes in reality: he believes, that is, in the real solidarity of the real duality, *I* and *you*' (G p. 118; E p. 59). He believes in destiny and that it needs and awaits him. And he makes his way towards it, not knowing where it is but with his whole heart. He sacrifices his unfree lesser will for the sake of his greater will. Not interfering, but also not just letting things happen, he listens and watches for what develops, not to be carried along by it, but so that he may give it the reality it asks of him through human spirit, human deed, human life, and human death.

He believes. That is to say, he encounters. For to live arbitrarily is to be without belief or encounter. It is to be concerned only to exploit the world to one's own advantage. What the arbitrary man calls destiny is really whatever facilitates his exploitation. He has in fact no destiny, no greater will, and is quite incapable of sacrifice (though he talks a lot about it). He interferes continuously, prompting 'destiny' whenever he can. Unbelieving and arbitrary, he sees around him nothing but unbelief and arbitrariness. For him, existence amounts to a fixing of aims and a devising of the means to attain them. 'Without sacrifice and without grace, without encounter and without presence, his world is a world of ends and means. It cannot be otherwise. And this is called fate. Thus, in all his arbitrariness he is inextricably caught up in unreality. And he knows it whenever he reflects on himself' (G p. 118; E p. 61). Which is why he takes the greatest pains not to do so.

Yet, if he were to permit himself to meditate on the real and the unreal *I*, and to sink into the depths of what is known as despair but which is in reality the ground out of which self-annihilation and rebirth grow, this would be the beginning of his *teshuvah*.

———

How does the *I* become unreal? Whether in relation, as in '*I* see *you*', or out of it, as in '*I* see the tree', surely it remains equally real in its self-affirmation, even though the act of seeing may be not equally real?

The answer is that the words themselves prove nothing. I can say *you* out of habit to what is really *it*; and I can say *it* to a *you* whose presence is as it were recalled from afar. Similarly, 'I' can be merely an indispensable pronoun. And self-affirmation? If *you* is truly intended in the one sentence and *it* in the other, and if therefore *I* is truly intended in both, is it the same *I* from whose self-affirmation both are said?

The *I* of *I–you* is different from the *I* of *I–it*.

In a stand of irrelation, my *I* is an Egotist[4] aware of itself as a subject engaged in experience and use. In a stand of relation, my *I* is a Person aware of itself as subjectivity. The Egotist appears inasmuch as it sets itself off against other Egotists. The person appears inasmuch as it enters into relation with other Persons. The purpose of setting oneself off against others is experience and use, and the purpose of these is 'life'—lifelong dying, that is. The purpose of relation is itself—contact with *you*.

One who 'is there' with another, and to whom the other 'is there', participates in a reality, in an existence that is neither merely his own nor merely extraneous to him. 'All reality is an effectivity [*Alle Wirklichkeit ist ein Wirken*] in which I participate without being able to make it my own. Where there is no participation, there is no reality. Where there is appropriation to the self, there is no reality. The more immediate the contact with *you*, the more perfect the participation' (G p. 120; E p. 63). The *I* does not lose its reality when it moves out of *I–you* relation back into the world of *it*. The participation endures within it, even when the presence of relation fades, as it must inevitably do. This, furthermore, is the juncture at which a longing takes shape for an even higher relation. It is in this condition of simultaneous consciousness of relation and irrelation, nearness and remoteness, that a yearning arises for perfect participation in being.

The Person is aware of itself as participating, coexisting, and hence as existing. The Egotist is aware of itself as being thus and not otherwise. This is not to imply that the Person surrenders its uniqueness in any way, but it does not focus on it. The Egotist, by contrast, is a glutton for itself, or for what it thinks itself to be, for the image is largely one of its own invention.

These are two poles of humanity rather than two types, for no one is purely Person and no one purely Egotist. 'None is wholly real and none

---

[4] *Eigenwesen* is the word used by Buber, and without Kees Waaijman's researches in the Martin Buber Archive in Jerusalem it would be hard to know how to translate it. R. Gregor Smith opposes 'individuality' to 'person', and Walter Kaufmann 'ego' to 'person'. Buber's own advice to Smith is that 'individuality' in this context sounds as though he had something against it, which was not true. But whereas 'individuality' is an objective idea relating to a personal quality, *Eigenwesen* is intended to allude to relationship within the self. Buber also wrote to Smith: 'I am very disturbed that "Eigenwesen" is rendered as "individuality", but I know of no better word. In French, there is the word "égotiste", which approaches close to what I mean, but the English "egotist" unfortunately means something else. Would "egotical being" be possible?' See Kees Waaijman, *De Mystiek van ik en jij* (Bijleveld, 1976), 186, n. 294.

is wholly unreal. All live in a dual *I*' (G p. 122; E p. 65). Nevertheless, some are so distinctly Person that we may call them Persons. And others are so distinctly Egotists that we may call them Egotists.

The more influential the Egotist becomes in private and public life, the more deeply the *I* slides into unreality. In such times, the Person goes underground, to lead a hidden existence there until the time comes for it to spring back into activity once again.

The word 'I' is humanity's shibboleth.

How discordant is the *I* of the Egotist! But how lovely the *I* of Socrates, the *I* of a man engaged in unceasing dialogue with his fellows! He believed in their reality and was present with them in reality. The *I* of Goethe, the *I* of communion with nature, is also beautiful. He believed in nature and could say to a rose, 'So, it is *you*!' taking his stand beside the flower within the one reality. And to anticipate by presenting an example from the sphere of absolute relation, how

powerful and even overpowering, how right and even self-evident, is the *I*-saying of Jesus. For it is the *I* of absolute relation in which a man addresses his *You* as Father in such a way that he can only be son and nothing other than son. When he says *I*, he can only mean the *I* of the holy basic word which for him is elevated to the absolute. If ever irrelation touches him, the bond of relation is greater, and he speaks to others from out of it. In vain will you try to reduce that *I* to something powerful in itself, or that *You* to something dwelling in us, and once more deprive the real—present relation—of reality. *I* and *You* remain. Each can say *You* and is then *I*. Each can say Father and is then son. Reality remains. (G p. 123; E p. 67)

What of those whose mission, whose attachment to some cause, obliges them to forgo *I*–*you* relation? What of the *I*-saying of Napoleon?

Napoleon clearly knew nothing of the *you* dimension. For him, people were values to be assessed and used. Impossible to classify as either Person or Egotist, he belonged to a third type, Daemonic Man, to whom millions say *you* and who answer only with *it*, 'to whom relation leads a thousandfold, yet from whom, nothing; who participates in no reality, yet in whom there is immeasurable participation as though in a reality' (G p. 124; E p. 68). On the other hand, Napoleon, unlike the modern Egotist, was not concerned with himself except as a necessary point of departure. His *I*-saying was not deceptive but merely the grammatical subject of his statements and commands. Certainly, an age whose ideal is Daemonic Man misunderstands him. Enthusing over his imperiousness and endeavouring to imitate his attitude towards his fellow beings, it fails to realize that he was not impelled by any lust for power but by his destiny and a desire to fulfil it. It mistakes his rigorous devotion to his cause for ebullient self-awareness.

Napoleon said 'I' without being able to enter into relation but as an achievement. Whoever tries to ape him, merely reveals the wickedness of his own self-contradiction.

What is self-contradiction?

It is when the *a priori* of relation, the inborn *you*, fails to be realized in the external world and strikes inward, developing on the *I*, the very place where there is no room for it at all. The result is a confrontation within the self which cannot be relation but only self-contradiction.

Sometimes a man will shudder over the alienation of his *I* from the world and it will seem to him that something should be done. Yet although he may know which direction to take, the path leading to *teshuvah* by way of sacrifice, he rejects this knowledge. Turning to reason instead, he exposes his wretched *I*, which is always empty no matter how much he fills it with experience and use, and reason paints pictures for him. In one of them, the earth emerges from the stars and man emerges from the earth and history bears him along through the ages. Underneath is written, 'One and all'. Another shows the soul. A woman spins; and the orbits of the stars, the life of all beings, the whole history of the world, is a spun thread called, not stars, creatures, words, but perceptions and psychological states. Underneath is written, 'One and all'. From then on, when the alienation frightens him, he looks at one picture and sees his *I* embedded in the world, and that there is in fact no *I*, so the world cannot harm it. And he is comforted. If he shudders on another occasion and the *I* causes him anxiety, he looks again at a picture, and whichever one he sees, the empty *I* is stuffed full of the world or else the world flows over it. And he is comforted. 'But a moment comes and is near, when shuddering the man looks up and sees in a glance both pictures at once. And then an even deeper shudder seizes him' (G p. 127; E p. 72).

PART THREE

The third and final section of *I and You* defines what Buber means by 'the everlasting *You*' and how he conceives of relation between it and the human *I*. It also indicates how such perfect relation is to be achieved, what it entails, and what are its effects.

The extended lines of relation meet in the everlasting *You*. With each *you*, we catch a glimpse of the everlasting *You*.

With every particular *you*, the basic word (*I–you*) addresses the everlasting *You*. From this mediation of the *you* of all beings fulfilment of relation comes to them and unfulfilment. The inborn *you* is realized in each but perfected in none. It is perfected only in immediate relation with that *You* which cannot by nature become an *it*. (G p. 128; E p. 75)

The everlasting *You* has been called by many names and to start with they have all meant *You*. But as people were driven to think and talk about their *You*, the names became part of the language of irrelation. Nevertheless, they remain holy, for in them God has not only been expressed but also addressed.

Some feel that the word 'God' should be avoided because it has been so misused, but what do all the mistakes concerning God's being and deeds matter beside the fact that by 'God' people have meant their everlasting *You*? 'For whatever the delusion in which he may be held, whoever utters the word "God" and really has *You* in mind, utters the true *You* of his life that can never be limited by another, and to whom he stands in a relation that includes all other relation' (G p. 128; E p. 76). But also, whoever addresses the *you* of his life with his whole being as one that can never be diminished by another, even though he may imagine that he hates the name 'God' and regards himself as God-less, he addresses God.

———

It is a grace that I encounter a *vis-à-vis* but an act of will that I say *you*. To enter into relation is to be chosen and to choose, passivity and activity in one.

The activity of a whole and unified person is where there is nothing isolated, particular or partial, but where the whole of him, at rest and contained in his wholeness, is active. To have gained stability in such a condition is to be able to go out towards supreme encounter. For this, there is no need to reject the world. On the contrary, we have to lift the barrier which divides us from it. But is it possible to say what is required for supreme encounter? Not in the sense of an instruction. 'Nothing of anything that has ever been contrived or devised through-out the ages of the human spirit by way of instruction, preparation, training, or meditation has to do with the most simple fact of encoun-ter' (G pp. 129–30; E. p. 77). All of this belongs to the *it*-world and leads not a single step out of it. The one way to indicate what is required is to draw a circle excluding all that is not itself. Then we can see that what is needed is a total acceptance of presence and of present time. The greater our remoteness from present relation, the more radical a *teshuvah* such an acceptance will demand. We shall have to surrender, not our *I* as mysticism generally supposes, but our false instinct of self-assertion which leads us to take refuge from the unreli-able, tenuous, transient, and dangerous world of *you* in a possession of things.

———

All real relation in the world is exclusive, but in relation with *You*, absolute exclusiveness and absolute inclusiveness are one. It is not to look away from all else but to see all else in him.

We do not find God by remaining in the world. We do not find God by leaving the world. He finds him who is not to be sought who goes out towards his *You* with his whole being, bearing with him the whole being of the world . . .

If you explore the life of things and conditionality you arrive at the insoluble. If you deny the life of things and conditionality you find yourself faced with nothingness. If you sanctify life, you encounter the living God. (G p. 131; E p. 79)

———

With the withdrawal of every particular *you* into the remoteness of *I–it* and with the disappointment which this brings, man's *you*-sense aspires beyond but not away from them all to a *You* that will remain for him everlastingly *You*. Not as though searching for something: how foolish it is to turn from one's way of life to search for God when there is nothing in which he cannot be found. He merely goes on his way hoping that it will be *the* way.

And when he has found, his heart does not abandon the *you*s encountered on his journey. He blesses every cell that has harboured him in the past and will harbour him again. For to find the everlasting *You* is not to arrive at the end of the road but at its everlasting midway point.

It is a finding without a search. His *You* was present from the beginning to his *you*-sense but its 'presence had to become entirely real out of the reality of a sanctified world-life' (G p. 132; E p. 128).

For God is not to be ascertained or deduced from other given facts or circumstances. God is that 'being that confronts us immediately, most closely and lastingly, that which may properly only be addressed, not expressed' (G p. 132; E p. 129).

––––––

The essential element of relation with God is not, as some maintain, a feeling, and specifically a feeling of dependence. Feelings are liable to be overtaken, outdone or cancelled out by other feelings. Also, every feeling derives its colour and significance from its opposite. To reduce absolute relation, which includes all relative relation, to an isolated and limited feelings, is to relativize it.

Perfect relation can only be understood as a *coincidentia oppositorum*. Dependence is certainly felt, but so is freedom. We certainly need God, but God also needs us. Creation happens to us and we tremble and submit, but we also 'take part in it; we encounter the Creator [*dem Schaffenden*]; we reach out to him as helpers and associates' (G p. 133; E p. 82). To attempt to construe pure relation solely as dependence is to deprive one of the partners of that relation, and therewith relation itself, of reality.

––––––

The same happens if the essential element of the act of religion is seen as a turning inward into the self, either by ridding it of the *I*, or by considering the self to be that which alone thinks and is. In the first case, appeal is made to the saying of John, 'I and the Father are one'; it is supposed that God enters into the *I*-less being or merges with it. The second depends on the teaching of Sandilya, 'The All-Embracing is my Self in my inmost heart,' and identifies *I* and *You*. The consequence of the first belief, therefore, is that relation between *I* and *You* ends with one partner engulfing the other, and of the second, that relation between them is likewise abolished because in fact no *I–You* duality exists.

That appeal to the words of the Evangelist is without foundation must be clear to anyone who reads them with care and impartiality. It is the Gospel of pure relation *par excellence*:

> Father and son, the essentially alike—we may even say God and man, the essentially alike—are the irreducibly real Two, the two conveyors of that primordial relation which from God to man entails sending and commanding, from man to God, watching and listening, and between them both, knowing and loving; in which the son, although the Father dwells and works in him, bows down before the 'Greater' and prays to him. (G p. 135; E p. 85).

What about the mystics and their reports of unity without duality?

The explanation is that we can become unaware of duality in two kinds of circumstances and mysticism is apt to confuse them. The first is when a person becomes gathered into a concentrated and effective whole, a unity. His powers and abilities fused into one, 'he stands alone within himself and, as Paracelsus says, rejoices in his exaltation' (G p. 135; E p. 86). However, this is an event that takes place in himself and not between himself and God.

The second situation in which we may lose sight of duality is that unfathomable act of relation when we imagine that two become one, that *I* and *You* submerge and humanity becomes absorbed into divinity. But what the mystics term 'union' is not union at all. It is the enrapturing *dynamic* of relation, like that which characterizes sexual love, when unity is so strongly felt that the *I* and *you* between whom the relation exists are forgotten.

The other claim concerning the identity of Universal Being and the self finds an answer in the Upanishad story of how Indra, prince of the gods, went to Prajapati, the Creator Spirit, to ask how he was to recognize the self. When a man rests dreamlessly in profound sleep, he was told, 'that is the Self, the Immortal, the Sure, that is Universal Being'.

Indra was dissatisfied. In such a state, a man can distinguish neither himself nor others. 'He has fallen into annihilation. I see no profit here.' 'Lord,' replied Prajapati, 'it is indeed so' (G p. 137; E p. 88).

In so far as it makes an assertion about true being, the teaching has nothing in common with one thing—lived reality—since it is obliged to reduce it to an appearance. And in so far as it sets out to conduce to meditation on true being, it leads not to lived reality but to an 'annihilation' without consciousness or memory, experience of which may be acknowledged as of non-duality yet not proclaimed as unity. 'In lived reality, there is no unity of being. Reality consists only in effective

action . . . and the strongest deepest reality is where everything enters
into effective activity, the whole man without reserve and the all-
embracing God, the unified *I* and the unbounded *You*' (G p. 138;
E p. 89).

In lived reality there is a unification of the *I*, an assembly of the
powers into one. But where the doctrine of submergence within the
self demands the preservation only of what is pure and the intrinsic,
and that the rest be eliminated, true unification, aiming at the whole
and undiminished man, 'esteems the instinctive not too impure, the
sensual not too peripheral, the emotional not too transient' (G p. 138;
E p. 89).

The doctrine of deep meditation promises communion with that
which thinks, with that by which the world is thought. But in lived
reality, there is no that-which-thinks without a that-which-is-thought.

Buddha, the perfected one who makes perfect, declined to assert
that there is, or is not, unity. For him, there was no 'thus', and no 'not
thus', but only an indissoluble 'thus-and-otherwise'. His desire was to
teach the Way, not an opinion. He disputed one statement: that there
is no doing, no deed, no power. And he made one assertion only:
'There is, O monks, an Unbecome, an Uncreated, an Unformed'
(G p. 139; E p. 91).

Otherwise, the Way would have no goal. This being so, the Way has
a goal.

If we are to remain true to reality, we can follow Buddha thus far but
no further. For we know that if this is one of the goals, it cannot be
ours. And if it is *the* goal, it is wrongly described.

We cannot tell whether future existences await us, but if we could,
we would still not seek to escape them but would ask only to be able to
utter in each of them 'the everlasting *I* of the perishable and the
everlasting *You* of the imperishable' (G p. 140; E p. 92). Whether
Buddha's Way leads to this goal, we do not know. It certainly leads to
an intermediate goal that concerns us, the unification of the soul,
though again, it entails an evasion of reality, an averting of the eyes
from the 'deception of form', which for us is not deception but the
world.

Moreover, rather than leading nearer to relation with *You*, it points
away from relation altogether. That Buddha was familiar with *you*-
saying is obvious from his intercourse with his pupils; but he did not
teach it. He was also certainly familiar with *You*-saying to a First Cause
beyond all other 'gods', but he said nothing about it.

All doctrine of self-immersion is grounded on the gigantic delusion of man bent back on himself that spirit is in him, whereas it is not in him but between him and what is not him. When it denies its relational nature, spirit is obliged to draw into man what is not man, to move God and the world into the soul.

The beginning and end of the world are not, as Buddha proclaims, in me. They *are* not, in any case. They 'happen continuously; and their happening pertains to me, my life, my decision, my work, my service' (G p. 141; E p. 94). Also, they do not depend on my attitude towards them, but on my deeds, on how I put that attitude into practice. If I merely redeem myself within myself, I do the world neither good nor ill. To affect it, I must believe in it. And if I do this, I cannot be Godless.

I know nothing of a 'world' or 'life in the world' which might separate us from God. A life so described is life with an alienated *it*-world of experience and use. Whoever truly goes out to the world, goes out to God . . .

God comprehends the universe and is not the universe; but he also comprehends myself and is not myself. It is by reason of this, the ineffable, that I can say *You* in my language, as every man can say it in his; by reason of this that *I*, *you*, dialogue and speech exists, and spirit whose primordial act it is; by reason of this that in all eternity the Word exists. (G p. 142; E p. 95).

Man's religious situation, 'his being-there [*Dasein*] in the Presence' (G p. 142; E p. 95), is distinguished by the essential paradox that all is entirely out of his hands and yet depends on him.

The paradox is insoluble. It cannot be tampered with, or synthesized, or relativized. No theological artifice can be allowed to provide an abstract reconciliation between thesis and antithesis. The meaning of the religious situation is that the paradox has to be lived. But in the reality of a life of standing-before-God, necessity and freedom are seen to be one.

How fugitive is the presence of *you*! Take the domestic cat. I look at it, and suddenly its eye catches mine, lights up, and without a doubt it begins to ask, 'What is this? What is it that is coming from you to me? What is it? Are you saying something to me?' Then just as quickly, the relational event is over. 'I relate this tiny episode, which I have experienced several times, for the sake of the language of this almost imperceptible rising and setting of the spirit's sun. In no other have I been so profoundly aware of the transitoriness of actuality in all relation with living beings' (G p. 144; E p. 98). Other relational incidents have a day, however short, between their morning and evening, but in this case, beginning and end flow pitilessly one into the other.

So much can never break through the crust of thing-ness at all, but even when it can, how inevitably brief is the time in which our *vis-à-vis* is nothing but *you*. It is not relation itself that fails, but its actuality. Even love is bound to alternate between actuality and latency. Only in one relation, the all-embracing, is latency nevertheless actuality. 'One *You* alone never by nature ceases to be *You* to us. Whoever knows God, knows also remoteness from God and the grief of aridity in a troubled heart, but not loss of Presence. It is we who are not always there' (G p. 145; E p. 99).

———

All real relation in the world is exclusive. Only in relation with God are absolute exclusiveness and absolute inclusiveness one.

All real relation in the world depends on individuation. It is this that enables us to know one another, and it is also the reason why perfect knowing and being-known are denied to us. But in perfect relation, my *You* comprehends my self without being my self. My 'limited knowing merges into a boundless being-known' (G p. 145; E pp. 99–100).

All relation in the world is alternately actual and latent. Only the everlasting *You* is by nature everlastingly *You*. It is our nature that obliges us to draw it into the *it*-world and into the language of *it*.

———

The world of irrelation coheres in space and time. The world of relation coheres in neither. Its point of coherence is in the Centre, the everlasting *You*, in whom the extended lines of relation meet.

The privilege of pure relation annuls the privileges of irrelation in that *I–You* relation furnishes a *you*-continuum: individual moments of relation combine to form a life of relation. Also, *I–You* relation lends to *you*-relation formative powers which can penetrate and transform the world of *it*. Finally, *I–You* relation preserves the *I* from alienation from the world and from losing its reality.

Teshuvah, the return to perfect relation, is a re-recognition of the Centre. In this act of being, our powers of relation acquire new life and in so doing renew the life of the world.

And perhaps not our world only. For we may surmise that the metacosmic, indwelling primordial form of duality (the human form of which is a duality of attitude, basic word and world-aspect) is a turning aside from the First Cause by virtue of which the universe sustains itself in becoming, and a turning back to the First Cause by virtue of which the universe redeems itself in being. (G p. 146; E p. 101)

———

In every relational act—with nature, with other human beings, with immaterial essences—we look towards the hem of the everlasting *You*. We hear its breath in each. With every *you*, we address the everlasting *You*. 'The one Presence shines through them all' (G p. 147; E p. 101). Yet each can be deprived of presence. The 'physical' world (consistency) can be removed from life with nature; the 'psychical' world (sensibility) from life with our fellow-beings; the 'noetic' world (validity) from life with the immaterial essences. They then lose their transparency and with it their meaning. Though invested with names such as Cosmos, Eros, and Logos, they become usable and opaque.

The truth is that man has a Cosmos only when the universe becomes his home, with a holy hearth on which to offer sacrifice. And man has an Eros only when living beings become for him images of the Everlasting and communion with them revelation. And man has a Logos only when he addresses himself to the Mystery with work and service in the spirit. (G p. 147; E p. 102)

Every *you* is a gateway to the Presence of the Word. But when perfect encounter takes place, the gateways come together to form the One Portal into real life, and you no longer know by which one you have entered.

———

Of the three relational spheres, the human is special because it is the only one in which *I–you* not only signifies relation but is actually uttered. Here alone, it is expressed in speech, as address and response.

This sphere is the main gateway into which the two side-gates lead. Here alone, as a reality impossible to lose, is there a seeing and being seen, a knowing and being known, a loving and being loved. 'Relation with man is the parallel proper of relation with God. In it, true address receives true response. Except that in God's response, all, the All, manifests itself as speech' (G p. 148; E p. 103).

———

But isn't solitude also a way to the Mystery? Aren't those who no longer cling to other beings particularly worthy to confront Being?

If solitude means renouncing an association with things entailing experience and use, this is the prerequisite of all relation. But if solitude means dispensing with relation, 'God raises up whoever is forsaken by those to whom he truly says *you*, but not him who forsakes' (G p. 148; E p. 104).

To cling to others is to be greedy to use them. To realize their presence is to be bound to them. But only one who is bound to others in this way is ready for God, for he alone confronts God's reality with a human reality.

Further, if solitude is a place of purification to which we turn before approaching the All-Holy or during our ordeals—to this we are disposed by nature. But if it means an isolation that will allow us to concentrate on communing with ourselves, 'this is the downfall proper of the spirit into spirituality' (G p. 149; E p. 104).

We can even become so infatuated with ourselves that we imagine that God is in us and that we speak with him. 'But however true it is that God encompasses us and dwells in us, we never have him in us. And we speak with him only when speech within us has come to an end' (G p. 149; E p. 104)

————

One modern philosopher maintains that we all believe either in God, or in idols such as money, power, sex, etc., and that the idols need only be exposed as a relative good assuming an absolute value, for the diverted religious act to return to its proper end. But this is to assume that relationship with a finite idol is the same as relation with God, for how else can the one simply replace the other?

Relationship with an idol understood in this sense is always directed towards acquiring, having, and holding an *it*, an object. To be dominated by an idol is to be 'possessed by a desire for possession', for which there is no remedy except *teshuvah*.

But how can someone make his *teshuvah*, return to perfect relation, when relation itself is unknown to him? For can 'a servant of Mammon say *you* to money'? (G p. 150; E p. 106).

Those who suffer from possession are healed by having their relational powers re-awakened and by being taught how to live in the world of *you*, not by being led in their sick state to God.

Whoever has substituted God for his idol 'has' a phantom to which he gives the name of 'God'. 'But God, the everlasting Presence, does not permit himself to be "had". Woe to the possessed who thinks he possesses God!' (G p. 150; E p. 106).

———

Some speak of the 'religious man' as one who is able to do without relation because he has outstripped 'social' man, influenced and determined by external forces, by virtue of a force operating entirely from within. Social existence can however have two connotations. It can mean community built on relation; and it can mean the massing together of human beings in conditions empty of relation. Community is the product of the very same energy as that which operates in relation between man and God, the All-relation into which every other relation flows without running dry. A man cannot, therefore, divide his life between real relation with God and unreal *I–it* relationship with the world. 'He cannot pray genuinely to God and make use of the world' (G p. 151; E p. 107).

Whoever envisages the world as an object to be made use of, does the same to God. His prayer is merely an unburdening of himself and it falls into the ear of the void. It is he who is Godless, not the atheist who calls on the Nameless One out of the night of his longing.

Some say too that the 'religious man' can approach God as a single, isolated being, because he has outdistanced 'moral' man, still tied to his obligations to the world. He has moved away from the tension between right and wrong, to a tension between the world and God, where 'should' dissolves into an absolute 'is'. He is commanded to disencumber himself of the agitation of responsibility and of demands made upon him, and to submit to what is ordained. In the context of his relation with God, the world and all he does there counts for nothing. 'But this is to suppose that God created his world for an illusion, and his human creatures for ecstasy' (G p. 151; E p. 108).

The truth is that for one who approaches the Presence, the world itself becomes so fully present that he can 'in one word say *you* to the being of all beings' (G p. 151; E p. 108). He is not relieved of responsibility, but exchanges a concern with temporal effects for a profound involvement with the world before the Face of God. 'Moral' judgements are finished with forever as far as others are concerned. But his own right behaviour has to be evaluated unceasingly. What he does in the world is then not without value but 'intended, asked for, needed and part of creation' (G p. 152; E p. 109).

––––––

The everlasting and primordial phenomenon of what is known as revelation is that a person does not come from supreme encounter the same as he entered it. Something is added. He has something more. He receives Presence as strength.

This Presence and strength comprise three effects which, though not distinct, may be considered separately. The first is that he becomes aware of being bound in relation without knowing how, or to what, and without his life being lightened in any way. On the contrary, it becomes heavy with meaning. The second is that he knows that this meaning is sure, that nothing can ever be meaningless again, and that the meaning has to be done, not expounded. The third is that he knows that the meaning concerns this life and not another life, this world and not a world 'beyond', and that it must be proved true through the unity of his being and in the unity of his life.

No instruction can lead to encounter with *You*, and none can lead out of it. For it to happen, we need only a total acceptance of Presence and presence. Similarly, we need the same acceptance of Presence after supreme encounter is over. We reach it saying simply *You*; and we leave it saying *You*.

That before which, within which, out of which and into which we live—the Mystery—remains what it was. It has become present to us and with its Presence declared itself to be salvation. We have 'known' it, but have no knowledge of it that might lessen or moderate its mysteriousness. We have drawn near to God, but no nearer to any unravelling or unveiling of existence. We have sensed redemption [*Erlösung*] but no 'solution' [*Lösung*]. We cannot go to others with what we have received and say, 'This is what you should know; this is what should be done.' We can only go and prove it to be true. And even this is no 'should'. We can and we must. This is the everlasting revelation present in the here and now. I know of none whose primordial phenomenon is not the same. I believe in none. I believe in no self-naming of God, in no self-defining of God before men. The word of revelation is, I AM THERE SUCH AS I AM THERE. That-which-reveals is that-which-reveals. That-which-is, is there. Nothing more. The everlasting source of strength flows on. The everlasting touch lingers. The everlasting voice sounds. Nothing more. (G pp. 153–4; E pp. 111–12)

––––––

The everlasting *You* can never become an *it* because it cannot by nature be measured or circumscribed; because it cannot by nature be conceived as a sum of qualities; because it cannot be found either in the world or out of it; because it cannot be thought; because it cannot be experienced. Yet although we by nature, and not arbitrarily, continually make God into an *it*, a 'something', this course of the God-thing through religion, this course of religion away from the living God and back to him, 'the changes from Presence to investment with form, to objectification, to conceptualization, to disintegration, to renewal—are a way, are *the* Way' (G pp. 154–5; E p. 112).

How does it happen that the Presence and strength of revelation—for all religions have their origin in some kind of revelation—become asserted knowledge and a prescribed code of behaviour?

Man longs to have God. He longs to have God continuously in time and space and his desire is not satisfied by pure relation. Wishing to extend his God-having in time, and not content with the alternate latency and actuality of the human ability to say *You*, he makes God into an object of faith. He prefers the duration of an *it* believed in, and the security it offers because of his belief, to living with the intermittent remoteness and nearness characteristic of pure *I–you* relation.

Likewise, wishing to extend God-having in space, he longs for a community of the faithful united with their God and therefore makes God into an object of a cult, which initially supplements relation with *You* but eventually tends to take its place.

But temporal continuity of *You*-relation can only be ensured by realizing the everlasting *You* in the world. Time then becomes so rich in relation that moments of *You*-encounter appear, not as momentary flashes of brilliance, but 'as the rising moon on a dark and starry night' (G p. 156; E p. 115).

Similarly, spatial continuity of *You*-relation can only be ensured by being attached to others, not in order to participate in a central *You*, but because each one is attached to *You*.

The purpose of encounter with *You* is not that we should concern ourselves with God but that we should verify to the world the meaning we have perceived. By bending backwards towards God, we turn away from him. No *You* confronts us any longer. In such a position, we can only install God into thing-ness as an *it*, believe in him and talk about him as an *it*. For what seems to be a turning towards the First Cause is actually part of the metacosmic movement away from it. And what seems to be a turning away from God on the part of one who fulfils his mission in the world is actually part of the metacosmic movement towards him.

These two movements—turning away into self-enlargement and turning back to relation—find their supreme human form in the history of man's relation to God. In *teshuvah*, the word is born on earth. As it extends and expands, it changes into the chrysalis of religion. In a new *teshuvah*, it acquires new wings.

The mighty revelations to which the religions appeal are all essentially identical to the quiet revelations continuously given everywhere. The mighty revelations are no other than the everlasting revelation. But the human 'mouths' that voice them are not instruments but organs, and they modify what they hear in accord with their own nature and time.

There is a qualitative difference to every historical era. In some, the true element of the human spirit waiting hidden underground is so ready to break into new life that for it to leap out, stamped with a new form of God in the world, it needs 'but the touch of him who touches' (G p. 158; E p. 117).

Thus throughout the ages, and throughout all the many transformations of the human element, fresh material from the world of the spirit has been raised again and again to divine form. We never see God without the world. We only see the world in God. But as we do, we unceasingly shape God's form. The form is a mixture of *You* and *it*. In faith and worship it can rigidify into an *it* yet become repeatedly present through the essence of relation enduring within it. But also, prayer can so degenerate in religion that it becomes more and more difficult for the whole and undivided *I* to pray *You*. A person must then withdraw from the false security which religion offers and make for the hazards of the infinite before he loses sight of his true *objectivum*. 'From a community whose roof is the Dome of the Temple but not the sky, he must go out into final solitude' (G p. 159; E p. 118). When religion's movement towards self-enlargement suppresses the movement towards relation known as *teshuvah*, God's form dies and everything built around it falls into ruins. 'And it is part of what then happens that, in the dislocation of his truth, man no longer sees what then happens. What happens is the decomposition of the Word' (G p. 159; E pp. 118–19).

The Word has its essence in revelation, is active during the life of the divine form, and becomes currency[5] during the dominion of the dead form. 'The times in which the essential Word appears are those in which the bond between *I* and world is renewed. The times in which the active Word governs are those in which understanding between *I* and world is maintained . . . The times in which the Word becomes currency are those in which reality is lost, *I* and world are alienated and fate comes into being' (G p. 159; E p. 119). But the course is not a circular one. It is the way. With each new age, fate becomes more oppressive and *teshuvah* more explosive.

And the theophany draws always *closer*. It draws away closer to the sphere *between* beings. It draws closer to the kingdom hidden in our midst, the Between.

History is a mysterious drawing closer. Every twist of its way leads at once into deeper corruption and a more fundamental *teshuvah*.

But the phenomenon known in its worldly aspect as *teshuvah* has a divine aspect known as redemption. (G p. 160; E pp. 119–20)

---

[5] Kees Waaijman notes that in Buber's original manuscript, *geltend* (his eventual choice) is given as *fiktiv*. He also points out that Buber advised R. Gregor Smith to translate *geltend* not as 'influence' but as 'currence (or validity); Geltung hier wie Gültigkeit einer Geldsorte' (Martin Buber Archiv, Jerusalem): Waaijman, *De Mystiek van ik en jij*, 241, n. 522. Buber's remarks show, incidentally, how unsuited he was to control the Englishing of his work!

Select Bibliography

Works by Buber in German are listed in order of publication; works by Buber in English are listed in alphabetical order of title, as the date of publication does not necessarily bear direct relation to the date of composition.

WORKS BY BUBER IN GERMAN

Collections

Werke, 3 vols., Kösel–Lambert Schneider, 1962–4: i, *Schriften zur Philosophie* (1962); ii, *Schriften zur Bibel* (1964); iii, *Schriften zur Chassidismus* (1963).
Briefwechsel aus sieben Jahrzehnten, 3 vols., ed. Grete Schaeder, Lambert Schneider, 1973–5: i (1972), ii (1973), iii (1975).

Single works

Der fünf Bücher der Weisung, Jakob Hegner, 1953.
Bücher der Geschichte, Jakob Hegner, 1955; Lambert Schneider, 1979.
Bücher der Kündung, Jakob Hegner, 1958; Lamber Schneider, 1978.
Begegnung: Autobiographische Fragmente, Kohlhammer, 1960.
Die Schriftwerke, Jakob Hegner, 1962; Lambert Schneider, 1980.
Der Jude und sein Judentum, Josef Melzer, 1963.
Nachlese, Lambert Schneider, 1965.

WORKS BY BUBER IN ENGLISH

At the Turning: Three Addresses on Judaism, Farrar, Strauss, and Young, 1952.
Between Man and Man, trans. R. Gregor Smith, Fontana, 1961.
Biblical Humanism, ed. Nahum Glatzer, Macdonald, 1968.
Daniel: Dialogues on Realization, trans. M. Friedman, McGraw-Hill, 1965.
For the Sake of Heaven, trans. L. Lewisohn, Meridian, 1958.
Good and Evil, trans. R. Gregor Smith, Scribner, 1953.
Hasidism, trans. C. and M. Witton-Davies, Philosophical Library, 1948.
Hasidism and Modern Man, trans. M. Friedman, Horizon, 1958.
I and Thou, 2nd edn., trans. R. Gregor Smith, Scribner–T. & T. Clark, 1958.
I and Thou, trans. W. Kaufmann, Scribner–T. & T. Clark, 1970–1.
Images of Good and Evil, trans. M. Bullock, Routledge & Kegan Paul, 1952.
Israel and the World: Essays in a Time of Crisis, Schocken, 1963.
Kingship of God, trans. R. Scheimann, Harper & Row–Allen & Unwin, 1967.
Meetings, trans. M. Friedman, Open Court, 1973.

Moses, East and West Library–Harper Torchbooks, 1946, 1958.
On Intersubjectivity and Cultural Creativity, ed. S. N. Eisenstadt, University of Chicago Press, 1993.
On Judaism, ed. Nahum Glatzer, Schocken, 1967.
On Zion: The History of an Idea, trans. S. Goodman, T. & T. Clark, 1985.
Paths in Utopia, trans. R. F. Hull, Routledge & Kegan Paul–Beacon, 1949, 1958.
Pointing the Way, ed. M. Friedman, Harper Torchbooks, 1963.
'Replies to my Critics', in P. Schilpp and M. Friedman, eds., *Scripture and Translation*, by Martin Buber and Franz Rosenzweig, trans. Lawrence Rosenwald and Everett Fox, Indiana University Press, 1994.
Ten Rungs, trans. Olga Marx, Schocken, 1973.
The Knowledge of Man, trans. M. Friedman, Harper & Row–Allen & Unwin, 1965.
The Letters of Martin Buber: A Life of Dialogue, ed. Nahum N. Glatzer and Paul Mendes-Flohr, Schocken, 1991.
The Philosophy of Martin Buber, Open Court, 1967, 689–744.
The Prophetic Faith, trans. C. Witton-Davies, Macmillan–Harper Torchbooks, 1960.
The Tales of Rabbi Nachman, trans. M. Friedman, Souvenir, 1974.
The Tales of the Hasidim: Early Masters, trans. O. Marx, Schocken, 1947.
The Tales of the Hasidim: Later Masters, trans. O. Marx, Schocken, 1948.
The Way of Response, trans. and ed. Nahum N. Glatzer, Schocken, 1966.
Two Types of Faith, trans. N. P. Goldhawk, Routledge & Kegan Paul–Harper Torchbooks, 1961, 1961.

BOOKS AND ARTICLES ON BUBER

Hans Urs von Balthasar, *Martin Buber and Christianity*, trans. A. Dru, Harvill, 1961.
S. Ben-Chorin, *Zwiesprache mit Martin Buber*, Bleicher, 1966.
Jochanan Bloch, *Die Aporie des Du—Probleme der Dialogik Martin Bubers*, Phronesis 2, Lambert Schneider, 1977.
Moshe Catanne, *A Bibliography of Martin Buber's Works (1895–1957)*, Bialik Institute, 1958.
Arthur A. Cohen, *Martin Buber*, Bowes and Bowes, 1957.
——, ed., *The Jew: Essays from Martin Buber's Journal, Der Jude, 1916–1928*, University of Alabama Press, 1980.
Margot Cohn and Rafael Buber, *Martin Buber: A Bibliography of his Writings 1897–1978*, Magnes Press/K. G. Saur, 1980.
Malcolm L. Diamond, *Martin Buber: Jewish Existentialist*, Oxford University Press, 1960.
—— *Contemporary Philosophy and Religious Thought*, McGraw-Hill, 1974, 101–29.

Paul Flohr, 'The Road to *I and Thou*', in *Text and Responses* (Festschrift for Nahum Glatzer), Brill, 1975, 201–25.

Maurice Friedman, *Martin Buber: The Life of Dialogue*, 3rd rev. edn., Chicago University Press, 1976.

—— *Martin Buber's Life and Work*, 3 vols., E. P. Dutton, 1983.

—— *Encounter on the Narrow Ridge: A Life of Martin Buber*, Paragon, 1991.

Hermann L. Goldschmidt, *Abschied von Martin Buber*, Hegner, 1966.

Haim Gordon, 'A Method for Clarifying Buber's I–Thou Relationship', *Journal of Jewish Studies*, 27 (1976), 71–83.

—— *The Other Martin Buber: Recollections of his Contemporaries*, Ohio University Press, 1988.

Haim Gordon and Jochanan Bloch, eds., *Martin Buber: A Centenary Volume*, Ktav for Ben Gurion University of the Negev, 1978.

Will Herberg, ed., *The Writings of Martin Buber*, Meridian Books, 1965.

Aubrey Hodes, *Martin Buber: An Intimate Portrait*, Viking, 1971; also published as *Encounter with Martin Buber*, Allen Lane/Penguin, 1972.

Rivka Horwitz, *Buber's Way to 'I and Thou'*, Phronesis 7, Lambert Schneider, 1978.

—— *Buber's Way to 'I and Thou': The Development of Buber's Thought and his 'Religion as Presence'*, Jewish Publication Society, 1968.

Karl-Johan Illman, *Leitwort-Tendenz-Synthese. Programm und Praxis in der Exegese Martin Bubers*, Abo Akademi, 1975.

Steven Kepnes, *The Text as Thou: Martin Buber's Dialogical Hermeneutics and Narrative Theology*, Indiana University Press, 1992.

Hans Kohn, *Martin Buber: sein Werk und seine Zeit*, 2nd edn., Melzer, 1961.

Werner Licharz, ed., *Dialog mit Martin Buber*, Haag and Herchen, 1982.

Paul Mendes-Flohr, *A Land of Two Peoples*, Oxford University Press (New York), 1983.

—— *From Mysticism to Dialogue: Martin Buber's Transformation of German Thought*, Wayne State University Press, 1989.

Donald J. Moore, *Martin Buber: Prophet of Religious Secularism*, Jewish Publications Society of America, 1974.

Roger Moser, *Gotteserfahrung bei Martin Buber*, Phronesis 5, Lambert Schneider, 1979.

Maren Ruth Niehoff, 'The Buber–Rosenzweig Translation of the Bible in German-Jewish Tradition', *Journal of Jewish Studies*, 44 (1993), 258–79.

Roy Oliver, *The Wanderer and the Way: The Hebrew Tradition in the Writings of Martin Buber*, East and West Library, Cornell University Press, 1968.

Stephen M. Panko, *Martin Buber*, Word Books, 1974.

Grete Schaeder, *The Hebrew Humanism of Martin Buber*, trans. N. J. Jacobs, Wayne State University Press, 1973.

P. A. Schilpp and Maurice Friedman, eds., *The Philosophy of Martin Buber*, Library of Living Philosophers, Open Court, 1967.

Gershom Scholem, 'Martin Buber's Interpretation of Hasidism', *Judaica*, i, Suhrkamp, 1963, 165–206; repr. in *The Messianic Idea of Judaism*, Allen and Unwin/Schocken, 1971.

—— 'Martin Buber's Conception of Judaism', *Judaica*, ii, Suhrkamp, 1970, 133–92; repr. in *On Jews and Judaism in Crisis*, Schocken, 1976.

Christian Schütz, *Verborgenheit Gottes: Martin Bubers Werk—Eine Gesamtdarstellung*, Benzinger, 1975.

Pedro Sevilla, *God as Person in the Writings of Martin Buber*, Ateneo University Publications, Manila, 1970.

Lawrence J. Silberstein, *Martin Buber's Social and Religious Thought: Alienation and the Quest for Meaning*, New York University Press, 1989.

Shemaryahu Talmon, 'Martin Buber's Ways of Interpreting the Bible', *Journal of Jewish Studies*, 27 (1976), 195–209.

Paul Tillich, 'Martin Buber', in J. Bowden and J. Richmond, eds., *A Reader in Contemporary Theology*, SCM Press, 1967, 63–7.

Pamela Vermes, 'Martin Buber: A New Appraisal', *Journal of Jewish Studies*, 22 (1971), 78–96.

—— 'Buber's Understanding of the Divine Name Related to Bible, Targum and Midrash', *Journal of Jewish Studies*, 24 (1973), 147–66.

—— 'Martin Buber's Correspondence', *Journal of Jewish Studies*, 25 (1974), 444–50; 29 (1978), 200–3.

—— 'Man's Prime Peril: Buber on Religion', *Journal of Jewish Studies*, 28 (1977), 72–8.

—— 'The Buber–Lukács Correspondence (1911–1921)', *Leo Baeck Institute Yearbook*, xxvii (1982), 369–77.

—— 'The Buber–Schweitzer Correspondence', *Journal of Jewish Studies*, 37 (1986), 228–45.

—— *Buber*, Jewish Thinkers, Peter Halban/Grove Press, 1988. Published in French, trans. Flore Abergel, intr. Emmanuel Levinas, Albin Michel (Présences du Judaïsme), 1992; in Italian, trans. Piero Stefani, Edizioni Paoline (Tempi e Figure), 1988.

—— 'Buber, Martin (Mordecai)', *The Blackwell Companion to Jewish Culture*, Blackwell, 1989, 116–18.

Kees Waaijman, *De Mystiek van ik en jij*, Bijleveld, 1976.

Index to Biblical, New Testament, and Rabbinic References

Index

Buber's writings are indexed under 'Buber, Martin Mordechai, works', rather than as independent entries in the index, with the exception of *I and You*, which is indexed both under Buber and in more detail as an independent entry.